Reality, Resistance, Rock and Roll

Recent World History in 110 Book Reviews

Ron Jacobs

Fomite
Burlington, VT

ISBN-13: 978-1-967022-23-6
Library of Congress Control Number: 2026930744

Fomite
58 Peru Street
Burlington, VT 05401
www.fomitepress.com

01/08/2026

Every review in this book first appeared in *Counterpunch* magazine, either online or in the (now defunct, a victim of inflation) paper magazine. I remain forever grateful to the editors Jeffrey St. Clair, Joshua Frank and the late Alexander Cockburn, the office staff and the readers of the magazine; the editors and staff for publishing my work and the readers for reading it. If you are not familiar with *Counterpunch*, (www. counterpunch.org) I encourage you to find it on the web and read it. Furthermore, I encourage you to subscribe to the stuff behind what is known as a paywall. It's worth it and there's really nothing else like it. That, and in this day and age, media like Counterpunch are needed more than ever.

Dedicated to library workers, teachers, bookstore workers, publishers and everyone else in the world who keeps the human endeavor of reading alive

Books Reviewed in This Collection

2003-2008

Chimes of Freedom: the Politics of Bob Dylan's Art—Mike Marqusee

The Meek and the Militant—Paul Siegel

Gate of the Sun—Elias Khoury

Subterranean Fire: A History of Working-Class Radicalism in the United States—Sharon Smith

Against the Day—Thomas Pynchon

The Darker Nations—Vijay Prashad

Guitar Army—John Sinclair

Hollow Land: Israel's Architecture of Occupation—Eyal Weizmann

Welcome to the Terrordome—Dave Zirin

Flying Close to the Sun—Cathy Wilkerson

Tales of the Out and the Gone—Amiri Baraka

Casualty Figures—Michèle Barrett

Long Shadows—David Giffey

GB84—David Peace

Che: a Graphic Biography—Spain Rodriguez

2009-2013

The Second Palestinian Intifada: A Chronicle of a People's Struggle—Ramzy Baroud

The Old Man: John Brown at Harper's Ferry—Truman Nelson

Afghanistan: The Untold Story—Paul Fitzgerald, Elizabeth Gould

The End of the Revolution—Wang Hui

What Really Happened to the 1960s—Ted Morgan

Orange Sunshine: the Brotherhood of Eternal Love and Its Quest to Spread Peace, Love, and Acid to the World—Nicholas Schou

Blood On the Tracks—S. Brian Willson

On the Ground: An Illustrated Anecdotal History of the Sixties Underground Press—Sean Stewart

It Started In Wisconsin—eds. Paul and Mary Jo Buhle

Why It's Kicking Up Everywhere—Paul Mason

The People's Pension: the Struggle to Defend Social Security Since Reagan—Eric Laursen

Leila Khaled: Icon of Palestinian Liberation—Sarah Irving

My People Are Rising—Aaron Dixon

The Catonsville Nine: A Story of Faith and Resistance in the Vietnam Era—Shawn Francis Peters

Islamophobia and the Politics of Empire—Deepa Kumar

The Global Offensive: The United States, the Palestine Liberation Organization, and the Making of the Post-Cold War Order—Paul Thomas Chamberlin

Empire of Ideas: The Origins of Public Diplomacy and the Transformation of U. S. Foreign Policy—Justin Hart

America's Deadliest Export: Democracy – The Truth About US Foreign Policy and Everything Else—William Blum

Out of Control: A Fifteen Year Battle Against Control Unit Prisons—Nancy Kurshan

Algerian Chronicles—Albert Camus

A Human Rights Manifesto—Julie Wark

2014-2018

Stokely: A Life—Joseph Peniel

The Phoenix Program: America's Use of Terror in Vietnam—Douglas Valentine

Technocreep: The Surrender of Privacy and the Capitalization of Intimacy—Thomas P. Keenan

An Indigenous People's History of the United States—Roxanne Dunbar Ortiz

Seizing Freedom: Slave Emancipation and Liberty for All—David Roediger

On Highway 61: Music, Race and the Evolution of Cultural Freedom—Dennis McNally

letter to jimmy (On the twentieth anniversary of your death)—Alain Mabanckou

War and Revolution: Rethinking the Twentieth Century—Domenic Losurdo

A Short History of Western Ideology—Rolf Petri

Culture and Politics: The Selected Writings of Christopher Caudwell—Christopher Caudwell

Overripe Capitalism: American Capitalism and the Crisis of Democracy—Alan Nasser

2019-2025

Palestine: A Four Thousand Year History—Nur Masalha

Our History is the Future—Nick Estes

Israel: A Beachhead in the Middle East—Stephen Gowans

This Land: How Cowboys, Capitalism, and Corruption are Ruining the American West—Christopher Ketcham

Why No Confederate Statues in Mexico—Ishmael Reed

My Lai: Vietnam, 1968, and the Descent into Darkness—Howard Jones

Guitar King: Michael Bloomfield's Life in the Blues—David Dann

Shakespeare's Tempest and Capitalism: The Storm of History—Helen Scott

Burn it Down! Feminist Manifestos for the Revolution—Breannne Fahs, ed.

Steeped in the Blood of Racism: Black Power, Law and Order, and the 1970 Shootings at Jackson State College—Nancy K. Bristow

Taking Children: A History of American Terror—Laura Briggs

Feminist City: Claiming Space in a Man-Made World—Leslie Kern

The United States of War: A Global History of America's Endless Conflicts, from Columbus to the Islamic State—David Vine

The Fall of America: Journals 1965-1971—Allen Ginsberg

Build Bridges, Not Walls: A Journey to a World Without Borders—Todd Miller

A Different Kind of War: Uneasy Encounters in Mexico and Central America—J. Malcolm Garcia

King Kong Theory—Virginie Despentes

We Are the Land: A History of Native California—Damon B. Akins and William J. Bauer Jr.

The Wretched Atom: America's Global Gamble with Peaceful Nuclear Technology—Jacob Darwin Hamblin

Cronies, A Burlesque: Adventures with Ken Kesey, Neal Cassady, the Merry

Pranksters and the Grateful Dead—Ken Babbs

The Aesthetics of Resistance—Peter Weiss

Rising Fascism in America: It Can Happen Here—Anthony DiMaggio

Gwangju Uprising: The Rebellion for Democracy in South Korea—Hwang Sok-yong, Jai-eui Lee, and Jeon Yong-Ho

Fighting Times: Organizing on the Front Lines of the Class War—Jonathan Melrod

Natural Consequences: Intimate Essays for a Planet in Peril—Char Miller

Waging a Good War: A Military History of the Civil Rights Movement, 1954-1968—Thomas Ricks

Organize, Fight, Win: Black Communist Women's Political Writing—Charisse Burden-Stelly, ed.

War by Other Means: The Pacifists of the Greatest Generation who Revolutionized Resistance—Daniel Akst

Future on Fire: Capitalism and the Politics of Climate Change—David Camfield

The Whole World in an Uproar—Aaron Leonard

Endless Holocausts: Mass Death in the History of the United States Empire—David Michael Smith

The Fascist Groove Thing: A History of Thatcher's Britain in 21 Mixtapes—Hugh Hodges

Playing God: American Catholic Bishops and the Far Right—Mary Jo McConahay

The Poverty Paradox: Understanding Economic Hardship Amid American Prosperity—Mark Robert Rank

This Flame Within: Iranian Revolutionaries in the United States—Manijeh Moradian

Capitalism: A Conversation in Critical Theory—Nancy Fraser and Rahel Jaeggi

The Subversive Seventies—Michael Hardt

A Day in the Life of Abed Salama: Anatomy of a Jerusalem Tragedy—Nathan Thrall

Late Fascism: Race, Capitalism and the Politics of Crisis—Alberto Toscano

Marc Estrin's Fictions of Alienation

I was out in Berkeley, California in early October 2023. While I was there I visited the Freedom Archives. Founded in the late 1990s and maintained by a small dedicated paid and volunteer staff, this institution is an important repository in the world of revolutionary US history. It is one of very few archives devoted to maintaining a collection of documents from and about the numerous radical and revolutionary movements and organizations in the United States from the 1960s on. Copies of underground and leftist organization newspapers, books by and about revolutionary figures of the time, history books, film, video and audio recordings are kept there, digitized and made available for those interested. The collection focuses on anti-imperialist and national liberation struggles, anti-racist struggles, and prison struggles, among others. The reason I begin my book with this mention is because, while I was there I examined a recent exhibit the staff at the Archives had put together. It was titled 99 Books.

After Black Panther George Jackson was killed in San Quentin prison in 1971, prison officials cleaned out his cell. As they did so, they documented their findings. For me, the most important pieces of Jackson's property (as a prisoner's personal belongings are called when one is incarcerated) were the books in his possession. Although one may not be able to judge a book by looking at its cover, it is possible to understand much about a human being by the books they have on their bookshelf. When one has only so much space in which to collect those texts, the importance of each one magnifies. George Jackson had ninety-nine books in his prison cell when he was shot down by Sam Quentin guards. Each book was not only an insight into Jackson's interests, it was also a piece of his revolutionary education. When considered in these terms, this was a case of the sum being much greater than each of its parts. This statement is not to diminish the individual value of each book in Jackson's collection, but to emphasize the nature of the collection and its importance when considered in its entirety and as an education.

I have reviewed hundreds of books for *Counterpunch* magazine since 2002. After some conversations with my editors Marc and Donna at Fomite Books and upon Marc's suggestion, I have chosen one hundred ten of those reviews for this collection. This number was originally set at ninety-nine—inspired by the bookshelves in George Jackson's cell and is meant to honor him in its own way—but I kept on adding to the original ninety-nine. The books reviewed in these pages were, for the most part published since 2000; some are reprints of books published a few decades previous. The majority are non-fiction—history, political analysis, books about music and its social meanings, theory, and biography. The rest are novels. Topics range from the music and politics of Bob Dylan to the life of Kwame Toure, the nature of twenty-first century imperialism to the capitalist turn in China. There's a review of a book detailing the she-nanigans of Ken Kesey, Ken Babbs, the Grateful Dead and the Merry Pranksters. There's also a story of the Second Palestinian Intifada. I explore the humor and intricacies of Thomas Pynchon's *Against the Day* and am bedazzled by Peter Weiss's *Aesthetics of Resistance*. I hope the breadth of the selections is broad enough and the content deep enough to express my educational aspirations. When I was selecting these few dozen reviews, I tried to keep the idea of the reviews (and more impor-tantly, the books being reviewed) as part of an educational program in mind. I hope those who take the time to read the included reviews will walk away with a better understanding of the world we exist in and the possibilities for positive change that exist, even in the most hopeless of times. George Jackson lived inside a prison cell for most of his life, yet his optimism and belief that revolutionary change was possible in the nation he described as fascist remains the most important part of his legacy. Most of this book's readers will most likely never have to experi-ence the trauma that is prison, nor the psychological wounds being on the inside inflicts on most who spend time there. I state this to provide some perspective when despair and misery overshadow the possibilities for change in our modern circumstances.

Thinking about the number 99, I can't help but hear the electronic beat of the 1980s hit song by the German band Nena: 99 Luftballoons. The song is about a nuclear holocaust, the stupidity of war and the fantasies of the warmongers and the militaries and industries they are a part of. The line from the song, " Neunundneunzig Jahre Kriegs Ließen keinen Platz für Sieger" tells us there is no victory in the dust of nuclear apocalypse. The year the song was released was 1983. Europe was the theater for a confrontation between the Soviet Union and the United States in their cold war. The threat of nuclear annihilation was heightened by Washington's decision to place nuclear-armed missiles in countries across western Europe aimed at the Soviet Union. Massive protests took place across the global north, especially in Germany, the United Kingdom and the Netherlands against this arming for apocalyptic war. In the current moment, the possibility is perhaps greater than it was in the 1980s. For those who think about it, that makes it even clearer that it is not other nations that are our enemy, but the leaders of every nation (and those who line their pockets) who considers warfare a reasonable approach to international relations.

Books cannot change the world alone. However, they do have a power beyond the pages they are written on or the covers they are bound in. It is this belief that keeps me reading; it is also this belief that spurs me to write about them. These reviews stretch back to 2003. Some of the references and context is probably dated. I don't think this matters very much. Indeed, what is more remarkable is how so much of what is considered in the reviews and the books being reviewed is how so little has changed. I think it's helpful to consider this in one's perusal of the text. Names may have changed, but the situation is often frightfully similar and equally familiar.

Take your time. I hope this collection is merely an introduction to the texts reviewed herein.

2003-2008

The Politics of Bob Dylan

Chimes of Freedom: the Politics of Bob Dylan's Art—Mike Marqusee

Let me begin this commentary by stating clearly that I am a Dylan freak. That being said, I'm not going to go dig in his garbage like some others so identified have, nor am I going to assign any supernatural aspects to the man and his work. After all, he is a human, not a god. It's because of my obsession with the man's music that I read almost anything that is printed about him, though. Indeed, it is what drew me to the recent work on Dylan's Sixties persona by Mike Marqusee. This work, entitled *Chimes of Freedom: the Politics of Bob Dylan's Art,* places Bob Dylan squarely in the center (how's that for a Dylanesque image?) of the political and cultural upheavals of that age. Of course, this is exactly where Dylan and his work belong.

Marqusee is something of a Dylan freak himself and admits as much in his introduction. He is also the author of one of the best books out there written about heavyweight champion and poet Muhammad Ali: Redemption Song. In fact, he peppers his work on Ali with references to Dylan's songs and easily equates the two men's influence and impact on the decade.

Marqusee opens the book with a description of the so-called early Dylan-a political broadsider, activist and heir to the legacy of the obviously political wing of the folk music revival then underway in the US and Britain. Woody Guthrie was not only Dylan's model, Dylan was Guthrie reincarnated. His songs not only spoke of the anger that resided just underneath the hopes of civil rights activists-black and white-they pointed that anger not at an individual but a system. Even songs like "The Lonesome Death of Hattie Carroll," which tells the story of an African-American woman accidentally killed by a rich white slumlord for which she worked, does not point the finger at the killer. As Marqusee points out so eloquently, Dylan places that incident in the context of a system that not only encourages racism, but thrives on it. The final verse in the song points the blame at the system that gives the killer a mere six months for his crime of negligent homicide. This contextualization is further developed in the song "Only a Pawn in Their Game." For those unfamiliar with the lyric, this is a song about the system's tactic of divide and conquer-a tactic that keeps natural allies fighting amongst themselves for the crumbs that litter the floors where the rich and powerful sup.

In his discussion of these and other songs and their meaning, Marqusee equates Dylan's development with that many people (mostly young) were simultaneously experiencing individually and collectively. The largest left political organizations—SNCC and SDS–representing black and white youth respectively, were also coming to a realization that what they were up against in their quest for social justice was not just a few individuals but a racist system that needed war to survive. Dylan lost his innocence along with the rest of his generation. His reaction to this loss was also shared with his audience cum compadres. Sometimes it was raging cynicism, sometimes it was a retreat into drug-fueled fantasy, and sometimes it was insurrection. And sometimes it was all three. Perhaps Marqusee explicates this best in his thoughts on the song he titles the book after: Chimes of Freedom.

It is the author's contention that Dylan grew frustrated with being a mouthpiece for the left (This is a contention shared with most Dylan critics and even by Dylan himself). This frustration, along with a growing alienation from those who would attempt to define him, fuels a goodly amount of the next few years of Dylan's repertoire. Tired of being "a pawn in (anybody's) game," Dylan began to explore the politics involved in the liberation of the personal. These are the years for which Dylan is best known: the years that brought Bringing It All Back Home, Highway 61 Revisited, and Blonde on Blonde to the world's turntables. The songs on these albums redefined rock music, popular music, new left politics, and were essential to the creation of the ethos of the counterculture. Marked by excess and clarity, noise and poetry, Dadaism and Rimbaudian symbolism, these three albums stand alone in Dylan's tremendous output. Furthermore, argues Marqusee, they encapsulate the generation that Dylan never wanted to be a spokesperson for. It's not that these songs eschew politics; it's more like they move politics to a new level. Along with the efforts of the rest of those cultural workers writing and performing in the countercultural milieu, the new left politicos, and the freaks who inspired and responded to the former, there was a move afoot that hoped to make politics matter to the individual and the mass, and to change the world forever. Some of this was conscious and some of it just happened due to the confluence of action and thought.

Like other biographers/critics, Marqusee uses Dylan's fabled 1966 motorcycle wreck near Woodstock, NY as his next critical marker. While the rest of America (and a good part of Europe) were either joining the counterculture revolution or reacting against it, Bob was reclaiming some personal calm and rediscovering his musical roots. He and some friends (The Hawks, soon to be The Band) sat in the basement of a house soon to be known as Big Pink and jammed. Pulling influences from the country and R&B songs he'd listened to on the radio in Hibbing, Minnesota late at night as a teenager, the hillbilly and delta blues tunes culled from Harry Smith's Anthology of American Folk Music, and the rock and roll all of them had been listening to since their teenage years, these men recorded over a hundred songs which were soon in circulation as illegal bootlegs. At the same time, Dylan was slowly pulling together the songs that would make up the apocalyptic collection that he would name John Wesley Harding.

By the way, Dylan never has been a spokesperson; he has always been a poet. Marqusee places him firmly in the lexicon of music, performance and politics that marked the period known as the Sixties. He also notes the transcendent nature of his works, constantly reminding the reader of the current relevancy of so many of Dylan's forty-year-old (yes, forty) songs. Unfortunately, what this also means is that the political system that Dylan spent exposing in the Sixties is more entrenched than we thought. It also means that it's up to those of us opposing that system to not make the same mistakes again. For some guidance in that exercise, one might do well to listen (closely) to "It's All Right Ma, I'm Only Bleeding."

Religion and Political Power

The Meek and the Militant—Paul Siegel

In a time when it seems that religious justifications for the excesses of both revolutionary and reactionary impulses are the standard, Haymarket Books' republication of Paul Siegel's *The Meek and the Militant* is a useful resource for the individual looking for a rational analysis of the relationship between religion and power. The book, which was originally published in 1986, provides a historical overview of the world's five great religions and takes a look at their relationship to power both inside and outside of government and capital. Although Siegel utilizes a Marxist analytical framework in his work, the text is equally useful for the Marxist and non-Marxist alike. Unfortunately, Siegel died in 2004, which precluded any update before republication.

The Meek and the Militant is essentially a history of the world's great religions, with the most detail saved for Christianity and Judaism.. One of the things that makes the text valuable is that it turns the current assumption that religion shapes social forces on its head. Instead, the text rests on the premise that social forces shape religions. In a metaphor familiar to fans of the rock band Jethro Tull's Aqualung album—which examined the relationship of humanity to religion– The Meek and the Militant asserts that man created God in his image. After making this assertion, Siegel takes it several steps further, arguing that once created, the powerful among men re-created that god in their image and used that newly created god to maintain the servility of the rest of humanity.

However, because of the nature of religious belief and the incredibly powerful hold it has on the psyche of humanity. Religion also plays a role in movements opposed to the powerful's need to dominate. Examples cited in Siegel's work include the Puritan-inspired revolution against the King of England, the struggle against slavery in the United States and, more recently, the role of Catholic liberation theology in Central and South America, especially as regards the Sandinista revolution in Nicaragua. Because of the book's publication date, the role of radical Islam is barely scratched. Indeed, Siegel acknowledges its power but only in passing when he mentions the reactionary social forces of the Ayatollah Khomeini and their role in derailing the Iranian revolution of 1979. To his credit, however, he does discuss the all-too-common misrepresentation of Islam as a fanatical and warlike religion. Indeed, its history is no more or less so than the histories of Judaism and (especially) Christianity.

Despite the revolutionary power of religion–something that one should expect given the often radical nature of various prophet's pronouncements against their rich and powerful contemporaries–the historical fact is that when all is sorted out, religious forces usually end up on the side of power. This phenomenon is explored and instances of it are enumerated throughout Siegel's text, whether he is discussing evangelical Christianity and the robber barons in the US or Orthodox Judaism and Zionism in Israel.

Each and every time god was revived by those opposed to the power structure, whether it was the prophecies of Moses against the pharaoh and his gods or Jesus' Christian underground against the Pharisees' and their temples; to Mohammed's pronouncements against the excesses of Islam's monotheistic predecessors or Buddhism's proclamations against the Emperor's Confucianism; the oppositional religion evolves into that which it opposed. According to Siegel, this is due to religion's easy manipulation by the ruling classes—a manipulation that is facilitated by the contradictory nature of religion.

This contradiction lies in its promise of a life not of this earth. Consequently, its radical nature can be as easily defined to be otherworldly and in favor of keeping things as they are here on earth just as it can be utilized to effect change in this temporal state. Oftentimes, this transition occurs when an interpretation that turns a prophet's word of liberation inward–from the liberation of a people (the Jews, for example) to the liberation from sin of an individual being.

As mentioned before, this book was published in 1986. At the time,

11

Ronald Reagan was president of the United States, the Soviet Union still existed and was fighting the US-sponsored predecessors to Al-Queda in Afghanistan, and the Sandinistas were fighting a CIA-sponsored counterrevolutionary force in Nicaragua. The rise of the so-called Christian Right was just approaching its zenith and had just began to dramatically alter the face of US politics. Ronald Reagan, after all, was not George W. Bush. Not that the forces behind his throne were any different than those behind the current administration, but the parliamentary forces opposed to them were arguably more organized and considerably stronger than they are today. Part of the reason for that is the power that right wing Christians have in this country. This element of US religious power has essentially bludgeoned those in the US political arena that don't share their beliefs into submission. Indeed, it is as if they really did have the power to send us all to hell because we might oppose their design for world domination and eventual apocalypse. In addition, the role of radical Islam in all of its forms was as yet unrealized at the time of the book's publication. Consequently, the text suffers from its suspension in a time just before today's political reality, yet this does not detract from its true value, which is as a historical overview of religious history. Indeed, perhaps the most important lesson one can draw from this text is that religious belief can be a humanistic and revolutionary force just as easily as it can be manipulated against those forces. Furthermore, Siegel's historical commentary proves once again that the application of dialectical thought is quite useful in anticipating the future.

As we head into another year of uncertain carnage defined by Washington's belief in its own covenant with a god created in its own image and an enemy with elements of its leadership seeming at times only too willing to oblige in a comparable oppositional role, the historical insights of The Meek and the Militant provide a useful reminder as to the roles religious belief can play in a world of circumstances that cry out for revolutionary change.

"I Know I'm Not Dreaming, Because I Can't Sleep Any More"

Gate of the Sun—Elias Khoury

A few years back I was talking with a young socialist organizer about books. He had just asked me why I wasted my time reading fiction when there was so much non-fiction that needed to be read. Culture, I replied, reflects and illuminates a society just as much, if not more, than history or economics. Even when the fiction one reads is bourgeois fiction the story reveals the society within which the story takes place. If there is such a thing as proletarian fiction, it too reveals the lives and desires of that class. Peter Weiss's narrator in his marathon work The Aesthetics of Resistance, notes that "art could not be versatile and inventive enough…. Painter, poets, philosophers reported on the crises and confrontations, the concretions and awakenings of their time….one might social upheavals, yet in the multiplicity of mirrorings, of visual concentrations, one could always find a unity…."

In 1998, the Lebanese writer Elias Khoury published his novel *Gate of the Sun* in Arabic. This work is a powerful piece of literature that illustrates quite evocatively why fiction is important. The publication of the English translation in 2006 by the small Brooklyn, NY company Archipelago Books was an important event missed by much of the US cultural media. This is unfortunate for all involved. Although I do not read or speak Arabic (to my regret), I found reading the English translation by Humphrey Davies spiriting me into the soul of Palestine. Dream and reality flow back and forth becoming one. Fears, hopes, love and anger are more than theories on a page. Khoury's story makes these emotions real in the souls of the people and the Palestine they want to maintain.

Dr. Khalil, the narrator, is a former fedayeen who works as a doctor at a makeshift Palestinian hospital somewhere in Lebanon. It is sometime after the beginning of the first Intifada and the doctor is watching his adopted father die, having lost his blood father when he was very young when Israeli troops murdered him in the doorway of their home. Afraid for his life because of a threat on his life over a murky love affair, the doctor is also using the hospital as a hideaway. Since he has all the time in the world, he spends hours talking to his "father," a famous Palestinian fighter now in a coma. He is a man with many names, one of which is Yunes. This one-sided conversation is a collection of stories about the lives of the doctor, the fighter, the women in their lives, and the villages and camps where they have lived and fought. It is also a story of Palestine, its occupation and the struggle to free it. The doctor's tale covers the story of Palestine over the last seventy years. The story he tells reminds us that every side has its own history, indeed every individual on every side has their own. Despite this, the histories are more similar than they are different and all of them are filled with tears.

The comatose fighter to whom Dr. Khalil speaks is a hero in the sense that any fighter is heroic. Yet it is the women in the story whose heroism really shines through. They are the keepers of the stories and the carriers of the water. It is the mothers, grandmothers and wives that keep the memory alive of the lands from which they were driven. It is the women that carry the children and the old people as the Israelis drive them from one place to the next. Yes, there are women in this tale who are victims, but it is those that stand up to the tragedy constantly unfolding around them that provide hope in an otherwise hopeless story. Perhaps the best illustration of this is an episode where Nahilah, the wife of Yunes the fighter, is arrested by Israeli troops because she is pregnant. The troops know that she is married to Yunes and hope to extract his whereabouts from her. Despite torture and other abuse, she refuses to provide the information. Instead, she tells then that she is a prostitute and has no idea who the father of the child in her womb is. By risking shame and degradation, she protects Yunes' whereabouts and life. The Israelis finally let her go, not knowing what to do in the face of Nahilah's heroic lies.

What is nationhood? Why does it matter? These questions are seem to be a curse of humanity. The search for their answer is also what gives us hope and heroism. Khoury's narrator struggles with the meaning of these concepts on almost every page. Is it the land and the homes from which his people have been driven? Or is it the ideas and the culture that the people share? Is the loss of the land what makes the idea of a homeland even greater? Does the blood of battle render such an idea less sacred (if it was ever sacred in the first place)? These are the questions that Palestine represents and these are the questions that Khoury so eloquently asks in this tale of Dr. Khalil and his people.

The linchpin of this novel is the Lebanese civil war. More specifically, it is the massacre of Palestinians at the Shatila and Sabra camps in 1982. As most readers know, these massacres were carried out by Falangist forces with the assistance of the Israeli Defense Forces. The numbers killed are believed to be around 1500 women, children and old men. Dr. Khalil refers to these events in flashes of memory and as points of reference. He remembers the deportation of the fighters from Beirut and the eventual dissolution of the camps during an intrafraternal war he calls the battle of the camps. This episode is a metaphor for the greater reality of battle and suffering, Khalil tells the comatose Yunes, where the fighters fight and the women and children suffer and die. Is it so different from the story of the Jews in Nazi Germany, he asks?

Mr. Khoury has written a modern Exodus in a period of history that has seen way too many such stories. He has done so with an eye for the truth that is hidden in memory. Not always completely accurate in matters of sequence and detail, tales like Gate of the Sun relate the truth of the human condition better than any government or non-governmental agency. Perhaps it is a historical irony that the location of Khoury's contemporary Exodus is also the location of the one so many humans are familiar with from their holy books. Perhaps it's just a cruel coincidence. This book is art that illustrates what Peter Weiss called a "multiplicity of mirrorings" in his aforementioned novel. It is also a work that achieves the unity Weiss says we seek from such art. Either way, it is not only a story that is worth reading, it's a story one shouldn't miss, if only for how beautifully it is told.

From San Diego Up to Maine, In Every Mine and Mill

Subterranean Fire: A History of Working-Class Radicalism in the United States—Sharon Smith

I finished reading Sharon Smith's latest book, *Subterranean Fire: A History of Working-Class Radicalism in the United States*, on May Day 2006. Rather appropriate, I thought as I turned the last page of text, especially since this working class holiday began in the United States during one of its headier periods of working class solidarity and rebellion. Even more appropriate when one considers the resurgence of May Day protests in the US this year thanks to the movement to make undocumented workers legal.

Smith's book is exactly what its title suggests. This is the story of class struggle in the United States–a story told from the perspective of a radical leftist. Consequently, it's a history most folks who went to school in the US do not know. Why? Because the powers that run this country don't want them to. Smith has done an outstanding job telling it. Well-researched and well-told, Subterranean Fire informs the reader with lively writing and unembellished facts of oppression, exploitation and the fight against such phenomena.

Ms. Smith begins the book by detailing the history of US labor prior to the War Between the States. At that time, the US economy was primarily agrarian in nature and depended on the enslavement of Africans and their descendants for its strength. Subterranean Fire not only acknowledges this, but discusses the essential role that slavery played in the creation of the US economy. Like others before her, Smith analyzes the international slave trade, the economics of Southern plantation growers, its repercussions for white-skinned workers, and the economic aspects of the US Civil War.

Furthermore, Smith keeps an eye on the reality that racial discrimination has played in the history of US labor throughout the book. Whether it was the use of African-Americans as scabs or the constant tactic of divide-and-conquer based on skin color by business or the refusal of the unions to allow black members, the role that the uniquely US racial situation plays in keeping the working class in constant uncertainty is detailed here. In addition, this history proves via its descriptions of various strikes and radical unions (most notably the IWW) that when workers ignore the prejudices of society and unite across racial and ethnic boundaries, they are more likely to win. The current struggle for immigrant rights in the US could learn from this lesson, especially among those US workers that believe it is the immigrant that drives their wages downward, not the corporation.

Today's news constantly runs stories about workers taking concessions and massive company layoffs. Smith's analysis holds that this is directly related to the conscious retreat from class-based struggle and the purge of leftists from US unions after World War Two. It is this historical fact that is also responsible for the continually falling numbers of union members throughout the United States. This model of unionism, known as economism by various leftists, helped prevent the development not only of a labor party in the United States, but also of politically oriented unionism. Instead of demanding that the government represent the majority of Americans–that is, the workers of the country–unions and their members got involved in providing pensions and health care to their members. In other industrialized countries where the labor movement is represented in the legislature by various labor and leftist parties, such issues are the duty of government. Of course, in today's neoliberal/neoconservative world, workers in those countries are finding their health care and pensions under threat from governments taken over by big business.

Speaking of worker's parties, the specter of the various anarchist, socialist and communist groupings looms in the background of Smith's text. She details the twists and turns of the Socialist Party, USA and the US Communist Party (CPUSA). It is her conclusion that the two organizations failed the workers of the country. The Socialists did this by acceding the leadership to the party's right wing, while the CPUSA stumbled in the wake of its Popular Front politics before and during the Second World War–politics that were determined by the Stalinist regime in Moscow more than by the situation in the workplace and on the ground in the United States. The anarchists failed, writes Smith, because of their determination not to be vanguardist. It was the latter's organizing and anti-capitalist politics, however, that insured the worker's movement would maintain its radical spirit and politics. This, writes Smith, is why they were targeted for deportation, harassment and elimination by the State and Big Business.

There are stories in this book that should be part of every textbook in the United States. The attacks on the miners in the Appalachians, the Ludlow massacre of women and children in Colorado, the police and military attacks on striking textile workers in Gastonia, NC, the remarks of various capitalists regarding their opinion of those that made them their riches, the persecution of labor and other radicals throughout the past 150 years, and the manipulation of the public by the two-party system–a manipulation that means the worker gets screwed no matter who he or she votes for. Women on the barricades and the Wobblies. Likewise, the tales of racial and ethnic prejudices that caused strikes and solidarity to fall apart should be told. This latter aspect of US labor history is very important today as immigrants flex their political muscle in the streets of the country and the power elites attempt to create and widen divisions between these immigrants and those US workers that were born here. If workers don't learn from history and oppose these attempts to divide us, Subterranean Fire makes it abundantly clear that all workers will suffer. And only the bosses will win. When lessons from our history are common knowledge we can move ahead in a manner that will bring a movement back onto US soil that protects the lives and rights of the working people in this country.

Smith's book is the perfect vehicle for such an endeavor. It is a readable, lively tale of the worker's movement in the United States. A collection of statistics and anecdotal stories combined with a critical analysis, it is at times despairingly downbeat and at other times exhilaratingly hopeful. Subterranean Fire's a piece of agitational literature. If there's one message that exists in its pages, it is this: Don't just read, organize.

Back in the Aether Again

Against the Day—Thomas Pynchon

Thomas Pynchon's *Against the Day* is the story of a quest. Perhaps for a reason; perhaps for reasons beyond reason. Perhaps for an understanding of the human experience. The story of a family named Traverse, which must be more than a mere family name. The father, Webb Traverse, ostensibly an itinerant miner in North America's West a couple decades after the US civil war, he is also a bomber whose sympathies lie with those opposed to the robber baron capitalists that populate the estates and boardrooms of the United States. The men whose general perception of the men from whose sweat and blood they make their millions is a perception that sees those workers as unworthy of life. Pynchon doesn't exactly condemn capitalism as much as he describes the inevitable progression of that system of economics to its ultimate expression in war and bloodshed. Which is condemnation enough. To the robber baron Scarsdale Vibe, Webb Traverse is somehow different. He is considered not just an opponent, but an opponent that must be sought out and killed. Once dead, he is brought to a place that is beyond boot hill, beyond Tombstone–a place where vultures of the human and avian type rule. Reading this particular section, I was reminded of William Burroughs' grotesque visions of the western lands. As it turns out, the youngest Traverse is provided an education by the same robber baron that ordered Webb's death. The daughter, meanwhile, marries the trigger man. Of course, the desire for justice cum revenge reveals its head along the plot line. Indeed, two of the brothers begin their travels with exactly such a thought. The Traverse family finds itself part of every facet in the tale. Mathematics and monopoly capitalists. Anarchy and anal sex. Airships and manned submarines built by Italian anarchists. Meteors that change the earth and murders accompanied by grotesque tortures that defy belief. It is not a pretty world provided here, but it is an interesting one that is full of adventure and surprise.

In the distance of time, a foreboding of human catastrophe lurks. Sometimes it is spoken of by travelers from the future. These are travelers who bend time and live in their own as well as the past. Other times, the coming catastrophe is spoken of by clairvoyants and con men. Above and beneath it all is the search for an ancient place, a holy grail, known as Shambhala. There resides a secret of life. Meanwhile, a weapon that destroys everything is for sale. It appears to be entropic in nature from the clues Pynchon provides. The Chums of Chance–a Tom-Swiftian group of adventurers that fly above the earth in a cloaked airship, call these travelers The Trespassers. The Chums, who introduce the entire work, believe at first that it is The Trespassers who are bringing on the coming apocalyptic event: an event that we readers have the luxury of history to tell us is World War I. The Chums fly on, taking orders from men they do not know and meeting many of the other characters in the novel. Eventually, they become aware that they are being used by forces they resent. Indeed, this is the case for most of the folks in the story. The sexually unusual Cyprian, the youngest Traverse, Kit. Even the gunmen and the women. As the reader, we of course have the advantage of seeing this, although even we are being manipulated. Isn't that the nature of art?

Ah yes, the women, not femme fatales but often very femme–the major ones being the sensuous and sexually adventurous mathematician and enchantress of unknown origin, Yashmeen; the strikingly attractive American girl Dahlia (or Dally), equally at home with street urchins and princesses, who grows into a woman over the course of the novel; and the Traverse women: Mayva the matriarch, Lake, her father's silent storm who marries his killer, and Stray, lover of both Frank and Reef Traverse and the mother of Reef's first child. She then reinvents herself as an adventurer, trader and friend of the Mexican anarchists. Women that are intellectually stimulating and physically desirous, they inspire all sorts of intrigue and shenanigans of every nature. Like other Pynchon tales, one could state that the novel itself radiates out from the few women who appear throughout the story.

Light is another radiant character here. Light bifurcated by pieces of crystal spar and light bent by mirrors that create likenesses as real as the thing or creature reflected. The abnormal bluish light and eerie glow that covered the planet in the wake of the Tunguska event of June 30, 1908 and the light of love, especially that of the unusual threesome of Reef Traverse, Cyprian and Yashmeen. Light that can destroy anything if manipulated in that way. Light that is the fundamental element of the mysterious Q-weapon and the Interdikt line that anarchists hope to destroy in order to prevent the war that is on its way. Light of mystery and mystical light.

Mathematics plays a starring role, much as it did in Pynchon's 1973 novel Gravity's Rainbow. It's a mathematics beyond the accountants books and the ledgers of the rich. Mathematics full of symbols and a language of its own. A language whose meaning provides clues to the meaning of existence and how the world exists. Mathematics whose various approaches creates devotees in the same way as religious cults. It's a math that always somehow leads to suffering and death. Yet we pursue it anyhow for the power it might provide us. Or for the pure beauty it provides—a symmetry of description that puts the world that is chaos in an order we believe we crave. It's a math where the sum of the angles of a triangle are greater than 180 degrees because the earth is curved not flat. Non-Euclidean and the gateway to Einsteins Theory of Relativity. Mathematics that strives to include the fourth dimension—time. Once included in the formula, time as we know it ceases to exist. We are here there and elsewhere all at once. Then again, so is everyone else. Mathematical poetry and magic, not to mention the tarot.

The ancient Greek concept of the Aether is the firmament on which much of this story resides. The stuff of alchemists and their creations, it is the Aether that transfers light and energy. Beyond that, it holds all matter together. Firmament that is not solid. This aether was believed to be the substance which filled the region of the universe above the terrestrial sphere. Aristotle included it as a fifth element distinct from the other four, Earth, Water, Air, and Fire and its Platonic solid, according to Plato, was the Dodecahedron. Humanity that likewise refuses to maintain its former shape and concepts. The age of invention. Tesla discovers an energy source in the ground capable of providing free electricity once it is properly harnessed. Of course, the robber barons do not want Tesla to succeed These capitalists have discovered the incredible profits to be made when they allow the profit to accumulate through acquisition and murder, thereby allowing them to accumulate even more. Anarchists and Bolsheviks understand the same process and hope to destroy it.

The situation described in these pages is one of present and future danger. It is a danger descended from technology and its (mis)uses. It is also a danger precipitated by the worship of and desire for profit and more profit. Individuals live their lives as if they are theirs to live but all the time wondering if they are merely puppets controlled by forces greater than even those who pay their bills. At times almost primitivist in nature, the opposition to this world one finds in these pages stems from a belief that science is wrought with danger. This belief doesn't come from the lack of scientific knowledge that is often the basis for religious fears of science, but from an overwhelming knowledge of science's potential. Indeed, it is the place where find ourselves today.

In Riemann geometry, there are no parallel lines and x is infinite when it's a negative number, but finite when it's a positive one. In Against the Day, only the number of pages is finite. The possibilities considered are without end. It is an adult Tom Swift series of adventures; a piece of historical fiction that is also an adventure with the requisite subplots of love and intrigue. This book is a marvel of lyrical descriptions of everything from various appearances of the sun to sexual practices frowned upon by "normal" society and the machinations of the parallel world of espionage, revolution and counterrevolution. The writing is what we have come to expect from Pynchon: sentences that loop toward a conclusion one can hardly wait to arrive at. Despite this desire, one finds oneself lingering–sometimes because the loop reads like one of the mathematical formulas trying to explain the unpredictability of human or geologic events. Other times one lingers on a sentence or phrase because the words assembled are structurally so complete they stand alone like a Taoist epigram. There must be a meaning behind the symbols on the page. Despite Pynchon's imploration to the contrary in his pre-publication blurb (found on Amazon and elsewhere), one can not help but think of the present day, with conflicts breaking out around the world and corruption and greed a way of life among certain classes.

Some critics will gripe that the novel is incomplete; that it leads nowhere, but this is not the case. This novel leads to the beginning of the human catastrophe we now call history-the Twentieth Century. Just as Gravity's Rainbow provided a uniquely subversive and anarchistically creative perspective on the world created in the destruction of World War Two, Against the Day provides us with a similarly subversive perspective on the opening act to the drama in which that war was Act Two. Despite the bleakness of the times that these tales are told, an indomitable beauty resides within them, thanks in large part to the characters Mr. Pynchon creates, the stories that they live, and the approach to the telling by the author.

Remembering and Re-examining the Third World

The Darker Nations—Vijay Prashad

Becoming politically aware in the 1960s and 1970s, one heard and read a lot about the Third World. Not only did the national liberation struggles of the Third World inspire many in the New Left to take action, those struggles also informed how us what form that action took. In fact, one of the terms used to describe various organizations–derogatorily or in praise–was "Third-Worldist." For example, the Weather Underground was considered Third Worldist and the Revolutionary Union wasn't. Those US leftist groups that were defined by their race and/or ethnicity went a step further and identified themselves as members of the Third World. This was not much of a leap, given the similarities between the exploitation of non-white members of the US population and seemed especially true in the case of the black population of the United States. Malcolm X was one of the first leaders of the 1960s to express this view and the Black Panthers and others picked up the concept after Malcolm's death. Not only did the idea of an internal black colony have a certain appeal, it made a certain amount of historical sense. In addition, it placed the black freedom struggle in the United States in an international perspective.

For those coming of political age after the fall of the Soviet Union, the concept of a Third World might seem antiquated. After all, as Vijay Prashad explains in his new book *The Darker Nations*, the concept derived from the so-called two-camp theory put forth by the United States after World War Two. This theory held that there were only two superpowers in the world–the United States and the Soviet Union. Every other nation would be best served by aligning themselves with one or the other of these camps. Naturally, both capitols would do their best to include as many nations as possible in their camps, since this served their needs for protection and expansion of markets and resources. This is not to say that there was not a difference between Washington's need to expand its capitalist enterprise and Moscow's desire to have some kind of socialist world, but to point out a fundamental understanding that runs through Prashad's book: the Third World saw nonalignment to either capitol as most beneficial to its own goals of independence and local development so they formed a movement of non-aligned nations. These nations shared a viewpoint that countered the view that the first and second world were somehow better. At times, according to Prashad's account, this was the only view they shared. Still, it was the view that united them.

Prashad divides his book into chapters titled after cities that represent milestones in the growth and demise of the Third World The titles are a shorthand travelogue of the third world's history. Some represent formative meetings that were held in those cities. Others represent meetings and incidents that precipitated the project's demise. Those meetings that took place early on in the non-aligned movement's (NAM) formation between the likes of Egypt's Nasser, India's Nehru, and Yugoslavia's Tito reminded me of today's meeting's between Venezuela's Chavez and Ahmadinejad; or those between Chavez and Bolivia's Morales. In other words, they were attempts to create a united front against the imperial power of the United States, despite the differences between those countries looking to form that front. As Prashad makes clear throughout his work, although the Third World nations insisted on independence from both the US and the Soviet camp, the predominant view among those nations was that US imperialism was the bigger threat to their independence. Time has proven them to be tragically correct.

Naturally, many of the nations considered part of the third world were birthed in national liberation struggles against their colonial masters–Britain, France, and the Netherlands, among others. While these movements provided real material leadership and support to the peoples they were determined to free from colonialism, they also provided inspiration to millions of others around the world. Unfortunately, it was their failure to make a transition from national liberation movement to democratic government that added to the difficulties these nations faced in the wake of victories that were usually accompanied by the enmity of Washington. When those national liberation struggles were military in nature, that transition became even more difficult, especially when considering the major transformation required when shifting from a hierarchical military structure to an inclusive democratic one.

The hopefulness of the book's first chapters is soured by the time the chapter named after New Delhi arrives near the book's end. This chapter describes the end of the Third World project. Although the NAM summit described therein was a phenomenal event, with Fidel Castro leading the charge as the movement's outgoing chairman, it was a hollow celebration. Many of the richer nations involved in the project's headier days had already thrown in their lot with the US capitalists and their growing neoliberal project of capitalist globalization. The victories of the 1970s in Vietnam, Nicaragua, Grenada, Ethiopia, and the Portuguese colonies in Africa were either bittersweet memories or under direct attack from the United States and its forces. In the place of these victories and the hopes they had symbolized, the elites in many of the third world's governments had begun a sell-off of their nations' resources, labor and markets to the multinational corporations headquartered in the world's north–especially in the US. The descriptions Prashad provides of these elite's manipulations of ethnic and religious differences, their replacing of a nationalism informed by a third world united against imperialism with one defined by the religious/ethnic majority's chauvinism is a tragic tale. If one wants an example of this process in a relatively brief and bloody illustration, they need only look at Iraq in 2007. All of the elements Prashad details in his book are there: national elites incorporated into the neoliberal economic model, IMF austerity measures encoded into law, national identity obscured by religious and ethnic differences, and all of this instigated and encouraged by Washington,, which wants control of the country's resources and (some would argue) its soul.

Prashad's book is part of The New Press People's History Series. According to Howard Zinn's preface, the goal of the series is to "shake up readers' understanding of the past–just as common people have shaken up their always changeable worlds." Prashad does a great job in The Darker Nations–the series premiere. He chronicles the rise and fall of the Third World Project, and describes the contradictory hopes of the project's beginning and its implosion. His thesis that the project failed as much from Washington's aggressive opposition as from Moscow and Beijing's sometimes purposeful inattention and the movement's own social and political contradictions is well made and concretely supported.

Return of the Guitar Army

Guitar Army—John Sinclair

It's hard for some of us who were around to remember and even more difficult for those who weren't to believe, but youth culture was once considered to be a revolutionary phenomenon . Of course, we didn't call it youth culture (that was a media catch phrase), but looking back, that's what it was. Indeed, that's part of the reason why it didn't last like we wanted it to. We couldn't figure out how to maintain it once we got older. So, capitalism took over and turned the whole thing into a commodity. Some groups and individuals that were politically inclined understood the revolutionary nature of a culture that opposed imperial war and racism and, more importantly, that challenged these phenomenon with their bodies and minds in the streets. Their attempts to organize this varied from the somewhat fumbling attempts of the Weatherman to the humor inflected approach of the Yippies. Then there were the White Panthers.

The brainchild of John and Leni Sinclair and a dozen or so other residents of Ann Arbor, the White Panthers were a counterculture revolutionary kernel that understood that in order to change the system one needed to not only change the economics and distribution of power, one also had to change the culture. John Sinclair ended up in prison not long after the White Panthers were formed. He was sentenced to ten years for giving two joints of marijuana to a woman who was a undercover narcotics officer. The White Panthers (and their successor the Rainbow People's Party) worked in alliance with the Yippies and the Weather Underground and represented the aspirations of thousands of youth across North America during their brief existence. They put on rock concerts and festivals, managed the rock group MC5, operated food cooperatives and a newspaper, and yet their greatest lasting achievement is probably the book penned by John Sinclair himself–*Guitar Army*.

A collection of writings on rock and roll, youth culture of the 1960s and 1970s, the formation of the White Panthers and a myriad of other rants and reviews, Guitar Army is being re-released by Feral House Publishing of Los Angeles. This book is a freakin' manifesto of the times. Naturally, some of it is dated in terms of context and the language overblown at times, but the discussions of the potential of culture to change people's thinking and the corporate world's understanding of that still ring true. Any modern rock or hiphop artist who really believes in the power of music to change the world should read this book. And, even more importantly, they should heed this book! So should those who listen and dance.

John Sinclair, who nowadays spends his time in Amsterdam and on the road with his band, The Blues Scholars, is a true believer in the power of rock and roll to change the world. Although the times have certainly changed since the first time such a thing seemed a political possibility in the western world, the fact remains that rock music changes lives every day. Think of the first time you heard the Rolling Stones' Beggars' Banquet disc. Or maybe it was "Hurricane" by Bob Dylan. Or maybe something even older by Mr. Dylan. Maybe it was the Clash's "White Riot" or a tune from Rage Against the Machine. Or Sly Stone and his band singing "Stand!" Or maybe even "Johnny B. Goode." Or something from the MC5. Whatever the song was, you gotta' admit that rock and roll changed your life.

The difference between these personal epiphanies and the program of cultural revolution that the White Panthers, and millions of others fought for thirty–forty years ago is that they made it into a political program with the goal of revolution the end. In the cultural realm of rock and roll this meant disconnecting the channels of distribution from the system of capital and the minds of the audience away from those of passive consumers. It meant connecting the record corporations to their holdings in the war machine and challenging them. It meant hooking up with the Black Panther Party and working in the white community for the liberation of blacks and other oppressed people in the United States. It meant taking it all into the streets and using the music as a means to change the way one thinks and the way the world works. It meant that while the music and the culture that it created was important, there had to be radical economic and political change, too. The answer to this assault on the powers that were was jail time for the organizers, big record contracts for the bands, police attacks on the concerts and communities where the counterculture gathered, and Richard Nixon and Spiro Agnew–two establishment guys who really, really didn't get it.

Guitar Army reads like a history book in this context. It begins with the dawning of the rock and roll age–Elvis and the rest–and takes the reader from the beat culture to the hippies and the political freak culture of the late 1960s and early 1970s. Cops busting concerts and peoples apartments. Riots in the streets over the war in Vietnam and solidarity with the Black liberation movement. John Sinclair thrown in prison for ten years for two joints of reefer and John and Yoko joining with the MC5 and others to free the man from what was clearly a political verdict. And the MC5 kickin' out the jams, motherfucker.

This book was published right around the historical moment that the political new left and the counterculture reached a critical mass in the minds of many youth and in the streets of the western world–especially the United States. Sinclair addresses the commodification of the counterculture by hip and not-so-hip capitalists, yet his words should resonate when he claims herein that the music still is the most important thing because no matter what, the people making the music still control the means of production.

A website connected to Audioslave/Rage Against the Machine guitarist Tom Morello and Serj Tankian of System of a Down called Axis of Justice has listed Guitar Army on its recommended reading list since the site went online several years ago. One hopes that the book's increased availability due to its republication will make these ideas that some consider naive and dated new again. Just in case the reader might be wondering what the book's message might sound like, the publishers have tucked a CD of rock music, poetry and rants in the book's back cover. Check out "The Motor City's Burning" by the MC5. It's not only time to free the music from the corporate machine, it's time to free the world from the war machine. Those of us in the belly of the beast have a role in this struggle. A rock and roll soundtrack always helps.

Architecture as Military Strategy

Hollow Land: Israel's Architecture of Occupation—Eyal Weizmann

The recent assumption of control in Gaza by Hamas (2006-7) may be more illusory than US media has represented it as. As Eyal Weizman makes clear in is fascinating and detailed book *Hollow Land: Israel's Architecture of Occupation*, there are innumerable and often invisible security apparatus set up across the region that ensure almost absolute control of the region's surface, airspace and subterranean acreage by the IDF and other Israeli security forces. The book, which takes the idea of an architecture of oppression written about by Mike Davis in his book City of Quartz and applies it to the paranoid security regime of Tel Aviv, is a tale of the intentional construction of a suburban security state. It is a state that provides an illusory reality of swimming pools and ranch housing for the occupiers and an increasingly barren, crowded life for the occupied.

Weizman is the Director of the Centre for Research Architecture at Goldsmiths College of the University of London, so he knows about architecture. His work with various NGOs and human rights groups in Palestine has given him the opportunity to observe Israel's ongoing campaign to disconnect (if not eradicate) the Palestinians from their land. As his book makes clear, this campaign is not accidental, nor is it something that only began because of the armed struggle waged by Palestinians against Tel Aviv's occupation. It is, in fact and deed, part and parcel of the Israeli project from its inception. Furthermore, this campaign has been waged in the military and architectural sphere in collusion with Israel's imperial cohorts–primarily the United States and Britain.

By banning certain materials and the construction of abodes by certain elements of the existing population of Palestine, the Israelis have been able to not only push Palestinians from their ancestral lands, they have also been able to borrow their aesthetic methods to construct a Jerusalem and Israel that looks like a television version of the Old Testament. Meanwhile, in the Occupied Territories, the settlers have built (with millions of dollars worth of government monies) suburban subdivisions with walls that block out the villages and camps around them. At the same time, these suburban settlements serve a role similar to the US Army forts of the Old West. In other words, they provide surveillance points and advance groupings of troops to keep the occupied indigenous people under control.

It is this juncture of civilian architecture and military strategy that provides some of the most interesting aspects of Weizman's work. A reader of US mainstream newspapers probably assumes that the Jewish settlers that set up their tents and trailers in the middle of a crossroads used primarily by Palestinians are acting alone and against the wishes of the Israeli government and military. Indeed, some folks probably even find these settlers lives to be slightly romantic, like the settlers of the Native American territories of North America. Yet, as Weizman makes clear, things are not necessarily as they seem. In fact, many of these settlements are begun where they are precisely because their presence serves a uniquely military purpose. Which brings us back to those US Army forts set up across so-called Indian Territory in the American Old West. These settlements are as much military outposts as they are living spaces. They are not innocent developments made just for people who want to live in peace in the land of their religion.

Because of their situation under occupation, the Palestinians find themselves in a double bind. In order for them to maintain a hope of return, they must maintain their refugee status as defined by the United Nations. In order to do this, they must not build anything that can be considered permanent. Consequently, there is never a sense of permanence in Gaza and the West Bank. On the other hand, this temporariness allows Israel to take continuous "security measures" whose main purpose is to permanently expand the borders of the Israeli state. This was seen during the Oslo negotiations of the 1990s when settlers and the military continued to grab land while the negotiations continued. It is also present in the never-ending incursions into Gaza and the West Bank by the Israeli military (despite the supposed withdrawal from Gaza in 2006.) Regarding those incursions, the Israeli Knesset is currently debating a bill that would declare Gaza a foreign entity. If passed, this law would allow the Israeli military to do whatever it wants to Gaza and its inhabitants and not owe them a shekel for reparations. Under the current status, Tel Aviv is supposed to pay the owners of the homes they destroy. Of course, this doesn't happen too often , nor does Gaza have true independence. Yet, this bill would make everything Israel does legal (and without any legal repercussions), just like the expulsions of Jews carried out by the Nazis and the arrests of undocumented immigrants in the United States.

In what can only be termed a postmodern attempt to control all dimensions of space, the Israelis have constructed a multilevel system of roads, checkpoints and walls in and around the Occupied Territories. These roads are restricted to Israeli traffic and provide the travelers with a means to get from one settlement to another without ever having to see a Palestinian. Meanwhile, the construction of the so-called Apartheid Wall (by its detractors) often prevents Palestinians from tending their crops and visiting their family that happen to be on the other side of the Israeli-constructed barrier. Of course, in order to build the wall, the Israelis found it necessary to destroy any houses and fields that lay in the path they had determined for its construction. It is a path, by the way, that continually shifts according to the needs of the Israeli military and various commercial enterprises hoping to develop certain areas not currently on the Israeli side.

In addition to the Wall, the Palestinians find themselves waiting hours at roving checkpoints set up by the Israeli military, often for no apparent reason other than to remind the Palestinians of the Israeli's control. Since the Palestinians can not use the Israeli roads, tunnels are dug under the roads so they can get from one point to another without setting foot on the road. Tunnels have also been dug by the Palestinians for the express purpose of getting past Israeli security. It is these tunnels that the Israelis destroy houses in Gaza to find. So. Like the NLF forces in Vietnam during the US war on their country, the Palestinians have also turned to a subterranean network to wage their resistance. This has furthered the perception of a multidimensional battle–the postmodern conception of space referred to above.

Regarding postmodernism, Weizman points out that the Israeli theorists behind much of the recent construction in Israel and the Territories are students of such postmodern thinkers like Gilles Deleuze and Guy Debord, whose concepts of non-linearity and critiques of postcolonialism have been turned on their head by the Israeli military and used to overcome the asymmetry of the Palestinian resistance and to reinforce the occupation of Palestinian lands. In short, the military has taken some of the principles of these social and cultural critics and reworked them to serve their needs.

Weizman's text is a dense, yet readable work. While a familiarity with the Israeli occupation and its history is useful to one's understanding of his claims, it is not essential. Nor is it necessary for the reader to be well-grounded in architectural theory. Fascinating in its detail and often alarmingly straightforward in its conclusions, Hollow Land lays bare the intelligent brutality of the Israeli occupation of Palestine and its architectural engineering. Furthermore, it reveals the nature of that occupation–a nature that can best be described by borrowing the title of a book written by Hannah Arendt about another type of engineering. What Weizman details within these pages is nothing less than a modern day example of what Arendt so aptly called "the banality of evil."

A Sports Nation of Millions

Welcome to the Terrordome—Dave Zirin

Dave Zirin loves sports. He is also one of sports' sharpest critics. And he's pretty damn funny. His newest book *Welcome to the Terrordome* exhibits all of these traits. It is a critical and unrelenting look at the place sports has played and continues to play in these United States and around the world. Zirin borrows the title from Public Enemy, the premier political hiphop group of all time (with KRS One and BDP a close second) and he opens the book with a look back on the terrordome that was the New Orleans Superdome in the aftermath of Hurricane Katrina. You remember the stories coming out of there about murders and rapes – stories that proved to be false. However, do you remember the origins of the Superdome in the destruction of a working class section of New Orleans – ethnic cleansing as urban renewal? In case you didn't, Dave Zirin reminds you of the ugly role money and greed played in that construction project. He goes further, critiquing the continuing construction of sports stadiums with public monies while the nation's educational and social services infrastructure disintegrates into nothingness.

And that's just the beginning. Naturally, Zirin addresses racism in sports. Indeed, it is his contention that sports is where the US struggles with race are played out on a daily basis. To make his point, he discusses the manipulation of hiphop culture by the National Basketball Association (NBA) to gain new fans only for that to be followed by a nasty attack on the culture's street roots. He also writes about the great baseball player Roberto Clemente's antiracist attitudes and the globalized racism inherent in Major League Baseball's (MLB) recruitment of Latin American and Caribbean players while the overall African-Americans presence in the sport continues to decline—not because of the rise of Latino players but because of MLB's decision to go where the talent is cheaper and easy to manipulate. Then, of course, there's Barry Bonds who is, according to some people the bogeyman of professional baseball because he may have used steroids. As Zirin points out, there are many other players not named Barry Bonds who have admitted to using steroids and they don't get half the grief Bonds does. To be fair, Barry isn't by most accounts the most pleasant man, but that is no reason to treat him like the Boston Strangler. Zirin rightly argues that MLB and the team owners are as much (if not more) to blame for the steroid era in professional baseball as any player or group of players.

Whenever I think on the role of race in US sport, I go back to the opening pages of Ralph Ellison's masterpiece The Invisible Man. It is there that we find Ellison's protagonist – a nameless African-American man – in a room filled with cigar smoke and fat white men drinking alcohol. The white men are there to be entertained. They tell the narrator (Ellison's invisible man) and a few other black youths to don blindfolds and boxing gloves. A naked white woman with a US flag painted on her body dances in the room. The youths than proceed to fight each other for the white men's entertainment in what is termed a "battle royal." In the final round the invisible man, loses to the victor. The white men then throw a bundle of coins on the floor and the youths scramble for the money, only to discover that there is an electric current running through the rug that shocks the youths over and over and that the coins are not gold, but brass tokens advertising a car dealer. In other words, they have no value, despite their prettiness, much like the fancy cars and shiny bling worn by many of today's professional athletes.

Welcome to the Terrordome is a book that describes and analyzes the real world version of Ellison's "battle royal." Young men of color seem to dominate most professional sport at the major league level, yet the paying audience in most stadiums and coliseums is white and reasonably well off. The coins thrown at them are many, but they come with a downside. While it is not an electrical current, it is a demand that these athletes keep quiet and, in the NBA (and the Yankees), wear suits. It's not that wearing a suit is a big deal, but the demand that these young men and women not speak their minds runs counter to the American illusion of free speech. The few that do speak out run the risk of not only ticking off their employer, but losing their job and ending up far away from the highlight reels.

Yet, there are those that do risk their current gig as ballplayers. It is these men and women that Zirin champions throughout his book. These are his heroes. Men and women who play games well but also stand for something more than good statistics and bling. He writes about people from the past like Roberto Clemente and Jim Bouton and current players like Etan Thomas of the Washington Wizards and Sheryl Swoopes of the WNBA's Houston Comets. These and other like-minded athletes are anything but invisible.

The late Gonzo journalist Hunter S. Thompson once said something to the effect that sports journalism is the only place in journalism where a writer could use techniques more familiar to fiction. Dave Zirin's writing takes the essence of Thompson's thoughts on sportswriting and succeeds dramatically. In addition, his humor and leftist politics only enhance the points about modern sports Zirin wants to make. My son, who is one of the biggest sports fans that I know, will get a copy of this book. So will a friend or two who tell me that they could care less about sports, since there's a political struggle to be won. In the Hegelian framework, Zirin's book is the perfect synthesis for all of them.

For the Sake of a Future

Flying Close to the Sun—Cathy Wilkerson

One of the email lists I belong to is made up of a few former students at the University of Maryland. All of the members were involved somehow in the radical student movement at the university in the 1960s and 1970s. Much of the listserv discussion is over political questions of the day and the members arguing equipped with a variety of viewpoints across the spectrum. More interesting in terms of history, however, are the names that occasionally pop up when one or the other member is recalling their glory days. Some of those names include local heroes and renegades while others are the names of nationally known scholars and political figures.

One name that pops up regularly is Cathy Wilkerson. For those that don't recognize her, Wilkerson was among the leadership of the Students for a Democratic Society (SDS) during its heyday. She was the head of the Washington DC region for SDS and editor of the organization's newspaper New Left Notes. She was also a member of Weatherman/Weather Underground. It is because of that membership that she was living in her father's townhouse in Manhattan on March 6, 1970 when the building exploded as a result of a wiring mistake during the building of a bomb by fellow Weatherman members.

Wilkerson is also the author of a new memoir titled *Flying Close to the Sun*. This book is less about the Weather Underground and the bombing than it is the story of how a young person from a well-off family from the United states develops a political conscience. It is a personal look at how one's political growth is also part of one's personal development; how the development of a moral standard can drive one to accept and commit actions that seem contradictory to that conscience. It is also a uniquely personal take on the history of the radical movement in the United States from the early 1960s until the mid-1970s.

When I am invited to classes to talk about the Left radical movements of the aforementioned period, there are always those in the audience who seem to be looking for some kind of psychological flaw in the members of those movements. It's as if they are unwilling (or unable) to accept that people in the United States can become political radicals for moral and political reasons. This is especially the case when groups like the Weather Underground are discussed. While Wilkerson's narrative is strictly her narrative, it relates a trajectory not very different from most middle-class and wealthy members of US radical movements. It is the story of hopes dashed by elected leaders preaching democracy, frustration with supposedly democratic channels that do more to prolong war and racism than end those ills, and the growing awareness of the power of the people. Furthermore, it is the story of the moral dissonance created upon realizing your family's financial well-being depends on other families' misery. It's a tale of frustration with the fact that power in the United States is directly related to wealth and the amorality of that wealth and the pursuit of ever more wealth it requires to exist.

At times, exciting and at other times reflective, Flying Close to the Sun is always captivating. Wilkerson's descriptions of undercover police activities against SDS show the seriousness of the government's fear. The discussions of her internal emotional and intellectual conflicts complement the descriptions of the political discussions within the movement while simultaneously providing the reader with a different understanding of how the personal does become intertwined with the political. Like most activists of her age, Wilkerson's radical politics were directly related to the discovery that racism was not only entrenched in US society, but essential to its development. This realization came through her observation, then participation in the civil rights movement that eventually ended legal apartheid in the country. In the minds of many activists that came of age around the same time as Wilkerson, there was nothing that white skinned people could do that would be enough to end racism's bloody and terrible legacy.

While this perception is crucial to understanding the nature of the US economy and its accompanying governmental policies, the guilt-driven desperation this analysis often brought was part of what fueled the decision by many white activists to reject anything having to do with that legacy. It is a decision that Wilkerson acknowledges helped place her fellow revolutionaries in Weather outside of the movement. It's not that many in the movement didn't agree with the essential nature of Weather's argument that ending racism was core to ending oppression and creating a new world, it's that they didn't share Weather's frustrated rage that tended to go nowhere. Wilkerson takes a look at Weather's macho posturing and examines her reasons for going along with it despite her misgivings. She writes critically about the results of the lack of a structure in SDS and the resultant hierarchical relationship between the Weather leadership and the various cadre. In addition, she examines the nature of revolutionary violence and its validity in the long term.

There are several books out now that look at the legacy of the Weather Underground Organization. Some are histories by outsiders and some are memoirs (including the recently republished With the Weatherman by Susan Stern). All of them are good reads and useful to the serious and casual historian. In addition, they provide several relevant insights to today's radicals regarding the pitfalls of organizing in the belly of the beast. Wilkerson's stands out among all of these books for its thoughtfulness, carefully worded discussions and the fact that it is the narrative of a woman's involvement in this most interesting period of history. For those that don't like straight history but want to know more about this particular period, Flying Close to the Sun might be your best bet.

The Bebop of Baraka

Tales of the Out and the Gone—Amiri Baraka

Amiri Baraka has always played with the language and, by default, our minds. His poetry and his prose often reads and sounds like a jazz improvisation that Sun Ra and Coltrane could have created. Words become sounds and the sounds of the words take on meanings never before conceived. In terms of politics, Baraka's tales are about men and women who fought in the streets and about a politics that begins where every one else's end. Like Sun Ra, he understands the place of dark-hued people in the west to be akin to that of a brother from another planet. It's not because the brothers and sisters who don't have pink skin aren't human. It's because the pink-skinned ones treat them as if they weren't. Don't believe it? Look at the history, say Baraka. Then tell me it ain't true!

Baraka began his writing as one of the only Blacks lumped in with the Beat movement in American writing. Still running with his Christian name of Leroi Jones, his poetry stung and each sting acknowledged the poison of racism. Two of his 1960s theater pieces, The Dutchman and The Slave, threw the misconceptions of white racism in the audience's faces–liberal or not. Like his then-named compatriots H. Rap Brown and Stokely Carmichael, Baraka threw the racist aspects of integration back in the liberal sociologist's face. Your education is better because it takes place in suburbia? Bullshit! Your god is better than mine now that you got him all blue-eyed and pink? Bullshit! It wasn't pretty, but it made the point better than and in spite of Thurgood Marshall and the NAACP.

The recently released collection of writings from Mr. Baraka titled *Tales of the Out and the Gone* proves all of the above points and more. While it is always somewhat difficult to review a collection as a whole–and this book is no exception–there are some things here that are consistent. Most importantly is the language. Playful and pointed, Baraka takes the language of the beats into the language of the streets and back again, reminding us all that the original source of hip culture is the black culture of America's streets. Bird and Monk, Black Nationalism, Muslims and Marxists. Stories about GIs and hookers in Puerto Rico and one about a butler who takes a revenge worthy of Nat Turner. Lilting bebop exercises in poetical prose that bounce around the inside of your skull in a manner befitting John Coltrane's cadenzas on the Ascension recordings. Multiple dimensions on a two dimensional surface. Sun Ra, too, would understand.

Baraka divides the book into two sections. One he titles "War Stories" and the other contains the "Tales of the Out & Gone." Somewhat more linear in their telling, the war stories are of the times long ago. Protests and politics. Women and jazz clubs. Dudes who did it right and dudes who did it wrong. Women who loved and women who made love. Good stuff that's not always fun. The out and gone are exactly that. Words get shortened like the one you just read. Poetry that appears as prose and little fables about our lives in postindustrial capitalist America. Baraka writes in a way that makes you read some things twice and still hear something new the third time around. He carries a tune with his words much better than the average writer–poetry or prose.

It is this that makes this book so enjoyable to read. The subject matter is overwhelmingly dark like Raskalnikov is dark. The writing is overwhelmingly fun, even hilarious at times. There are moments herein when skin color and the accompanying racism are everything and there are other times when they are not. This is good stuff for today's world–a world that we are told is beyond racism and discrimination based on skin tone. A world where this lie is merely the correct way of saying whiteness is back on top. Racism isn't gone, no matter what Condoleeza Rice, Bill Cosby, or Barack Obama might say. And no matter what the leftists say, it ain't just about class in the US of A. It's about skin tone, too. Centuries of enslaving black people, killing red-skinned ones, and treating yellow and brown-toned folks like vassals or cattle doesn't go away just because some laws were passed (or not). The discrimination and oppression becomes more sophisticated and, yes, class becomes a more obvious part of the mix, but anybody who thinks that WEB DuBois color

42

line is a thing of the past is fooling themselves, no matter what part of town they hail from. The recent outbursts by various US comedians are but one more proof of this actuality. Then again, so are the recent figures regarding US residents in prison or on parole and probation.

Racism is not gone. It is, however, better disguised. Someone needs to remind us of this fact. Thankfully, Mr. Baraka does exactly that. Quite cleverly, I might add.

Shellshock and Redemption

Casualty Figures—Michele Barrett
Long Shadows—ed. David Giffey

By now most everyone is familiar with the phenomenon known as Post Traumatic Stress Disorder or PTSD. We associate this disorder primarily with veterans of combat. What many people do not know is that this disorder was included into the bible of therapeutic mental health disorders only after a long struggle by the Vietnam Veterans Against the War and some other US veterans organizations in the 1970s. Prior to that inclusion, veterans who were suffering from what was then commonly known as shell shock were left to their own demons or, in some extreme cases during wartime, executed by the military for cowardice under fire. Even today, some returning vets of the Iraq and Afghanistan engagements who have symptoms that suggest PTSD have been accused of faking these symptoms to get out of a third or fourth tour in those battle zones. In fact, in one recently publicized incident, the Surgeon General of the Army ordered military counselors to stop processing requests for psychological assistance from GIs returning from Iraq and Afghanistan.

Michele Barrett's new work from Verso titled *Casualty Figures* takes a look at the lives of five men who fought for the British military in the First World War and suffered some form of shell shock. The five vignettes that make up the bulk of the text include passages from the men's letters home to family and loved ones.

They also include brief sections of unpublished accounts by the men themselves regarding their battle experiences. Those experiences included battles where 10,000 of the German enemy and 3,000 British soldiers died in one battle. The stories also tell of men being holed up in trenches for days on end with nothing but corpses to keep them company and other tales of battlements being built from the corpses of the enemy. They relate moments of realization by the individuals portrayed that the war itself was pointless and served no soldier's interest, no matter who he was fighting for.

The two most interesting men portrayed by Barrett are Bombardier Ronald Kirth and Air Vice Marshall Sir William Tyrell. After Kirth refused to obey an order to bombard a church, he was demoted to a lower rank and lost his leave and some of his rations. This experience and his experience that caused the death of a friend when they were bombarded while manning a pill box led him to become a pacifist. The death of his friend and the events immediately following the bombardment when Kirth was catapulted several meters into the air caused Kirth to experience total amnesia. That episode would be the first of many such experiences. Realizing that he would not have suffered this if he hadn't been in the pill box (or the war), and understanding that the amnesiac episodes are his brain's method of coping with that he saw and felt, Kirth became opposed to all wars.

Tyrell, on the other hand, saw his bout of shell shock as a weakness that he must destroy by becoming tougher and more military-like. The rest of his life was spent doing exactly that, both in his professional military life and his personal life. The stories of these two men vividly illustrate the nature of a society steeped in militarism and its effect on individuals subjected to the militarists' propaganda and institutions. Likewise, the stories of the other three-two who died young and a third who lived within himself until he died-show the effects of those who fight the militarists' wars for whatever reason. Indeed, it is these three who may be more typical than either Kirth or Tyrell.

By telling these stories, Barrett brings home to the reader the pointlessness of modern war and the damage it inflicts on the survivors. Looking through the lens provided by Barrett's selection of these five men's stories, the reader is reminded quite graphically of the consequence of one of humanity's bloodiest adventures in human slaughter-World War I, the war to end all wars. Many of the men who ended up dead from wounds in World War I nowadays survive similar wounds thanks to medical progress. Unfortunately, this fact only seems

45

to make war more palatable to the politicians, generals, arms manufacturers and powerbrokers that depend on it for their livelihood.

Long Shadows is a book similar to Casualty Figures in that it relates the stories of men (and two women) who served in the military. The difference, however, lies in the fact that the individuals in Long Shadows decided to use their experience and the trauma it caused to work towards opposing future wars of power and empire. It wasn't always an easy path to that decision for these folks, but it is one that all of the individuals writing in this collection believe to be the best one they could have made. The nineteen veterans whose thoughts and memories appear in this book are all members of the Madison, Wisconsin Clarence Kailin chapter of Veterans for Peace, an organization of veterans with over 120 chapters throughout the United States. The collection's writers include a veteran of the Spanish Civil War, vets of World War Two, the Korean War, the war in Vietnam, an Israeli-American vet, and veterans of the Middle East and Asian wars that began with Desert Storm in 1990.

Evocative and often heartwrenching, these stories are a collection of epiphanies by men and women who discovered through personal experience how terrible and pointless war really is. While many of them are now pacifist, one or two are more specific in the wars they oppose. Specifically, they oppose wars of empire and conquest, while supporting the right of people to defend themselves from invasion and occupation. Coming from all walks of life-wealthy, poor, farmers, city dwellers, progressive and reactionary, white skinned and black-each of the individuals underwent a transformation either during their wartime service or in the years succeeding it that brought them to a point where they felt the only option was to speak out no matter what the cost. Some, like WW II vet Charles Sweet, came to this decision because of their children. Others, because of their need to deal with personal demons and guilt. One or two never would have predicted while they were serving that they would join the ranks of the antiwar protesters. Still others, like Will Williams, needed to find a place to transpose the anger within himself (an anger growing from the racism he experienced as a black American) into something positive.

If you don't tear up at least once while you read this book, then you are not capable of tearing up. Whether it's a veteran telling the story of seeing his buddy die or his attempts to deal with the torture and wanton killing he either took part in or was unable or unwilling to stop, the emotional level of these memories left this writer drained. Some of the vets herein were diagnosed with PTSD, but most were left to deal with their demons on their own. Still, the book is not all wretched sadness, Indeed, it is the hope for a more peaceful future growing out of the struggle these men and women have joined that is the overriding message in these pages.

As the friend of several members of living and deceased Vets for Peace, I responded immediately and positively to editor David Giffey's request to review Long Shadows. Having grown up in a military family during the Vietnam era, I think I understand something of what it is like to buck the expectations of relatives and society and take a stand against the military and its purpose. For those who actually wore the uniform to reject it and the brainwashing and come through that intact is worthy of respect. To use those experiences in support of preventing others from becoming veterans is even more noble. That, I believe, is the primary intention of the men and women appearing in this book. That is also why you should share this book with those currently serving or considering such a move. It might convince them to change their mind.

Riot Squads, Privatization and the National Front

GB84—David Peace

In 1984, the Thatcher regime and the British National Coal Board annulled an agreement reached after the 1974 British miners' strike. The Board told the British public that they intended to close 20 coal mines and privatize the previously nationalized industry. At least twenty thousand jobs would be lost, and many communities in the north of England and in Wales would lose their primary source of employment. The Thatcher government had prepared against a repeat of the earlier successful 1974 industrial action by stock-piling coal.

David Peace, a British crime novelist, was a teen at the time who lived in the region of Britain most affected by the strike. He became known to the British and US crime fiction reading public with his series of four books about the Yorkshire Ripper—a British serial murderer. These four books, known as the Red Riding Quartet, are as much about police corruption and criminality as they are about the serial murders. Cops on the take. Cops running prostitution rings and pornography outfits. A police chief that tells his select group of officers that since there will always be vice, then the cops should be the ones that control it. Murders of prostitutes and criminal opposition and the destruction of witnesses' lives. False arrests and frameups. There are no redeeming characters that survive in Peace's Quartet—only the most corrupt and evil. It is a bleak look at human life in the twilight of British capitalism and a despairing prediction of a future many of us now inhabit.

Maggie Thatcher was the Prime Minister than and her ruthless disregard for human life that did not serve her intended resurrection of capitalism and empire in colors that bled toward the fascist National Front is the underpinning of Peace's work. If there was one political event besides the ongoing trouble in northern Ireland (including the H Block prison situation, many spectacular bombings by the IRA and provocateurs posing as IRA, and the growth of the Protestant paramilitaries), it was the aforementioned miner's strike. Of course, Peace wrote a novel about the strike. It is a novel that reads best with Elvis Costello's first two albums, Billy Bragg's War and Peace EP, and maybe something by The Smiths playing in the background.

That book, titled *GB84*, is nothing short of stunning. Told in two parallel narratives, its portrayal of corruption, political machinations, and corporate and government heartlessness makes the desperate situation of the miners and their union superreal. One strain of the narrative is told by a striking union miner who details the lives of men on strike who lose their homes, their wives, their children, jobs and dignity. The other strain is the story of the union leadership, its government counterpart, and various police and corporate operatives that operate in different levels of secrecy. Some are M15 and some are private contractors with ties to the National Front. Some are double agents whose final allegiance lies with the government of the ultraright Maggie Thatcher. Like the Quartet, there are ambiguities in the story, but only in as much as there are ambiguities in real life. Interpretation, after all, is a part of the whole.

GB84 is about the savagery of capitalism. Jackboots and legalized police beatings of unarmed strikers. Secret hit squads and government/corporate sponsored organizations of police pretending to be miners whose job is to convince the strikers to scab. Democratic forms and fascist realities. The war of the super rich against the workers. This is David Peace at his best. There is no beauty here. Some of the union officials demand sacrifices of their members while they secretly hole away funds for a future after the union's demise. It is these leaders' distance from the travails of the members and their proximity to the slime intent on profit at the workers' expense that corrupts them. Indeed, it is as if they cannot help themselves as they fall into the abyss of selfish concern for their own future while the union crumbles under the onslaught of big time capitalists and their governmental conspirators whose ruthlessness knows no bounds.

The miner's strike was a symbol of resistance during the reactionary

1980s. It was simultaneously an example to corporate capitalists the world over of how the battle must be fought if they wanted to stay on top. No more negotiations with workers and no respect for their lives. Resistance to the will of capitalism should not be legitimized by negotiation but destroyed through violence. The defeat of the strike and the privatization of the national economy in Britain was a harbinger of the neoliberal future we now live in. It is a future that for many is as bleak and despairing as Peace's master work. It is also a future that more of us may soon be sharing. When the shock of economic collapse heightens, there will be nothing left to protect us. Like the miners worn down by the systemic strangulation of their union in the mid-1980s, the only response will appear to be one that increases our isolation from each other and, like so many fish fighting over a fisherman's chum, leaving us to fight among ourselves with the final victory being one that leads us to certain death at the hands of the fisherman. The only possible redemption might be in a rebirth of solidarity amongst those currently fighting over that chum.

Che Guevara Meets Trashman

Che: a Graphic Biography—Spain Rodriguez

Like many of my contemporaries, I grew up on comic books. From the mainstream graphic fiction starring Billy Batson and Archie to the alternative realities of the Zap Comix universe and the Freak Brothers, those stories with pictures entertained me and enhanced my world. Nowadays, comic-styled tales and interpretations of classic novels claim a popular space in libraries and bookstores across much of the world. Many of the graphic novels are geared towards a youthful audience and deal with teen angst, vampires and such. Others are designed to convince the reader of a certain point of view and are often published by an organization or group with a particular point of view. Then there are those that stand alone.

The recently released *Che: a Graphic Biography* stands among the latter. Drawn by one of the most political of all the underground comix artists from the 1960s and 1970s–Spain Rodriguez–Che is the story of the revolutionary Che Guevara. Spain's detailed drawing and direct storytelling is more than an introduction to Che Guevara. It is a classic of the graphic genre. In the past, Spain used his radical passion and artistic skills to tell the story of the Spanish anarchist military hero Buenaventura Durruti. He created one of the most interesting characters and scenario in comix fiction in his Trashman series and drew some of the most intricately beautiful singular panels that ever appeared in the Zap Comix series. The writer of the text in Che is Paul Buhle, a longtime radical, a founding member of the defunct journal Radical America and a writer who has at least two other radical comix to his credit: the 2007 release Students for a Democratic Society: A Graphic History and Wobblies.

Che is drawn in a manner quite similar to the Trashman comics. Quasi-proletarian in its styling, the story is told in a shorthand that emphasizes landmark moments in Guevara's personal and political life. The reader follows the journey told in Che's Motorcycle Diaries and watches as Spain points to incidents and people that educated Che to the ways of the capitalist world and moved his worldview towards revolution. From there, the reader is taken to Mexico where Che begins a commitment to the Cuban revolution. Key moments in that revolution and Che's role in it are drawn and told. From there Che goes to Africa and then to Bolivia where he meets his end at the hands of the CIA.

Spain was always the most politically radical of the underground comix artists. His work never shied from putting his belief in the need for revolution and freedom on the page. There's a panel in the first Trashman comic that features a billboard in the dystopian future inhabited by Trashman and the humans he fights for and against. The message on the billboard reads –in a clear reference to the behavior modification theories of B.F. Skinner made popular among some in the power elites in his book Beyond Freedom and Dignity–"Beyond Freedom and Dignity Lies Fascism." That message, delivered in the offhanded manner that it was yet in the context of the proletarian counterculture superhero Trashman fighting those who would use their money and power to control us all in their pursuit of profit, has remained with me as much as Marx's admonition to lose our chains.

Che was not a superhero. He was a man. Despite the current fascination with his image and its use by many around the world, that is the most important lesson of his life. He worked constantly to change himself into the new man he hoped to create in the world, but he existed still as a human being like the rest of us. Spain's comic biography of him reminds the reader of that fact. Simultaneously, it reminds us that we too are capable of creating similar change in ourselves and the among our fellow humans.

Comics like Spain's Che are more than pictures. They are more than the words put sparingly on the page. They are a medium designed to help their readers imagine a world defined by the ink lines of the artist in an effort to bring the story alive. In the case of Che Guevara, the dynamism of the story is more than enough to turn those lines from two dimensions into three. Combined with Spain's comparably dynamic artistic style, the contradictory force that was Che Guevara is truly brought alive in this work.

2009-2013

Remembering the Second Intifada

The Second Palestinian Intifada: A Chronicle of a People's Struggle—Ramzy Baroud

I finally got around to reading Ramzy Baroud's 2006 book *The Second Palestinian Intifada: A Chronicle of a People's Struggle* on the twentieth day of Tel Aviv's most recent attack on Gaza. While debating with various online acquaintances about the possible intentions of Israel's government and watching streaming video from Al-Jazeera inside Gaza, I began to read this volume. Hoping to understand what I can't understand–why Israel insists on what seems to be a path towards eternal war that will never guarantee its security–I was drawn into Baroud's description of the events leading up to the Al-Aqsa intifada that took place for some five years after Ariel Sharon took thousands of Israeli troops and police forces with him to the Al-Aqsa mosque in September 2000. In the days that followed hundreds of Palestinians were killed and wounded by Israeli security forces. Soon afterwards, the much criticized Palestinian strategy of suicide bombing began, bringing the death and destruction visited on the Palestinians into the cafes and shopping areas of Israel. These murderous acts were naturally responded to by further murderous acts by Israel, with the end result of hundreds dead and wounded on both sides, although the Palestinians took an exponentially larger number of those casualties.

Baroud, the editor of the Palestine Chronicle, is a partisan observer. He makes no bones about his belief that Palestine should be free and that the Israeli occupation of Palestinian lands is a crime. His description of events in this book are written with a passion and occasional anger that does not spare Israel or Washington's role in the ongoing oppression of the Palestinian people. Concurrently, he does not spare his criticism of the Palestinian resistance, the makeshift Palestinian governing body known as the Palestinian Authority (PA), or the strategies undertaken by these forces. Most telling in this latter regard is his discussion of the corruption of the PA and various Palestinian businessmen discovered selling Egyptian concrete to the Israeli companies building the separation wall that divides the Territories into sections Israel hopes to manage by destroying communities and livelihoods. He also roundly criticizes the morality and strategic sense of suicide bombings.

The question of Palestine is on one level a very simple one. It has the right to exist in peace. This means that its people have the right to conduct their own trade, decide on their own government, live free from the fear of attack, travel freely, and educate its children and give them hope for the future. This can only occur when it is no longer occupied. Israel knows this and, if our eyes are to be believed, has no desire to see such a scenario take place. After all, Israel refuses to acknowledge the results of Palestinian elections, ignores most agreements it has made with any of Palestine's leaders, refuses to allow Palestinians freedom of movement, restricts education in the West Bank and Gaza, and attacks the territories at will. As Baroud, points out, Israel does all of this not only because it can, but because it is allowed (if not encouraged) to by Washington and many European governments. Until this fact is no longer a fact, Palestine's future will be one that is defined by more of the same.

The Second Palestinian Intifada: A Chronicle of a People's Struggle is an eloquent and evocative book based in part on the premise that Palestine, like Israel, has the right to defend itself. Over and over Tel Aviv and Washington were told the world that the murderous attacks on Gaza a few weeks ago were justified because Israel "has the right to defend herself." Baroud's narrative makes a clear argument that Palestine also has that right. Indeed, it is Palestine that needs the world to help in its defense. Unfortunately, unless the people of the West see through the mythology of Israel as victim that pervades our media, Palestine's day is a long way off. Writers like Baroud take their task to separate the truth of the Israeli-Palestine conflict from the Washington-Tel Aviv mythology seriously. So should the rest of us who care about peace and justice.

Mr. Baroud published this book in 2006. Right before its publication, Hamas won a substantial number of seats in the Palestinian legislature in certifiably free elections. Israel and Washington quickly disavowed the results despite their demand for democracy in the Middle East and Israel began a blockade of the territories that is supported by the US and many European governments. Hamas and other resistance movements in Gaza fired several thousand rockets into Israel, killing a little over a dozen Israelis. Hezbollah stood its ground against Israel in a summertime war while the West Bank slipped further into economic and political despair. Israel pulled its troops out of Gaza, but left their siege intact via air force flyovers and surveillance. This siege culminated in the December 27th, 2007 air attacks on Gaza that preceded a ground invasion. This action by Israel killed around 1500 Palestinians, many of them women and children.

His Terrible Swift Sword

The Old Man: John Brown at Harper's Ferry—Truman Nelson

On the New York side of Lake Champlain sits the little town of North Elba. Outside of the town is the homestead of American anti-racist revolutionary John Brown. When I lived in Vermont, I made a trip across the lake one May Day to commemorate the man whose actions against slavery did more than all the words written to force the US to end that diabolical practice. The homestead is a National Historic Landmark now, yet in his heyday Brown was reviled by many of his countrymen, north and south. He was admired and respected by many others. For those few that might be unaware, John Brown's raid on the Federal Armory in Harper's Ferry, West Virginia was the spark that lit the raging inferno that became the United States Civil War. If the Civil War is the defining moment in the history of the United States and the historical moment that virtually every major domestic political moment since then hearkens back to, then the Harper's Ferry raid is that history's moment of apocalyptic creation. The raid itself failed due to miscommunication and misplaced hopes, but its place in history stands with the battles at Lexington and Concord that began the American colonists' war for independence from England.

Naturally, volumes have been written about John Brown, his life, dreams, anti-slavery escapades and the culmination of it all–the raid on Harper's Ferry, his trial and execution for treason. From WEB DuBois' biography to the fictionalized tome titled *Cloudsplitter* by US author Russel Banks, the number of words written about Brown rival those written about the man that history knighted to carry the war against slavery to its ultimate end, Abraham Lincoln. One of the best of these works is the recently republished *The Old Man: John Brown at Harper's*

Ferry by Truman Nelson. First published in 1973, when elements in the New Left had taken on Brown's mantle in their attempt to end US imperialism and racism by setting off bombs in buildings and black liberation fighters were being hunted down by the federal government and its allied forces, Nelson's work focuses solely on the raid in Harper's Ferry and its aftermath.

It is a riveting story told in a captivating narrative that takes the reader into that small town in the West Virginia mountains. The physical details are here–the planning, recruiting, purchase and smuggling of arms, and the training. So is a discussion of the political philosophy behind Brown's endeavor. It is a simple philosophy and one still worth striving for–a nation without slavery and with equal opportunity and choice for all.

The Old Man describes a nation splitting apart. Anti-slavery legislators attacked in Congress by men whose very lives are bound to the practice of the bondage of other humans. Men who would never consider breaking a law tired of waiting for the political system to end slavery deciding to fund Brown's insurrection. The Christian churches split between those who would use the Bible to justify slavery and those whose interpretation forces them to conclude that enslaving other humans is the work of Satan. Financial interests looking after their own interests who care little about the morals of slavery but only about the money that can be made by supporting it or ridding the nation of it.

Through it all, John Brown's terrible swift sword remained true. He saw slavery as the abomination it was and understood the northern capitalists who did not align themselves with the abolitionists to be the opportunists they were. His vision of a post-slavery United States did not see the black man or woman as a lesser being but as a genuine equal. This was something that was even beyond the thought process of many abolitionists. Yet, it mattered not to Brown. Some called this madness, yet it was merely the single mindedness of a man with a just mission. Compromise rarely extended to Brown's approach and never to his principles. Nelson tells us that he was not unreasonable, just certain of his reason for being on earth.

The raid on Harper's Ferry was to be the first salvo in the fight to free the slaves. Indeed, in a harbinger of the coming War Between the States, it was future Confederate General Robert E. Lee whose unit was sent to quell the Harper's Ferry insurrection. Despite the arrest of Brown and most of his co-conspirators and their hanging, that raid served its purpose. The foul institution of slavery was wiped from the United States. We continue to deal with its legacy. As the recent refusal by a federal appeals court in Georgia to commute Troy Davis' death sentence and the ongoing mockery of justice known as the trial of the San Francisco 8 continues in California make clear, the bonds of slavery have been removed, but the forces that represent the slavers' legacy have not disappeared. As for the meaning of John Brown's armed attempt to free slaves in Harper's Ferry, it continues to prove its meaning to the oppressed in the United States.

The Untold Story of Afghanistan

Afghanistan: The Untold Story—P. Fitzgerald;E. Gould

In the first week of 2010, five US soldiers were killed in Afghanistan. The last week of 2009 saw the deaths of eight CIA agents there. Several more Afghan civilians were killed during this period, including the apparent executions of several young boys by persons either in the US military or working with them. In addition, insurgent forces targeted a Karzai government in official in eastern Khost and launched rockets at the site of a future US consulate in Herat. It was reported on January 6, 2010 that the Obama administration was sending 1,000 more US civilian experts to the country to help in so-called reconstruction projects. This news was greeted with skepticism from Afghans both in and out of the government. The Afghan ambassador to the United Nations noted that few Afghans trusted these so-called reconstruction endeavors and that the US might do better if they hired Afghans to do the rebuilding instead of shipping in US citizens to "create parallel structures that would ruin (the Afghan government's) efforts." The ambassador must be quite aware that the history of US reconstruction in either Afghanistan or Iraqis is a legacy of corruption, poor construction and failed endeavors that benefited no one but the foreign companies that garnered the contracts.

Despite the aforementioned situation and the eight years of comparable failure that preceded the weeks described above, the Obama administration is sending at least 30,000 more US troops into the Afghan fray. In addition, there will be an untold number of mercenaries added to the numbers of occupying troops. Like his imperial predecessors in Washington, London and Russia, Barack Obama is convinced that his army can somehow shape Afghanistan into a nation that will do the bidding of the empire he leads. As the authors of *Afghanistan: The Untold Story* make clear, his chances for success are slim. History is not on his side.

This book, published soon after Barack Obama's election in 2008, is a look at Afghanistan's history with an emphasis on the past one hundred years or so. The nature of Afghanistan's place in regional and international struggles for power and control in Central Asia are the primary subjects. From Alexander the Great to Barack Obama and General McChrystal, Afghanistan has spelled frustration and in every case so far, it has also meant defeat for the invader. The authors, journalists Paul Fitzgerald and Elizabeth Gould, present the reader with the details of Great Britain's perennial failure to subdue the armies of Afghanistan no matter who was ruling that nation.

According to Fitzgerald and Gould, the primary reason for this was the debate over the Pashtun dominated areas(Pashtunistan) that were claimed by Britain under the Durand agreement yet were considered by Afghan nationalists to be part of Afghanistan. Even as it was losing its empire, London ensured a continued struggle over these lands and people when they created Pakistan out of the Indian subcontinent and split Pashtunistan in two.

After World War Two the United States moved into Great Britain's former colonies, forming defense and economic pacts in its desire to encircle the Soviet Union. Like Great Britain before it, Washington's interactions with Afghanistan exhibited an ignorance of Afghanistan's historical desire for non-alignment. This ignorance was combined with an insistence that any expression of that desire proved that Moscow was influencing Kabul's politics. Fitzgerald and Gould write that this was not an accident. In fact, it was the logical outcome of a 1950 national security directive known as NSC 68. This directive, written by the anti-communist and militarist wing of the US foreign policy establishment, insisted that the Soviet Union was intent on establishing world hegemony and that the only way to defeat this was for the US to do so first. The essence of the philosophy motivating this directive was simple: one was either on the side of Washington or one was the enemy. The direct result of this directive was the creation of a permanent war economy and the creation of a national security state. In practice, some of what this meant was that national liberation struggles and national desires for non-alignment were perceived to be Soviet-inspired and therefore part of the enemy camp. Furthermore, US residents who opposed the policies of the US were considered to be potentially traitorous.

In the Muslim world this view led to the beginnings of Washington's courting of the Islamic right. A fundamental reason for this alliance was the Islamic right's hatred of Marxist philosophy. In addition, certain US powerbrokers, like William Casey of the CIA, considered the Islamic right to be their spiritual brethren, at best ignoring their misogynist and murderous methods and at worst tacitly endorsing those practices. The alliance began with the British MI5 and CIA's surreptitious assistance to elements of the early Muslim Brotherhood in its struggle against Egyptian nationalist Abdel Nasser and found its ultimate expression in the arming of the Afghan mujahedin under Carter and Reagan.

The US involvement in Afghanistan that began under Jimmy Carter was not an accident. It was the result of a concerted effort by the US Right to regain its power in the wake of the US defeat in Vietnam. Led by neo-cons Zbiegniew Brzezinski and Richard Pipes and aided by liberals like Barney Frank and Paul Tsongas, this ultimately successful effort represented a resurgence of the pro-militarist wing of the policy establishment as the primary architect of US foreign policy. According to the authors, what it meant for Afghanistan was that Washington "was (now) backing a class of mullahs and landowners that had been fighting any social reform for generations" and was involved in a "process that drove social evolution in Afghanistan back to the Stone Age." The mujahedin war and what followed destroyed the social progress made under previous Afghan governments. Women and girls were relegated to second-class status and fundamentalist intolerance became the order of the day.

The history told within these covers is the story of an ancient nation whose intention in the past century or so has been the creation of a free and tolerant society. It is also a history of a nation whose geography has placed it in the middle of many a battle for control by greater powers intent on colonization. The struggle for tolerance and fairness has taken place under monarchies, socialist regimes, autocratic capitalist regimes and democracies. It is the authors' contention that this struggle erupted into

63

a civil war when the US began arming warlords and reactionary religious forces in its war against the Soviets. The chaos that has occurred in the wake of this decision resulted in the destruction of the forces working in favor of modernity and the rise to power of the forces of reaction. At this point in time the chaos in Afghanistan has devolved into a battle among powerful warlords and the Taliban, with the US siding with various war-lords in the fight against their progeny-the Taliban. This book puts the responsibility for Afghanistan's desperate situation directly in the laps of US policymakers: the corruption of the Karzai government, the Taliban, the acid-in-girls-faces, the warlords, the heroin trade and so on. It also asks whether or not this was the intention of those policymakers all along.

If there is a shortcoming to this text, it is not in the writing or the history, but in the implication that it is solely the neoconservative elements in the US power structure that are responsible for Afghanistan's recent past and current situation. One might go along with this implication if it weren't for the historical record. Every Congressional vote to fund US aggression in Afghanistan has been anything but close, while the US mainstream media has rarely if ever questioned the war or the reasons given for that war. Indeed, when Ronald Reagan was posing for photos with the mujahedin, they were hailed as freedom fighters in every mainstream outlet. The policy of the US in what is now termed the AfPak war is not a policy of the right or the liberals, but of most of the Washington establishment. The muted response to Barack Obama's recent escalation of it is but the latest evidence of this fact.

Afghanistan: The Untold Story ends with a set of recommendations for Barack Obama. The first and the last of these recommendations are their essence. Number One is simple: stop killing Afghans. The last one is a little more complex. Fitzgerald and Gould recommend that the debate over the United States national identity be reopened. According to them, this debate was closed down on December 7, 1941 when the Japanese attacked Pearl Harbor and the national security state became ascendant. From where I sit today, it looks like Mr. Obama has considered neither of these recommendations. Indeed, his policies are essentially a continuation of the past. If one wants proof, I suggest they read Obama's speech justifying the escalation of the war in Afghanistan and the news stories regarding the ongoing killing of Afghan civilians by US forces.

End of the Revolution

The End of the Revolution—Wang Hui

Back in 1989, the world was captivated by media images of hundreds of thousands of Chinese students and workers camped out in Tienanmen Square in Beijing. Most were horrified as they watched elements of the Chinese People's Army attack and kill hundreds of these protesters. The series of protests that are now summed up in the words Tienanmen Square were but the most public presentation of the struggle between the Maoist legacy and the move towards capitalism that has been going on in China since the 1970s. For many Chinese, it represented the end of a popular democratic urge for greater political freedom and its replacement with an authoritarian capitalist paradise (for the capitalists and their government facilitators). In other words, the result of the protests and the government reaction was that the only freedom that would be allowed in the post-Mao China was the freedom of global capitalists to exploit the Chinese people and reform its society to their benefit.

Chinese writer and Professor of Chinese Literature Wang Hui was one of those hundreds of thousands in Tienanmen Square in 1989. He is a critical observer of Chinese culture and politics and is a member of what various western media call the Chinese New Left. His newest English release, titled *The End of the Revolution* is a collection of essays mostly dealing with the effects of China's pugnacious pursuit of an essential role in the global capitalist order on its people and politics. Academic in its approach, Wang Hui's text details the demise of Maoism and its replacement by a political structure and culture that is socialist in name only. He discusses the separation of the democratic impulse from the pursuit of profit, the resulting curtailment of political freedom and an

65

explosion of what passes for personal freedom in the capitalist nations of the West–the freedom to consume.

The End of the Revolution is more than a study of the new China. It is also a captivating study of the effects of global capital on a nation. Many of the situations described by Wang Hui could easily be describing the situation in almost any nation that is part of the neoliberal world of the twenty-first century. In addition, it is a discussion of the meaning of modernity in the world of capitalism and a convincing argument that the world of neoliberal economics is a world whose mechanics thrive best under authoritarian governments. According to Wang Hui, democracy is not a beneficiary of this economic system, but a hindrance that the financial world believes it must undermine to survive. Furthermore, it is Wang's contention that China is the ultimate laboratory for hypothesis.

What about that protest in Tienanmen Square? Did it represent a true desire for democracy? Wang says yes, it did. However, like so many grass-roots popular uprisings around the world, the symbolism of the moment was appropriated by some of the same powers that the original protest opposed for other purposes. The impulse for freedom and democracy mutated into a free market that ends up only freeing the pocketbooks and wallets of the managerial class while relegating the workers on the shop floor to poverty and in some cases a life of near slavery. The peasants, meanwhile, are forced by economic conditions to leave their villages for a life that cycles between low paying wage slavery and unemployment. When the work ends they are left to find their way back home or fend for themselves in urban streets. Tragically, the modern worker's plight often resembles the industrial workplaces of Charles Dickens' England. This is the nightmare of modernity Mr. Wang boldly questions.

Can the phenomenon Wang calls modernity exist together with democracy? What about political freedom and personal freedoms not defined by the marketplace? It is the opinion of the author and millions of others that they can but will require a fight by those opposed to the domination of the market. The global capitalists will tell us that this coexistence is already in place, but the truth contradicts that. In fact, the global capitalists have little taste for democracy when it gets in the way of their profits, which they believe it often does.. In China, this goes so far as censoring the Google search engine and forbidding Bob Dylan from performing. It also means that certain municipalities (Shenzhen being the best known) have become surveillance states on a par with the most fantastic of science fiction writer Philip K. Dick's most paranoid tales.

The discussions Wang Hui presents are discussions that all of us should be having. They do not apply only to China. Indeed, it is easy to conceive that the aforementioned Philip K. Dick surveillance states that exist in China are mere test runs for the future US metropolis. The march of corporate capitalism is not a benevolent one. As any observer who has not bought the myths of the capitalist faith can see, those who sit in the boardrooms of finance and industry seem intent on expanding their ever-growing control of the planet, no matter what the cost to human freedom, life or the environment.

Framing the Sixties

What Really Happened to the 1960s—Ted Morgan

The 1960s continue to open and salt wounds in the US political and cultural psyche over forty years later. From the holiday celebrating a domesticated Martin Luther King, Jr. to the hysterical hype around the Black Panthers and Weather Underground, the actual history of that period continues to be manipulated and misrepresented by popular journalism, Hollywood and TV, creating a scenario where fiction becomes fact and facts become harder and harder to discover. The skeptical observer might ask if there is some kind of conspiracy afoot to obliterate the radical reality of that time period.

Author and historian Edward Morgan doesn't go that far in his recently published study of the 1960s and the media, but he does raise interesting and pertinent questions regarding the nature of the fifth estate's (and its fictional counterpart in Hollywood) representation of that period's popular struggles then and now. According to Morgan, it's not that the media didn't cover the movements against racism and imperial war in the period known as The Sixties. It's how they covered them. Of course, one might argue that any coverage was better than the almost complete lack of media attention most progressive grassroots movements experience today.

Like many other historians that focus on the period, Morgan accepts an understanding that the mainstream media sees the Sixties historically as being divided into two primary periods. First, there were the "good" Sixties. This was when African-American and white Americans battled racist laws and those who upheld them in America's south. Their tactics were nonviolent and their cause was morally unimpeachable. A complementary part of this history puts men like the Kennedy brothers and

Lyndon Baines Johnson at the front of this struggle against segregation and for racial justice. Morgan points out that this retelling ignores the very real facts that the mainstream media was not as supportive of the anti-racist movement during that period as it claims it was now. Furthermore, both the Kennedys and LBJ were forced by events to support civil rights legislation that was opposed by the very powerful Southern wing of their political party. They did not carry the torch of civil rights until it was politically necessary.

The "bad" Sixties, then, were composed of Black Panthers, urban riots, radical students fighting police and blowing up buildings, and so-called hippies like Charles Manson. Morgan calls these elements "media outsiders" and contends that the portrayal of these "outsiders" as such was related to the media's role in defining the parameters of dissent–parameters which had been transgressed repeatedly by 1968. In addition, it was the combination of those parameters: the "outsiders" desire to get their message across to the broader public, and the media's portrayal of those attempts as spectacle that combined to limit the appeal of those whose protests targeted the roots of the war in Vietnam and racism in the United States. In other words, truly radical and anti-capitalist/anti-imperialist debate was considered foreign by the mainstream media (liberal and conservative) and would be treated as such, no matter what.

Morgan provides example after example. Martin Luther King Jr was a true hero of the media until he publicly spoke out against the US war on the people of Vietnam. Betty Friedan and her Feminine Mystique were palatable once one finished reciting the standard jokes about feminists. The more radical elements of the women's movement, on the other hand, were portrayed (and consequently perceived) as men-hating witches and lesbians. The Beatles were positively presented until they made it known that they took LSD and considered themselves to be part of the counter-culture. And so on.

Behind the delightfully vivid discussions of iconic and not-so-iconic events, people and movements that occurred during the period we call the Sixties is Morgan's underlying premise that capitalism and democracy are mutually exclusive. Acknowledging that this premise goes counter to the standard tale we are told by those who rule the United States, Morgan points out that "capitalism and its companion political theory, liberalism, are grounded in a view of humans as essentially self-interested beings" who need political society and its laws only to curb the excesses that such self-interest might create. Democracy, on the other hand, "rests on a foundation different from the self-interested individualism of capitalism." It's not that humans are not self-centered; it's that they are so much more than that. It is the latter actuality, argues Morgan, that informed the popular grassroots movements of the Sixties and continues to inform similar movements today. Likewise, it is the former supposition that informed (and informs) those in power and their media accomplices. Therefore, there was bound to be a conflict between those popular movements that depended on participatory democracy and the established power structure. After all, the fundamental impetus of grassroots democracy is that the people have the power, not some representatives chosen from the power elites or the corporate interests they represent.

If one considers this when studying media representations then and now (of the Sixties and today), it becomes clear that the media understood its role to be one of protecting the powers that be. Although this was occasionally difficult, especially when the images presented were impossible to reinterpret in a manner favorable to the power elites, in general the corporate media was able to perform its task. When images were impossible to explain away, the media merely explained them in such a way that the overall structure of power was unperturbed, while regressive elements that conflict with the necessities of corporate America were rendered to the (often well-deserved) dustbin of history. No better example comes to my mind than the video of Birmingham police and their dogs attacking civil rights protesters. The time for legal apartheid had come to an end in the United States and the media was doing its part by pointing to reactionary politicians and police in the US South as the only racists in the nation. By doing so, the deeper question of racism's role in building the modern US economy and its continued existence throughout the US could be whitewashed away. Then the riots in Watts and other US cities proved otherwise, as did Malcolm X and groups like the Black Panthers. However, true to their role, these phenomena were presented in the media as spectacle without context. This rendered them meaningless or, even worse, criminal. As noted above, this scenario replayed itself over and over (and does to this day). When it came to the war in Vietnam, those who portray(ed) it as a colossal mistake and not an imperial exercise were (and are) given play in the mainstream media, while those who understand things differently are not.

What Really Happened to the 1960s is a look at the role the media played in the presentation and interpretation of the struggles of the 1960s. Simultaneously, it is a consideration of the meaning of democracy in a society where the media is owned by corporations and elites who consider democracy antithetic to their hegemony. The nature of democracy is an important element of this book. Indeed, the need to struggle to regain some democracy in the world is an important element of this book. It is Morgan's contention that understanding how corporate media helped and hindered the democratic movements of the Sixties will help us develop today's grassroots movements. His text does an excellent job of developing that understanding.

Orange Sunshine and the Sixties

Orange Sunshine: the Brotherhood of Eternal Love and Its Quest to Spread Peace, Love, and Acid to the World—Nicholas Schou

The popular history of the 1960s includes a number of stories that are rife with rumor and unsubstantiated tales. From the possibility of conspiracies that killed two Kennedy brothers, Malcolm X, and Martin Luther King, Jr. to the rumors begun by a college student in 1969 that Beatle Paul McCartney was dead, the period was an amalgamation of truths and exaggerations. Its history is the same even today.

One of the groups whose history has been always shrouded in mystery is the Laguna Beach, California-based spiritual and drug operation known as the Brotherhood of Eternal Love. Intimately connected to acid guru Timothy Leary and–through circumstance, LSD and money–the Weather Underground and Grateful Dead, this band of Southern California street toughs took LSD and became proselytizers for a new world based on love and spirituality. Their story was the subject of many a stoned conversation, DEA report, and partially informed newspaper article. Given the fact that the folks involved in the Brotherhood were smuggling, manufacturing and distributing illegal substances, it's easy to understand why no members wanted to talk about the group.

Investigative reporter Nicholas Schou has changed all that. In his recently published book *Orange Sunshine: the Brotherhood of Eternal Love and Its Quest to Spread Peace, Love, and Acid to the World*, Mr. Schou provides the most complete history of this 1960s phenomenon to date. Based on numerous interviews, research, and driven by an apparently intense interest in the subject matter, the story told in Orange Sunshine captures the idealistic beginnings of the Brotherhood and its disintegration into just another drug operation with guns, egos and greed.

While reading Schou's book, one can feel the genuine desire of the group's founders to change the world through marijuana, LSD, and an alternative way of living outside of the technological suburban nightmare they perceived all around them. The transformation of these founders from pot dealers, addicts, street toughs and surfers who obtained their first acid by robbing a Hollywood personality at gunpoint to a group led by John Griggs– a man Timothy Leary called the holiest man in the world– reads like a novel under Schou's pen. So are the story's next chapters as the Brotherhood develops a scheme to smuggle hashish from Afghanistan into the United States and use the profits to set up a utopia in the canyons of southern California, manufacture Orange Sunshine LSD and turn on the world.

About That Orange Sunshine

During its heyday, rumors about Orange Sunshine were as rampant as rumors about Bob Dylan playing at Woodstock. Some were true and some you just hoped were true.

The second time I ever ate acid was in 1971 and the source was a friend of mine who had gone to boarding school in New England and then come to Germany to stay with his parents (who worked for some US corporation). It was a summer afternoon in Gruneburg Park in Frankfurt am Main. My friend took out a little leather bag and produced two orange wafer thin tablets and a piece of green blotter paper that had a drawing of the R. Crumb character Mr. Natural on it. The orange tabs, this guy began, are Orange Sunshine made by a guy in California who used to be Owsley's apprentice. You only need half a tab. In what was probably one of the saner decisions I ever made when it came to LSD, I took his advice and only ate half a tab. Then the melting began. My buddy R saw the Grateful Dead in 1971 at the shows that would later be culled into the Skullfuck album and insisted until his death that people on the stage at the Fillmore East were shooting balls of paper filled with Orange Sunshine tablets into the audience.

Even the Village Voice got into the Orange Sunshine circle when it ran an article in the spring of 1971 about a guy who went by the name of Sunshine John. It seems John was somehow connected to the Brotherhood and, as part of its mission to spread Orange Sunshine around the world, was one of its primary distributors on the US east coast. According to the story (and Schou, as well), there was an acid drought in late 1968 because of the arrests of the primary US manufacturers of the drug. Then, along came Orange Sunshine. Tens of thousands of hits began to appear on the streets, at rock concerts and in rural communes. Most of them were given away for free as part of the Brotherhood's mission to spread peace, love, and acid. As the experiences related above make clear, the acid continued to be manufactured and distributed well into 1971 at least.

The Beginning of the End

Naturally, all this LSD drew the attention of the authorities. Until the early 1970s, most of the anti-narcotics work concerning the Brotherhood had been carried out by local police in Laguna Beach. One officer in particular, Nicholas Purcell, was behind most of the arrests and harassment of the Brotherhood and those who distributed its acid and hashish. With the intensification of the war on drugs under Richard Nixon's White House, Purcell and his cohorts were able to involve California and federal agencies in their mission to destroy the Brotherhood.

Meanwhile, the Brotherhood continued to smuggle marijuana products and distribute LSD. Simultaneously many of them were moving to Maui after the ranch in the canyons was raided, Timothy Leary was arrested and their leader John Griggs overdosed on synthetic psilocybin. In addition, the mission to spread peace and love via LSD was foundering. Like so many other spiritually-inclined endeavors, when the Brotherhood lost their spiritual leader, the mission became confused by the more earthly desires of some of those next in line.

Egos and easy money transformed enough of those involved into just another bunch of drug dealers with guns and cocaine. Drugs, too, had ceased to serve a liberatory function. After those first few years of revelation and communion, they were now often just crutches or, even worse, tools of the oppressor.

I knew this when acid and pot dealers I knew began considering guns a necessary tool of the profession. When old-time hippies who had always considered themselves providers of a sacrament began thinking only in terms of dollars, the signs of decay were there. Greed became the watchword for some of its biggest dealers and cynicism replaced the hopes of just a few years earlier. To borrow a phrase popular at the time, like so much of the counterculture, the Brotherhood had become part of the over-the-counterculture. It had succumbed to the all powerful capitalist god of cash.

The story of the Brotherhood of Eternal Love is simultaneously the story of the southern California 1960s counterculture and a metaphor for the phenomenon in its entirety. The story of Orange Sunshine LSD could easily be the story of the later years of the 1960s US counterculture. Perhaps the lesson to be learned here is that money, ego, and law enforcement trumped everything else in that period known as the Sixties in America, despite the most positive intentions.

Stopping the Train, Stopping the System

Blood On the Tracks—Brian Willson

In a world where the violence of war can be safely ignored by most of the population because it occurs in faraway lands the need for moral witness has never been greater. When the recipient of the Nobel Peace prize unabashedly claims that the violence of war is sometimes necessary and then pursues a policy dependent on increasing that violence, the need for those who oppose such a philosophy to speak up would seem essential to human survival. When the economy of the world's richest nation goes into free-fall because it insists on destroying lives and land in at least three different nations under the guise of fighting for their freedom, the need to put one's life on the line to end those wars and the economy that creates them has never been clearer.

Unfortunately, in recent years, the number of people actually willing to do so seems to have diminished to a relative handful. Of that handful, even fewer are known outside their own circles. Even this latter group finds it difficult to be acknowledged by the greater population. Much of this inability to get publicity can be attributed to the mainstream media machine whose sole purpose is to gear the population up for the next invasion and accompanying repression of rights at home. Occasionally, however, an act so dramatic and courageous creates a situation that not even the corporate media machine can ignore it.

One of those instances occurred on September 1, 1987 outside of the Concord Naval Weapons Station (CNWS) in Concord, California. It was on that day that military veterans Duncan Murphy, David Duncombe and S. Brian Willson sat down on some train tracks outside of CNWS as part of an attempt to block trains carrying weapons and other materials bound for Central America. In Central America, these materials were being used by the El Salvadoran military to kill revolutionaries and their civilian supporters. In Nicaragua and Honduras those materials were being used by US-funded paramilitaries and the Honduran military to destroy the popular government of Nicaragua. Protests like the one that took place that day in 1987 had been going on for weeks. The trains had always stopped before reaching any protesters on the tracks and waited for local police to arrest the protesters.

On September 1, 1987 the train did not stop. In fact, it sped up as it headed towards the three men. Two of the men were able to extricate themselves from the tracks at the last moment. Willson could not. In seconds his legs were crushed and his skull pierced. His body bounced around under the still moving train as the men driving it continued on their way back on to base property. If it had not been for the medical knowledge and quick action of Willson's fellow protesters, he would have died. Given the impact the attempt on Willson's life had in the national media, one can be fairly certain that there were those involved in waging the US wars in Central America who wished he had died.

As it turned out, Willson lost his legs, but otherwise recovered. He was hailed as a hero by the Nicaraguan people and became something of a moral beacon for the anti-intervention movement in the United States. His memoir, *Blood On the Tracks*, was recently published by PM Press. The tale he tells is one that is not completely unique to Wilson, although the specifics certainly are. Born in a small town in the eastern US, he played sports in high school, went to college, went into the military and served in a war. His particular war was Vietnam. Like most of his fellow GIs, Willson never seriously questioned or understood why he was being sent to Vietnam before he was in country. However, once he got there, the murderous contradictions began to challenge his very core. When he wondered aloud why civilians were being killed and labeled as the enemy, he was told to shut up. When he didn't shut up, his tour was shortened and his military life was essentially over. Thus began what would become his future as an antiwar activist, even though he did not know it at the time.

Willson's narrative is a deeply personal story contextualized by a growing awareness of the avaricious and murderous history of the country he always called his own. This growing awareness created a situation quite common amongst Willson's compatriots of the 1960s and 1970s–a situation best described as cognitive dissonance. In other words, everything he had been led to believe about his nation was a lie. Furthermore, he was complicit in living and perpetrating that lie. His (and our) complicity is so complete that even if we do nothing to support Washington's wars and Wall Street's rapaciousness, we remain complicit by the fact of our citizenship. Willson's realization is what motivated him to untangle himself from the web of complicity all US citizens are tangled in. Like so many others, his journey involved opposing the wars of his nation. Unlike so many others, it cost him part of his physical body.

S. Brian Willson doesn't just acknowledge his and our complicity; he demands that we challenge it. Even more, he demands that we work to end it. As anyone knows, this is not an easy or necessarily desirable path. Yet, in the moral universe of Willson, there is no alternative to certain destruction unless every U.S. American confronts their role in maintaining the machinery of death and greed we call America. Like the revolutionary Mario Savio told a crowd at UC Berkeley in 1964, "There's a time when the operation of the machine becomes so odious it makes you so sick at heart that you can't take part. You can't even passively take part. And you've got to put your bodies upon the gears and upon the wheels, upon the levers, upon all the apparatus, and you've got to make it stop. And you've indicate to the people who run it, to the people who own it, that unless you're free, the machine will be prevented from working at all!" Blood On the Tracks is the story of one man's attempt to change the direction of that machine or, failing in that, preventing it from working at all.

Drawing Conclusions on the Wall

On the Ground: An Illustrated Anecdotal History of the Sixties Underground Press in the US--ed. Sean Stewart

There were two types of media my high school friends and I truly looked forward to on our colonial outpost in what was then West Germany. The first was the appearance in the post exchange of the latest album from our favorite band. The other was when one of us received the latest issue of an underground paper from the US. Since we came from towns and cities all over the nation those of us that we're so inclined could read undergrounds from all over the nation. I always had a few hidden away in my bedroom to peruse: Quicksilver Times, Kaleidoscope, Berkeley Tribe and Barb, Georgia Straight from Vancouver, BC, and so on. These papers served a multitude of purposes. Like those record albums mentioned above, they kept us abreast of what was going on back in the States culturally (counterculture, that is), politically, and otherwise. In addition, they helped us frame our understanding of our situation in an overseas US military community. They also inspired us to create our own media and protests.

There have been a number of books written about this underground press. The granddaddy of them all is most certainly Uncovering the Sixties: The Life & Times of the Underground Press by retired Northwestern University professor Abe Peck, who began his journalism career as a member of Chicago's groundbreaking underground called the Seed. More recent endeavors include John McMillan's Smoking Typewriters: The Sixties Underground Press and the Rise of Alternative Media in America and the just-released *On the Ground: An Illustrated Anecdotal History of the Sixties Underground Press in the US* Edited by Sean Stewart, On the Ground is essentially an oral history that features the recollections of several people that were involved with underground papers from around the United States. Unlike McMillan's work which runs toward the academic side of things, Stewart's text has a populist feel to it. The recollections are straight from the speakers' mouths; sometimes angry, sometimes humorous and always honest.

The best part of the book are the graphics. As I read through the memories of the folks Stewart spoke with for On the Ground I was repeatedly surprised at how well I remembered various illustrations and photographs Stewart reprinted throughout the text. Like the papers his interviewees are remembering, the most striking thing about On the Ground is the layout. Even though I know the book was composed on a computer screen, the book looks as if it were laid out via the old cut and paste method by folks possibly stoned on weed and a day or two with minimal sleep–just like many issues of almost every paper Stewart discusses.

Being in the Movement and the counterculture was generally an upbeat experience. So was being in the Sixties underground media. Most folks were young and full of hope and those that were not necessarily young in years were where it counted–in their approach to life. Reporters did not cover stories as much as they took part in them and then wrote about it afterward. As Abe Peck says about working at The Seed: "We were very determined and unless something terrible happened–like [the murder of] Fred Hampton–up, just pretty upbeat." Politics was omnipresent, whether it was at a very political paper like The Black Panther or a paper that had a more counter cultural bent like The LA Free Press. This was because, as far as the authorities were concerned, everyone involved with the underground press–writers, printers, cartoonists, sellers and readers–were on the wrong side of the law and had to be watched. Sometimes, they were dealt with by methods legal and otherwise. This meant things the stores selling papers being harassed by police and vigilantes; the withdrawal of advertising because of pressure from the FBI and other agencies; and assaults against persons involved by cops and others.

When Richard Nixon took over the White House in 1969 the repression of the Movement and counterculture intensified. Naturally, this meant that the media that represented these phenomena would be under greater attack. Black Panther papers were destroyed enroute to cities across the country and even to military bases overseas. Storefronts that newspapers worked out of were firebombed by vigilantes and shot at by police. Obscenity charges were brought against newspapers that then tied up the papers' funds in court costs. High school underground press writers were thrown out of school and administrators suspended students selling and reading those papers. Although the reasons given for the expulsions usually had to do with attendance and other disciplinary infractions, the reality was that high school disciplinarians resented the threat to their authority and power. A friend of mine in Montgomery County, Maryland was suspended from the progressive John F. Kennedy High School for selling The Washington Free Press on campus. The issue in question featured a cartoon of a judge that had been involved in efforts to shut down the paper. The drawing showed the judge masturbating. Underneath the drawing was the phrase (made popular by the TV show Laugh-In) "here com da judge." The cartoon was a response to a series of rulings made by the judge forbidding the distribution of the Free Press on high school grounds. These rulings and the school board decisions that preceded them were being challenged by the ACLU.

As the 1960s turned over into the 1970s, many folks that had been on the front lines began to retreat for the sake of their sanity. Others just fell into the trap of individualism and self-satisfaction–an easy trap to fall into in the US of A. By 1974 or thereabouts, the curse of identity politics had taken over much of the political discourse on the left and effectively limited the reach of the Movement as people separated according to their gender, sexuality and ethnic origins. Intentionally or not, this trend hastened the demise of the underground press and the movements it was a part of. However, its legacy remains. There are many websites and even some print journals that are more than observers of the protests and movements they report on. Journalist Alice Embree notes that "The underground press was the connective tissue; it spread the news …" When the papers began to fail, the connectivity was lessened. The underground press was a vital part of what happened in the sixties. Sean Stewart's wonderfully edited text On the Ground lets the reader know how and why that remains true. The striking graphics and compelling recollections in this text are at once a popular history and an inspiration.

Sparks and Wildfires

It Started In Wisconsin—eds. Mari Jo & Paul Buhle
Why It's Kicking Up Everywhere—Paul Mason

It was about a year ago that the protests against the anti-worker legislation in Wisconsin were reaching their zenith. What had begun as a concerted effort by the Teaching Assistants Association at University of Wisconsin, their supporters and some other activists grew into the largest pro-union/pro-worker movement in decades. The use of tactics not seen since the 1960s, including building occupations, was essential to its organizational success. Unfortunately, the right-wing majority in the state government was equally determined to end collective bargaining rights for public workers and on March 9, 2011 passed the legislation in the dark of night.

However, the spark was lit. The eruption of popular protest against the neoliberal corporate agenda that most of the world had already experienced by the winter of 2011 had finally reached the nation most responsible for that agenda—the United States. The rest of the year would see the expansion of that protest across the United States grow in dimension and breadth. From further State Capitol occupations to the occupations of city parks, the masterminds and profiteers of the neoliberal economy were put on notice. Meanwhile, protest from like-minded citizens of the rest of the world also continued to spread. Politicians scrambled as they figured out how to respond to what was clearly a left-oriented popular movement against those who had bought and sold them long ago.

Naturally, there have been millions of words written and published about this wave of people power. A very recent collection of some of those words edited by Wisconsinites Paul and Mari Jo Buhle, is titled *It*

Started In Wisconsin. Essentially a collection of essays written by various participants and organizers of the Wisconsin protests, It Started In Wisconsin provides a reasonable and objective look at the movement. By discussing its structures and organizational strategies, the politics of the movement are also examined. Like the Wisconsin movement itself, the parameters of the discussion tend to remain limited to the parameters of the liberal-progressive spectrum. The book begins with the first essayist attempting to place the protests firmly in the tradition of the great Progressive Robert LaFollette. However, the very fact that the movement ended up being confined to the traditional Democrat-Republican contest made even the more left elements of the Progressive philosophy irrelevant in the final outcome. It Started In Wisconsin tends to examine the uprising and its politics from a generally anti-corporate perspective but, like the movement itself, never truly challenges capitalism at its roots as an essentially unequal system that by its nature requires growing levels of inequality.

There is one essay that stands out from the rest of those that analyze the movement in that it does look beyond the façade of neoliberalism. That essay, titled "The Role of Corporations" by Roger Bybee, is the most radical in the book. Radical, that is, in the fundamental definition of the word: "of or going to the root or origin." The essay is a clear and straightforward description of how neoliberal capitalism works, who it benefits and, to put it bluntly, who it screws. No other analytical piece between these covers quite approaches the clarity and depth of analysis like Bybee's.

Yet, this book is not really about analysis. It is a collection of stories from those that participated in one of the most inspiring movements to erupt in the US heartland in decades. Those stories provide the observer from afar with a fairly universal and nuanced look at the daily lives of those involved in organizing, occupying, reporting and otherwise participating in those weeks of popular democracy. Interspersed between the tales of the workers, students, farmers and other protesters are a number of photographs and comics. The inclusion of these graphics truly enhances the overall effect.

One of the last two essays in It Started In Wisconsin discusses the position of the Wisconsin uprising in the global insurrections of the past eighteen months. The authors of this short essay, Ashok Kumar and Simon Hardy, briefly discuss the possibilities and take a quick look at the lessons they see to be learned. In addition, and most importantly, they broach the subject of the differences between the radical grassroots and the more conservative entrenched union and political leadership. It is here, they hint, that the real direction of this global movement will be determined. In Wisconsin that outcome has already taken one turn with the shifting of the uprising's momentum into the recall efforts against Governor Scott Walker. The outcome of this turn to electoral politics is still being hotly debated by many of the uprising's organizers, with some of them refusing to endorse the Democratic candidate opposing Walker because they see him as just more of the same.

Moving from the local to the global, let us consider another recently published text that takes a look at the international manifestations of this movement. This book, titled *Why It's Kicking Up Everywhere* is authored by journalist Paul Mason. Like the Buhles' effort, Mason's book describes the movements against neoliberal intolerance and authoritarianism that have become part of the collective imagination this past year. Likewise, Mason's text examines the politics of the movement from what can only be termed a new left viewpoint. What this means is that he places the emphasis on the cry for freedom implicit in these protests while under-emphasizing the economic nature of the oppression the protesters are rebelling against.

Given the broader scope of Mason's text, there is also a broader discussion. Several different manifestations of the movement—from Greece to London to Cairo to Spain and other points in between—are reported on. These reports are good journalism. One feels as if they are present at the rallies, occupations and riots that Mason describes. The anecdotal tales he provides should remind anyone who participated in any kind of popular resistance in the past decades of the energy and hope one finds and feels at such events. These are the stuff that makes one join such movements.

When it comes to analysis, Mason's text provides some interesting possibilities. He spends a fair number of words discussing the desire for freedom this global movement represents. The Egyptians opposed to the harshness of the Mubarak authoritarian regime and the British student fearing the limitations a life without affordable education will create are examined through what Mason calls the social laboratory of the self. He emphasizes the role of social networking and the existence of a new dimension in organizing directly related to the existence of networking technology. He rightly questions the validity of the Left, but does not really examine what he means by the Left, choosing instead to adopt the mainstream media's definition that the Left is composed of political parties like Labour In Britain, various elements of the Democratic Party in the United States, and numerous sects espousing various versions of Leninism.

By dismissing the Left, even in its current splintered formation, Mason is also dismissing a more radical analysis of the true culprit in the global economic catastrophe. It is true, as Mason makes clear, that neoliberal policies are responsible for the numerous maladies the global uprising sprang from. However, what is unexplored in Why It's Kicking Up Everywhere is why neoliberal capitalism is the dominant economic regime on the planet. That explanation can only come from an understanding of the economic works of Marx and his theoretical successors like Nikolai Bukharin, Rosa Luxembourg and even Lenin. It was these thinkers and revolutionaries, after all, that studied and explained the stages of capitalism in the industrial world and how they would come about. So far, they have been pretty damn accurate. Mason has it right when he places the search for freedom and against the authoritarianism of a Mubarak or of neoliberalism in the context of Marx's discussion of the alienation of the human spirit under capitalism. However, by not taking a similar look at the analysis Marxist economics provides regarding the trajectory of capitalism, the analysis he provides falls short. It would be useful for Mason and the protesters he writes about if they knew that a Marxist anti-imperialist analysis does not mean that a Leninist solution is the necessary result.

Yet, Mason is not much different from the movements he describes. Rightly opposed to the excesses of neoliberal capitalism (which is merely another phase of monopoly capitalism as described by Luxembourg, et al.), the current movement runs the risk of merely removing the worst of those excesses. If this is the result, it will only be a few decades before an even harsher manifestation of capitalist greed subordinates the world. Unless, that is, the current movement undertakes a truly radical analysis that places the existence of capitalism itself at the core of the problem. I don't expect that capitalism will be removed from the planet. However, without an understanding that it is capitalism that is the root of the problems of inequality and sustainability we are currently facing, there can be no substantive change in the future we face. Then again, the very fact that many elements of the movement don't seem too concerned about the Left's role is a call to those on the Left to get active and make it clear that what passes for the Left in today's world is for the most part nothing of the sort. Indeed, it is a rejection of the Left's important and earth-changing history.

Despite the aforementioned shortcomings, these two publications are worthwhile and provocative reads. The authors and editors present the primary actors in the global uprising-students, workers and the marginalized—and describe their passion, joy and fears. They also begin to explain where the global movement against neoliberalism came from and where it is now. Reading them in this context will certainly help guide us through that movement's next metamorphosis.

Trying to Kill Social Security

The People's Pension: the Struggle to Defend Social Security Since Reagan—Eric Laursen

It seems like every few months alarms are sounded warning US workers that Social Security is going bankrupt. Oftentimes, the follow up to these alarms includes a warning that the only way to save the system is by turning all or part of the funds involved over to Wall Street investment houses like Goldman Sachs. Usually the alarms are sounded by right wing politicians from the Republican Party. In recent years however, this cacophony of lies has been assisted by more and more Democrats.

According to Eric Laursen in his new book titled *The People's Pension: the Struggle to Defend Social Security Since Reagan,* the desire to end what is Washington's most successful government program has been underway since Social Security's inception. It has only intensified in recent decades. As the title suggests, that intensification sharpened in 1981, the year Ronald Reagan became president. As anyone with an understanding of neoliberal capitalism and the role played by investment houses in this stage of capitalism knows, that year coincides more or less with an increased interest in Social Security funds by those houses. Why? Because their required growth requires more funds to invest and there are billions of dollars in funds sitting in the Social Security reserves.

Laursen provides the reader with a brief history of the philosophy behind Social Security. Harkening to the writings of 19th century anarchists and leftists, he describes part of the impetus behind Social Security as coming from the ideas of mutual aid; where every citizen is cared for. More specifically, he traces the institution of the social security system to the Townsend clubs begun in the 1930s by Dr. Francis Townsend of California. It was Townsend's idea that old people should be guaranteed an income based on their work and funded by taxes. His reasoning was simple, if senior citizens had an income, they could remain consumers, thereby helping stimulate the economy. Millions joined these clubs, exerting political pressure that led to the Social Security Act of 1937. Naturally, this act was fervently opposed by many corporate executives and the wealthy as being socialist and un-American.

Most of today's opponents are not so blunt in their assessment. However, their proposals to privatize the system suggests that they too oppose a government program that does not benefit their corporate benefactors. Instead, they would rather turn it over to the Goldman Sachs of the world. This desire is certainly related to the substantial campaign donations they receive from Goldman Sachs and their cohorts. One expects right wing politicians opposed to any government expenditures not related to benefiting private industry and the Pentagon to oppose Social Security. It is the Democratic opponents that deserve our real attention. Laursen's history is also a history of the gradual shrinking of support among Democrats and other so-called liberals.

The People's Pension puts the beginning of the current assault on Social Security in the lap of the Reagan administration. Laursen makes it very clear that the opponents of this program are not interested in saving money, a fairer distribution of benefits, or helping the elderly. They are serving an ideological agenda of social Darwinism. Furthermore, every attack on Social Security is nothing more or less than an attempt by the corporate world and its right wing supporters to end it once and for all. Laursen further points out that the arguments used by Social Security's opponents never address the economic consequences of ending the program; they only draw up flimsy prognostications of disaster should the program continue. Calls for privatization are nothing more than one more attempt by corporate America to take public monies and privatize the profits while insuring the continued socialization of the risks and loss. As Laursen points out, this is exactly what is done by the defense industry and any scheme to privatize Social Security would do the same thing.

A fact that is not very well known outside of certain circles is that the model for privatization promoted by the so-called supply side economists was developed in the fascist Chile of Augusto Pinochet. Championed by many Republicans and their banker/corporate sponsors, this model is ultimately more expensive than keeping things as they are and its greatest benefits are to the banking industry. Furthermore, this and other privatization schemes assume an ever-growing capitalist economy—a phenomenon less certain than it was before the crash of 2008. Despite this, politicians continue to include Social Security in their gunsights. Whether it is Alan Simpson calling Social Security a "Milk Cow with 310 Million Tits," or so-called Blue Dog Democrats suggesting that benefits be changed, the assault on the program never goes away.

Eric Laursen has written a comprehensive and exhaustive history of the Social Security program in the United States. The People's Pension is an honest, detailed and even eye-opening discussion of the program's origins and continuing efforts to provide elderly and disabled Americans with a livable income. Equally important, it is a discussion of the attempts to alter and ultimately destroy the program by forces whose only interest seems to be profit and the elimination of any government institution that guarantees every citizen worker an income in their old age.

A Tale From a Time of Heroes

Leila Khaled: Icon of Palestinian Liberation—Sarah Irving

There was once a time not so long ago when the world seemed to be full of revolutionary heroes. These heroes were both men and women. The actions and accompanying commitment of these individuals inspired millions of others to join movements and organizations dedicated to a vision of social justice and freedom that understood colonialism and racism to be their primary opposition. From Martin Luther King, Jr. to Rosa Parks; from Huey Newton to Assata Shakur; and Che Guevara to Leila Khaled, the list of such individuals is too great to recount here. Their enemies included secret and not-so-secret police, intelligence agencies dedicated to their murder, and governments both liberal and reactionary whose lot lay with the imperial powers in Washington, London and else-where in the North. The presence of such men and women made them targets for those opposed to their vision. Simultaneously, the fact of their stature provided them with a media presence created a public awareness of their cause which helped recruit adherents and supporters.

During the first Gulf war (1990-1991) I worked with an antiwar group in Olympia, WA. There was a young woman named Leila of Syrian heritage in the group. It was during a conversation about the Palestinians that the subject of Leila Khaled came up. After five min-utes of conversation or so, Leila mentioned that she was named after Khaled. I knew that Khaled's youth, beauty and media savvy had made her a media favorite during the hijackings and other actions she had par-ticipated in. I also remembered the spray painted silhouettes of Khaled that appeared on the walls of squats and at the Goethe Universitat in Frankfurt. However, this young woman was the first person I had met who was named in her honor.

Recently, Pluto Press published a small biography of Leila Khaled as part of its Revolutionary Lives Series. It is titled *Leila Khaled: Icon of Palestinian Liberation*. Authored by Sarah Irving, a freelancer who has written about environmental and Palestinian issues, this biography looks at Khaled's life from its beginnings in a Palestinian village occupied by the Israelis to her current activism. Culling information from her biography My People Shall Live, newspaper and journal articles spanning her life and recent interviews, Irving's book takes a comprehensive look at a life fully-lived.

For those who remember the hijackings Khaled participated in, Leila Khaled: Icon of Palestinian Liberation brings those events back to life. In addition, she provides the reader with Khaled's insights and descriptions of how those hijackings unfolded. Khaled also touches briefly on her emotions during those actions. Irving describes the determination of Khaled's enemies to kill her, a determination that resulted in her sister and sister's fiancé being murdered by mistake. She also describes the life of Khaled's family as refugees and relatives of a revolutionary wanted by Israel and a myriad of other governments. The Palestinian movement Khaled first entered was quite different than that which exists now. Religious elements had minimal influence. Indeed, the primary divisions in the movement arose in the political/economic arena. The primary organization, Al Fatah, was what was then termed a bourgeois nationalist movement, while the Popular Front for the Liberation of Palestine (PFLP) defined itself as a Marxist one. Khaled was (and is) a member of the latter, but seems to have been only minimally involved in the internecine warfare that occasionally erupted between the factions. Her discussion of the influence of Muslim culture in the Palestinian movement and how it effects the role of women in the Palestinian struggle is an important part of this book and worthy of further exploration. This is especially true given Khaled's long history in the movement and her lifelong insistence on the need for women to be involved. A sidebar to this discussion is her telling about incidents where some of the men pretending to be strict enforcers of the hijab in Gaza following Hamas' victory turned out to be informers for the Israeli military. This story points out the potentially reactionary nature of a nationalism that depends on cultural elements to define it while rejecting anti-capitalist economic analyses.

Khaled discusses the current situation in Palestine. In her opinion, the Oslo accords should never have been signed. The continued control of Palestinian economic, social and daily life by Israelis and their paid police insures the perpetuation of the Occupation. Her opposition to the Accords is often characterized by her enemies as being an opposition to peace. Khaled's response is simple. When there are no more Israeli soldiers, police, and other agents of the Tel Aviv government occupying the territories, then there will be peace. Until then, the struggle continues. As if to emphasize this, some events arranged by Irving's publisher to announce the book to the British reading public have been canceled because of threats of violence. This fact proves Khaled's continuing relevance, while also intensifying the need to publicize the book.

The struggle of the Palestinians is a different looking struggle than it was when Leila Khaled's name first became known to the world. Yet, it is the same struggle. Heroic figures like those mentioned above do not seem to be part of that struggle right now. However, their stories are important and need to be told. Leila Khaled: Icon of Palestinian Liberation does a great job of telling one such story.

The Black Panthers—No Bullshitting

My People Are Rising—Aaron Dixon

The Black Panthers were arguably the most important revolutionary organization in the United States in the late 1960s and early 1970s. Their presence was an inspiration to millions of men and women around the globe, especially those living in colonial and neocolonial situations. Furthermore, the Party was a key element in the movement in the United States against imperialism and its manifestations of war and racism. It was because of this latter truth that the Party was also the target of a brutal campaign of repression organized at the highest levels of Washington DC's security apparatus. Surveillance, false charges and arrests, the use of informants and provocateurs, and outright murder; nothing was out of the question when it came to destroying the Black Panther Party.

Begun in Oakland in 1967, the Panthers organized chapters in Los Angeles and Seattle, Washington soon afterward. The Seattle chapter would become one of the Party's longest lasting chapters and an integral part of the African-American and leftist community in that city. Founded and led by a young Seattle native named Aaron Dixon, the legacy of the Seattle chapter is still present in that city.

Like many young people discovering leftist politics in the late 1960s, my experience was greatly influenced by the Panthers. For better and worse, their leather jackets, berets and guns combined with a media presentation as badasses appealed to me and many of my compatriots. One instance in my political education that remains indelible in my mind occurred during the summer of 1970. I was attending summer school at the US high school in Frankfurt am Main, Germany. We had just spent a class discussing the very recent US invasion of Cambodia, the student strike, law enforcement murders of young people at Kent and Jackson

State, and the meaning of Nixon. Class had been dismissed and I was hanging out in Gruneburg Park next to the school. There was a lawn in the park where German hippies hung out and smoked hashish. Young travelers from around the world often ended up on this lawn, playing guitars and drums, smoking dope, meeting up, discussing politics and music, and just hanging out.

That afternoon my friend and I ended up in a circle of people discussing the Black Panthers. The discussion was more or less being led by an African-American man around twenty. I had seen him in the park before, but had never talked with him. As he continued to talk, about half of the people drifted away, either too stoned to listen to his politics or just too apathetic. I stayed. Eventually, there were only three of us; me, a Black girl I knew from high school and the aforementioned young man (who seemed old to my fifteen year old self). He took out some literature from his backpack and handed us each a packet. As it turned out, he was a GI recently discharged from the Army who was traveling around Europe. He had ordered several copies of Mao Ze Dong's Little Red Book and a quantity of other literature from the Panthers' Oakland office to distribute on his travels. He suggested a couple articles to read in the issue of the Black Panther newspaper he had given us and for the next several days, the three of us met in the park and discussed what we had read. He continued on his travels, and the girl and I stayed on, occasionally hanging out at school the following year despite the different circles we traveled in.

I relate the previous story as an example of the influence the Panthers had. The recently released memoir by Aaron Dixon tells a much more compelling story while providing a history of the Party through the eyes of one of its long-term members. Dixon was both a leader and a foot soldier; an intelligent black man in the mid-century United States who knew racism first hand and wanted to end it. As a young teen he occasionally participated in protests against racism while learning the streets of Seattle. His parents worked hard to maintain an approximation of a middle class life for their children while biting their tongues all too often when they ran into racism in their daily lives. Like many others of his generation, it was the assassination of Martin Luther King, Jr. in 1968 that convinced him that non-violent protest was no longer the only option.

If there was to be real change in the United States, it would have to be of the kind put forward by the newly found Black Panther Party. Dixon and several others traveled to the San Francisco Bay Area for a Black Student Union conference and he joined the Panthers. Simultaneously, he was made captain of the Seattle branch.

Dixon's book, titled *My People Are Rising*, goes on to tell a tale of protest, gunfights with police and their stooges, and political change. The reader is presented with a story full of action, love and politics. The Black Panther Party's rise and fall is revealed through the experiences of Aaron Dixon and those men and women he worked and lived with during his time in the party. Moments of victory and moments of defeat fill these pages, both personal and political. The narrative reads like an action thriller. Dixon's writing is even, descriptive and urgent. Whether describing the preparations for an attack by police on a Panther house or the organization of the Panther breakfast program in Seattle, My People Are Rising keeps the reader in the story, curious as to which way the events described will turn.

The Panthers eventually fell apart. The power they represented in the African-American community diminished midway through the 1970s in their primary base of Oakland and much earlier in other parts of the United States. Much of this can be attributed to the repression carried out by law enforcement under the aegis of COINTELPRO. Other factors that caused the disintegration of the party were related to the nature of the Party itself. During the heyday of their organizing drive, many people who joined saw the Panthers as just another street gang and used it accordingly: selling drugs and pimping women. When the Party leadership got wind of such activities carried out in the Panthers name, they dealt with it quickly and harshly. Indeed, when the Party began to shrink in size, Dixon was called to Oakland and became a member of one of the cadres that engaged in such activity. A questionable program was begun to chase dealers and pimps from the streets of Oakland's neighborhoods. I say questionable not because the pimps and dealers should have stayed but because the money, guns and violence involved invited corruption. Meanwhile, the political wing of the Party had involved itself in electoral politics, running and endorsing candidates for political office in

Oakland, California. Unfortunately, no Panthers were elected, although some of the candidates they endorsed did. By 1978, though, the party was essentially finished.

Coda: In 1978 a friend and I were hitchhiking in Oakland. We were headed to Santa Cruz. An African-American man driving a Buick Regal picked us up. Once we got in the car he asked us where we were headed. I told him Santa Cruz and he said he would take us there. First, though, he needed to stop at a house in the Oakland Hills. My friend and I shrugged our shoulders and went along for the ride. He found the house, went inside for fifteen or twenty minutes and came out in a hurry. We left that house and made our way to Highway 17 towards Santa Cruz. Once we were on the highway he pulled out a big joint and lit it. We smoked the weed and sat back. He handed me a pint of brandy and asked me to open it. After a few sips, our tongues loosened and we got to talking about Oakland. My friend and I had only been in California for five months and told him so. He told us he had grown up there. As the conversation somehow turned to politics, the subject of the Panthers came up. He dismissed them out of hand. I objected, telling him the story I related at the beginning of this piece. He chuckled and said; yeah he was like that once, too. After working for the Chairman, though, all he was going to say was that the Panthers had turned out to be nothing more than another bunch of gangsters. I didn't argue and I didn't agree. We changed the subject.

Aaron Dixon's memoir is the first of many Panther memoirs I have read that honestly addresses the demise of the Panthers. He discusses the role of COINTELPRO, the descent into gangsterism, and the end of the revolutionary aspect of the Party. He does not mince words, nor does he disavow what the Party meant to millions and means in history. In the book's final paragraph, Dixon apologizes for nothing, remembering the Black Panther Party as "men and women rising in unison to...write a new, bold future for Black America." That, I believe, is the truth found in this book and the truth revealed by history.

Burning Paper Instead of Children

The Catonsville Nine: A Story of Faith and Resistance in the Vietnam Era—Shawn F. Peters

Fire is a most evocative element. From Hell to the fiery tongues of the Christian Pentecost to the forges of Hephaestus and the Fire Demon of the Bhagavad Gita, the religious meanings attached to fire swirl around the concepts of death, punishment, and rebirth. On a more real level, fire is an all too familiar part of war, whether it is the Greek fire of Byzantine warfare, the crematoriums of Buchenwald, the firebombing of Dresden and various Japanese cities in World War Two or the searing death of napalm in Vietnam and white phosphorus in Iraq. The screams of the incinerated are impossible to fathom for those unfamiliar with the horror of war.

On May 17, 1968, several Catholics brought this fact home to US citizens when they stole almost four hundred Selective Service files and burned them with napalm in the parking lot of the Catonsville, MD draft board office. That act was to earn them damnation and praise; death threats and calls for sainthood; a trial and prison terms. I myself was a questioning thirteen-year old Catholic kid living twenty miles away from the pyre. That action made me see my faith in a new light. Maybe there were those in the Catholic Church who understood the example of Jesus to be a revolutionary example, not an affirmation of the patriarchy and the war machine. Maybe my occasional consideration of the priesthood might be the way to go. One didn't have to be like the conservative clerics banning books, movies and music from the pages of the Archdiocese newsweekly or the disapproving priests in our parish who read the Pope's 1968 encyclical on birth control with what seemed to be woman-hating relish.

I didn't become a priest, although the example of the Catholic anti-warriors and liberation theologians (and the conversation of some Jesuit seminarians and priests during high school) did lead me to spend a couple months in a seminary before I went off to try college at a Jesuit university. Within a year of that endeavor, my hope for the Church was gone, having washed away in a realization that if the Church didn't hate women, they surely did not trust them. Like most other anti-war organizers, I have worked with priests, nuns and other Catholics in a number of actions and committees and have usually found them to be sincere and committed people. It is their boss and his pronunciations I can't abide.

Anyhow, back to the Catonsville Nine. Their action in Catonsville had been preceded by a smaller action in Baltimore that included two of the Catonsville participants: Tom Lewis and Fr. Philip Berrigan. It was followed by a much larger action in Milwaukee that saw the destruction of thousands of draft records. The Catonsville participants went to trial in 1968 and, thanks to the arguments of their lead attorney William Kunstler and the understanding of the court, the defendants were allowed to bring the questions of the Vietnam War and the draft into the courtroom. The trial was covered by news organizations around the planet. Poet Daniel Berrigan (Philip's brother and a Jesuit priest) wrote a well-received play titled The Trial of the Catonsville Nine. The play modified the trial transcript and addressed the moral issues involved, alluding to other instances of the struggle between conscience and authority throughout history.

Until recently, only the play and a couple books told the story of the Catonsville Nine and their action. Another book has joined the list. Written by Shawn Francis Peters, who was born in Catonsville in 1966 and has two previously published books centering around religion and society, this comprehensive look at the Catonsville Nine is titled *The Catonsville Nine: A Story of Faith and Resistance in the Vietnam Era*. While sympathetic to the ideals that drove the Nine to break the law in such a dramatic manner, Peters does not skimp on detailing the criticism levied against the Nine from the outside. Nor does he whitewash the internal doubts and misgivings that took place within the group during the planning, execution and aftermath of the action. The reader is left with a tale of commitment, spiritual certainty, and human emotion.

Despair, anger, ecstasy, and determination are the ingredients of Peters' narrative and he combines these ingredients with the skill of a master storyteller.

The personal history of each member of the Nine is presented as a prelude to the central event in the book: the draft board raid and the subsequent trial. Their lives as children brought up in a Catholic church known for its dogma and rigidity is discussed. So is the effect of the liberalization of that church during the brief reign of Pope John XXIII and the Vatican Two conference. Equally important to many of the protagonists were the words of the Church hierarchy regarding the nature of modern war, colonialism and imperialism. It was during the post-World War Two period that the Catholic Church became more vocal in its opposition to war, the preparation for war and the inequality of the ever-growing world capitalist system. The combination of these words from the hierarchy, the liberalization brought on by Vatican Two and the desire of more and more Catholic clergy to engage in anti-poverty and antiwar work instead of just ministering to the spiritual needs of their flocks created a critical mass of activism within the Church. This included those members of the Nine whose previous work as missionaries in Latin America had revealed the disconnect between Washington's words of social justice and the poverty and repression of daily life under US-sponsored regimes. They realized they could no longer not participate in opposing those regimes.

This activism did not sit well with many more conservative church members. Peters relates this aspect of the Nine's tale well, intertwining the reaction to the Nine and other activist Catholics with the Nine's frustration with the Church to act on its words about peace and against war. Although the strongest opposition to the Nine came from law enforcement and those who supported the war, there were many in the Church who had nothing positive to say about the group, either. Indeed, for some members of the Nine, it was the negative response from the Church that bothered them the most.

The Catonsville Nine have always been identified with the Berrigan brothers, Philip and Daniel. In part, this was because the two men were the individuals that the media focused much of their attention on. Another reason was due to the sheer presence of both men. Not to be discounted was the fact that they were both priests, while the other members of the Nine were mostly laypeople, although David Darst was a Christian Brother. Peters' book does a wonderful job bringing the other seven members of the Nine alive. His well-researched tale makes each of these other activists fully three-dimensional. By doing so, he creates a picture of the Nine that presents the entity of the Nine as much a part of the actual story as the Catonsville action itself. While drawing this picture, he also provides the reader with a representation of the entire Catholic antiwar movement of the 1960s and 1970s.

The lasting legacy of the Catonsville Nine action is Daniel Berrigan's play, The Trial of the Catonsville Nine. First published in 1970, this play in free verse used the trial transcript of the Nine as its inspiration. It was produced around the world almost immediately after its publication and was made into a film in 1972 produced by Gregory Peck. I recall seeing it performed on a military base by a community theater group made up of GIs and military dependents. Incredibly powerful and direct, it is still performed and was republished during the US occupation of Iraq in 2004. Like the draft board raid itself, the play forces the individual, no matter what their faith, to look at their role in the war economy we live in and it asks the audience member/reader what they are going to do about it. In its own way, The Catonsville Nine: A Story of Faith and Resistance in the Vietnam Era also forces the reader to deal with this modern contradiction. It doesn't call on the reader to become an activist; it presents them with the compelling story of individuals who did.

This is a must read for people of any faith, whether that faith is in a god or in humanity. Peters' compelling narrative renders the Catonsville Nine not as saints nor as villains, but as human beings who could no longer be silent in the face of injustice and war. They risked everything and, by doing so, gained much more than they ever could have lost. It is a story older than Antigone but, when told as masterfully as Peters does here, it is a story that never grows old. Nor should it.

It's An Anti-Imperialist Struggle, Not a Clash of Civilizations

Islamophobia and the Politics of Empire—Deepa Kumar

In the machinations of Empire, religious and ethnic differences are often used to justify wars and repression. Historical examples abound. Animosity between nations' ruling elites are framed in religious terms to rile up the populace and convince them the antagonisms between rulers over land and money are actually between the common people over religion. From there, the antagonism disintegrates into hatred and then war. Despite the conclusion of many religious adherents and teachers that all religions are merely different paths to the same godhead, people continue to cave into the fears propagated by other clerics and institutions that only their religion is the one true one. All others, therefore, are false and their followers are infidels. Once the flames of religious hatred are lit, it becomes very difficult to extinguish them. History has proven this over and over again.

Most recently, the world has seen this manipulation of faith take place against Muslims. This is not the first time Islam has been the focus of hate. Various Christian faiths have considered it a demonic religion over the centuries, from the Catholic Church to the small sect run by Terry Jones in Florida in the US. It was Islam, after all, that bore the brunt of the Catholic Crusades in the middle ages. It was also the Catholic Church that ravaged the lands of Spain during the Reconquista; and it was the Catholic Church that forced Jews and Muslims alike to renounce their faith or face death during that same period.

Like most prejudices that the ruling classes and their politicians stir up for their own ends, much religious hatred is based on ignorance and misunderstanding. This is certainly the case when it comes to Islam and its perception among many Christian churches. Despite the fact (or perhaps because of it) that Christianity, Judaism and Islam are all derived from the legacy of Abraham, the level of ignorance about this among believers is astounding. Indeed, it would leave one to think that perhaps that ignorance was intentional.

This is one of the points argued in Deepa Kumar's latest title, *Islamophobia and the Politics of Empire*. Kumar traces the history of anti-Islamic imagery in the Christian west: its equation of the religion with Satan and sorcery, mysterious sexual practices and perversions. From this beginning, Kumar draws a line to the development of Orientalist scholarship and its use by colonialist nations to justify their domination and exploitation of what they termed "the Muslim World." Orientalism is best described by the author of the best book on the subject, Edward Said. "Orientalism," he wrote, "is a style of thought based upon ontological and epistemological distinction made between "the Orient" and (most of the time) "the Occident Thus a very large mass of writers, among who are poet, novelists, philosophers, political theorists, economists, and imperial administrators, have accepted the basic distinction between East and West as the starting point for elaborate accounts concerning the Orient, its people, customs, "mind," destiny, and so on. . . . The phenomenon of Orientalism as I study it here deals principally, not with a correspondence between Orientalism and Orient, but with the internal consistency of Orientalism and its ideas about the Orient ... despite or beyond any correspondence, or lack thereof, with a "real" Orient."

In other words, Orientalism is a framework developed by the West to define the non-European part of the world that emphasizes the differences between these two artifices. It often has little to do with the reality of life and thought in the non-European world and is a methodology used to justify the occupation of those lands, the subjugation of their peoples, and the use of whatever means it takes to do so. In addition, it ignores essential facts that do not fit its framework that assumes the superiority of the West. Kumar discusses five myths Orientalism bases itself on and, in doing so, effectively dismantles those myths. While reading this particular chapter it felt like I was reading any number of news articles from the past fifty years explaining how Washington's enemies were less civilized, less worldly than Americans. Medievalist, sexist, less value placed on human life, incapable of democracy or rational thought; the rationales for opposing Islam are not much different than those given for slaughtering over a million Vietnamese. Kumar looks at these phenomena historically and provides a perspective rarely if ever considered by most Western commentators.

Much of Islamophobia and the Politics of Empire is an examination of the relationship between the ruling elites in Washington DC and the various elements of Islam, especially during the last twenty or thirty years. The text takes a look at Washington's relationships with state and non-state entities. This includes Washington's self-serving support of the Saud family in Saudi Arabia to the CIA coup in Iran that led to the tyranny of the Shah; from the arming of the Afghan mujahedin against the Soviet army to the endless war on the Afghan people and its expansion into Pakistan via armed drones. Kumar explains the economic, political and military reasons for the skullduggery and death waged in Americans' name in countries Kumar terms "Muslim majority." She never lets the reader forget that underlying the entire Islamophobia project is the desire for hegemonic control of the world by Washington.

After exploring the reasons for and the results of the Islamophobic project in the Empire's outposts, Kumar turns her eye inward to the United States. She chronicles the legal attacks on mosques and Islamic social service foundations under the guise of their "support" of terrorism and discusses the growth of anti-Muslim and anti-Arab sentiment stirred up by various right wing and Zionist individuals. Citing the example of the so-called "Ground Zero" mosque, she exposes the politics of the individuals and organizations behind the campaign to prevent the building of that structure. Although many readers identify Islamophobia with Zionists, the neocons and their Christian fundamentalist supporters (Kumar spends a fair amount of tine elucidating on this), the book makes it clear that this phobia is not limited to that particular mindset. In fact, Kumar labels the liberal version of this phobia and the policies it informs "liberal Islamophobia." This latter incarnation is one that pretends to understand Islam, while simultaneously accepting many of the same myths about the religion maintained by the aforementioned groups.

There's a lot in this book. Deepa Kumar takes a subject that is often intentionally misconstrued and brings a clarity that incorporates the multiple facets involved. Politics and religion are notoriously dangerous bedfellows, yet they have tended to define human history for as long as there has been such a thing. This phenomenon has only become truer as history moves on. While other books may explain the religion of Islam and its relationship to Christianity better, Islamophobia and the Politics of Empire stands alone in its exploration of the relationship between western imperialism and the Muslim-majority world, especially as regards recent history. If recent events in the Middle East and other Muslim majority regions are an indicator, this relationship may be on the verge of a substantial change. This makes reading and understanding Kumar's text even more essential.

The Difference the PLO Made

The Global Offensive: The United States, the Palestine Liberation Organization, and the Making of the Post-Cold War Order—Paul T. Chamberlain

April 1975. University of Maryland, College Park, Maryland. A friend and I sat at a literature table in front of the Student Union building. It was lunchtime and we were putting in our hours talking with people about the issues of the day. University cutbacks were the primary topic of conversation, but some folks who stopped by seemed more interested in the unfolding final scene of the US war in Southeast Asia. The final offensive of the national liberation forces was underway in Vietnam. Lon Nol's regime had just fallen. The forces of US imperialism were on the run. Things were heating up in Lebanon between leftist forces supported by the Palestine Liberation Organization (PLO) and various Maronites eventually identified with the right wing Phalangist militia. The literature on our table covered most of these issues. Nonetheless, we were still somewhat surprised when four guys walked up to the table, begin taking our pamphlets in support of the PLO and tearing them up. My cohort asked them what the hell they were doing. The biggest guy (who I actually remembered from high school) told him to shut the fuck up. My friend took that as a challenge and the next thing I knew the table was turned over and we were defending ourselves from physical attack. Fortunately, a few students that were hanging out came to our defense and the attackers left. After asking around, we discovered that the men who had confronted us were members of the local Jewish Defense League (JDL), a right-wing racist organization under the leadership of Rabbi Meir Kahane. They were also University of Maryland students. I have to admit that I was a bit taken aback at their angry actions. As the semester wore down, these men or other JDL members would stand near our literature table, looking menacing and keeping some interested passersby from engaging us.

In 1975, the PLO was the dominant force in Palestinian politics. It was a secular organization composed of nationalists, Marxists and others determined to bring about Palestinian statehood. Just like there were a variety of political trends in the organization, there were Christians, Muslims and atheists. Although the PLO had been in existence since 1964, its true rise to power began in 1967 after the Israeli defeat of the Arab nations in the June war. Today, it is a shell of its former self, weakened by the rise of Hamas, the death of its leader Yasser Arafat, and the failure of its diplomatic pursuit of statehood. Palestine is in straits all too close to those in which it found itself during the PLO's heyday. Under constant Israeli economic and military onslaught, the Palestinian people still in what remains of the former Palestine are mostly poor, and almost completely subject to the whims of the Israeli government and its armed forces. This is not an accident. Indeed, as Paul Thomas Chamberlain's new history of the *PLO, titled The Global Offensive: The United States, the Palestine Liberation Organization, and the Making of the Post-Cold War Order*, makes quite clear, Tel Aviv is determined to never give the Palestinians a nation of their own. The continued intransigence of Israel combined with an increasing stubbornness on the part of Washington to a just settlement has insured both the longevity and the nature of the conflict.

Chamberlain begins his book by defining a few of his terms. Because the PLO is historically identified with the word "terrorism," Chamberlain discusses the baggage associated with the term and explains his usage as being de-politicized. He also explains his position on the conflict between Israel and Palestine: he believes Israel has the right to exist and the Palestinians deserve a sovereign state on the lands of the West Bank and Gaza. By focusing his book solely on the military heyday of the PLO (1967-1975), Chamberlain avoids a discussion of later liberation groups such as Hamas. This focus also serves to deepen his exploration of the meaning of the PLO in the time period examined.

Placing the PLO directly in the context of the numerous struggles for national liberation occurring around the globe in the 1960s and 1970s, Chamberlain details the support the PLO and its fighters received from those movements. The PLO's alliances with many of these groups is also considered and explained. By providing this context, it becomes clear that the success of the PLO was in large part related to the time of its appearance in history. Without the revolutionary wave sweeping the world during the period, it seems unlikely that the PLO would have had the success it did. The same could probably be true for most of the PLO's revolutionary allies. Conversely, the military strength of Washington and Tel Aviv prevented much of the potential of that movement.

The PLO did not speak with a single voice. Although Fatah was the largest group within the organization and Arafat was Fatah's leader, smaller factions acted within the context of the PLO while simultaneously angering other elements. These factions included the Marxist Popular Front for the Liberation of Palestine and its offshoots, along with Black September (formed in the wake of the PLO's defeat by the Jordanian military). Perhaps the best known of these factions was Black September, whose spectacular terror attacks during the Munich 1972 Olympics and at the Lod Airport sealed its infamy. The Global Offensive chronicles the attacks, the battles and the differences within the PLO. In a similar vein, the text also details the differences in opinion over policy within the United States government. It also makes a point of discussing the minimizing of those differences once the Nixon-Kissinger team took over matters of war and state in Washington, DC. Chamberlain pulls no punches when he argues that Washington's decision to support Israel right or wrong beginning with these two men provided Tel Aviv with the only outside rationale it needed to continue its murderous and expansionist policies against the Palestinian people.

As I write this review, Kemal Meshal of Hamas is once again calling for the PLO and Hamas to join forces. Ever since the rise of Hamas over the last twenty years and the subsequent weakening of the PLO, these calls have become infrequent. In part, this is due to differences in the PLO charter and that of Hamas; other reasons for the dual existence include the role of religion in the struggle and the nature of the Palestinian state. It is difficult to state whether Hamas' renewed desire to join the PLO stems from a belief that it is currently in a powerful position vis-à-vis Fatah or if the opposite is true. The only thing that is certain is that Israeli and US intransigence is worse than ever.

Paul Thomas Chamberlain's book remembers a time when the world was in a popular left-oriented revolt against the forces of imperialism and colonialism. He places the PLO's global offensive squarely in that time. While relating the group's history, he tells the story of a resistance up against a pair of indomitable foes, determined to do whatever it took to prevent the PLO's survival. This book provides a history of the Palestinian-Israeli conflict with an emphasis on objectivity and clarity. It is not pro-Palestinian or pro-Israeli. While reading it, it becomes clear that the solution to the conflict lies in a real nation for the Palestinian people. Of course, this will probably not happen until the United States and Israel act in a manner that encourages such a solution. The story between these two covers is a narrative not only useful but essential to understanding the sphinx that is the Palestinian struggle.

American Overkill

Empire of Ideas: The Origins of Public Diplomacy and the Transformation of U. S. Foreign Policy—Justin Hart
America's Deadliest Export: Democracy - The Truth About US Foreign Policy and Everything Else—William Blum

A frequent target of antiwar protests when I lived in Frankfurt am Main, Germany was the local Amerika Haus. These buildings existed in several European cities and were essentially outposts of the United States Information Agency, which was part of the propaganda wing of the United States government and under the aegis of the CIA. As the US war in Vietnam grew in intensity and scope, their presence became a sore point among leftists and other war opponents in the countries that hosted them. At the same time, the Frankfurt Amerika Haus was where I heard Kurt Vonnegut give a lecture that did not support the war in Vietnam. A group of us involved with the theater department in the US high school put on a performance of Jean Anouilh's version of Antigone there.

In Justin Hart's new book *Empire of Ideas: The Origins of Public Diplomacy and the Transformation of U. S. Foreign Policy*, Amerika Haus and many other aspects of Washington's propaganda machine are addressed. This history of the origins of the current government propaganda machine in Washington covers the years 1936-1953 and presents the debates, uncertainties and ultimate use of that machine as an important tool in the proliferation and maintenance of US markets overseas.

After watching Michelle Obama's presentation of the award for Best Picture to a film praising the CIA from the White House, it's somewhat difficult to believe that there was a time when politicians and government officials questioned the usefulness of propaganda in the battle for

US hegemony. Yet, that is exactly where Hart's tale begins. In a rather interesting tale, he presents the beginnings of what is euphemistically called public diplomacy in Franklin Roosevelt's Good Neighbor Policy towards Latin America. It represented a new understanding that spreading US culture helped open markets overseas while simultaneously justifying the growing US Empire to the domestic audience, an audience which to that point was mostly isolationist in its outlook.

This new approach was not without its detractors. Most of them came from the extreme right, who saw propaganda as communist-inspired, given its use by the new Soviet government in Russia. This concern was also related to the fact that cultural diplomacy (another euphemism for propaganda) was championed primarily by liberals and progressives with Henry Wallace leading the charge. The presence of liberal and elements at the forefront of this movement lends further credence to the argument that it was liberals and progressives who were at the forefront of the US hegemonic endeavor. It's obvious from Hart's telling that the inclusion and acceptance of propaganda as a useful tool for those interested in building the US Empire (pretty much every official in Washington) was not without its ups and downs. However, by the time Harry Truman was president, it was clear that its role was accepted and certain to expand.

Of course, when propaganda failed, the iron fist became ungloved. By 1950, the US military was engaged in a brutal war in Korea whose aim similar to the efforts of the cultural propaganda committee. In other words, to keep the Soviets from expanding into markets Washington had defined as its own. Meanwhile, the Marshall Plan, hyped as bringing democracy, was underway in Europe and part of the same process. As William Blum makes clear in his latest collection, *America's Deadliest Export: Democracy – The Truth About US Foreign Policy and Everything Else*, the folks that truly benefited from the Marshall Plan were the US corporations that rebuilt Europe. Just like the so-called reconstruction funds apportioned to Kosovo after its "liberation" and Iraq after the US invasion, the truth about those reconstructions is that they were primarily a means to move taxpayer dollars from the US treasury into the coffers of a few giant corporations.

Blum's new book is a collection of commentary exposing the true nature of Washington's ongoing campaign to spread its democracy around the world. While reading it I was reminded of the t-shirt that shows a photograph of a US bomber plane dropping bombs on some city somewhere on planet earth. Inscribed above the photograph are the words "Democracy, We Deliver." America's Deadliest Export explores the lies involved in this campaign and exposes the brutality and associated arrogance. In his inimitable style, Blum rips into the lie of US propaganda and takes Hart's academic discussion into the streets, simultaneously pointing out the hypocrisy of US democracy and indicting it for the fraud it is, not only abroad but at home, as well.

While Hart's text looks primarily at the role of US propaganda overseas, Blum's tends to focus on how it is utilized to manipulate domestic public opinion. He takes the concept that Washington and its military act only for the good of the world and traces its history from the "Good War" to the "humanitarian" intervention in Libya, and the "liberation" of Iraq. Along the way, he not only shows the lie behind the concept but how that concept is accepted by most US citizens in the same way Christians accept the immaculate conception of the Virgin Mary.

These two books provide a complementary narrative on US foreign policy. While Hart's examines the development of the US imperial propaganda machine, Blum's looks at its growth and also the brutality of the military whose operations the propaganda seeks to misconstrue. As we move into an age where the only victims of US wars are those whom our propaganda claims to be freeing and the assumption of our national goodness is enforced and reinforced to the point of overkill, the understanding these two books provide is more crucial than ever.

A Microcosm of the Nation–Control Unit Prisons

Out of Control: A Fifteen Year Battle Against Control Unit Prisons—Nancy Kurshan

In the late 1990s and early part of this century I worked as a researcher and writer for the journal Southland Prison News. This small journal usually ran about thirty pages and was sent out to prisoners incarcerated primarily in the US South. Edited by an inmate in Virginia, each issue contained a digest of articles concerning prisoners and prisons along with a feature or two, some book reviews, some prisoner poetry and art. I stopped working for the journal when the funding dried up. Before that work, I had never spent much time working on prison-related issues. Sure, I had attended forums and rallies supporting various political prisoners and prisoner rights ever since the uprising and massacre at Attica prison in 1971, but my political work usually did not involve prison issues. Perhaps this came from a distaste acquired through various brushes with the law and the subsequent days spent in jail here and there.

The same cannot be said for Nancy Kurshan and the people whose work she so artfully chronicles in the recently released book *Out of Control: A Fifteen Year Battle Against Control Unit Prisons*. Kurshan, a lifelong political activist, (among other things, she is one of the founders of the Yippies) is an ardent opponent of the US prison system, especially those prisons known as control unit prisons. Her book tells of the genesis and growth of these units throughout the United States and of the battle to oppose them.

It is not a tale with a happy ending. According to the text's introduction, over 80,000 prisoners are currently locked away in control unit prisons in the United States. What this means is that over 80,000 prisoners exist in a world controlled almost completely by prison architecture and the guards those prisons employ. Living in cells smaller than many suburban bathrooms, the walls are painted white, lights are on most of the day, no windows or even bars, hardly any exercise, no reading materials and no visitors; that is the life of most prisoners in these units. Sometimes there are even further restrictions. Rarely are there fewer. These units are constantly watched by prison video feeds and prisoners are often beaten at will by the guards. If this doesn't bother you, then you probably shouldn't bother reading the rest of this review.

There are over 2,000,000 people locked up in the United States. That is more than any other nation in the world. Furthermore, the rate of incarceration in the United States is higher than that of any other nation. According to the NAACP, African American and Latinos comprised 58% of all prisoners in 2008, even though they make up approximately one quarter of the US population. This is not because Blacks and Latinos are more likely to be criminals. It is because US laws and the police that enforce those laws target these demographic groups. This fact alone lends credence to the argument made by the activists in *Out of Control* that there is a calculated plan to imprison black and Latino men in the US. The history of the US is one that required control of its Black population, even after slavery. Indeed, even more so after slavery. Prisons are part of that plan. It is with this as a fundamental part of that understanding that Kurshan tells her story of a movement (Movement to End the Marion Lockdown) built to oppose that calculation.

The reader is presented with detailed descriptions of the meetings, protests, legal campaigns, and other work the Committee to End the Marion Lockdown undertook over the fifteen years of its existence. This group was composed of leftists, religious clergy and laity, families of prisoners and other concerned humans. There are small victories and many defeats, primarily because of the complete lack of regard for prisoners' humanity displayed by the Bureau of Prisons, most politicians and other officials. There are also the small victories. After years of demanding a new water source be built for the Marion prison, headway was finally made. Occasionally, even a prisoner gets freed. Throughout, the narrative is told with a warmth and humanity that exists in direct contrast to the tales being told. Her description of the development of a friendship between her family and the Reverend Bruce Wright, whose book Black

Robes, White Justice was one of the first books to discuss in plain terms the role the US justice system plays in continuing the racism of US society, is the story of a friendship between unsung warriors.

Many of the procedures used in control unit prisons began in the 1960s when the United States government started locking up leftist revolutionaries and others as part of its COINTELPRO program. This time period is also when leftists began to consciously focus on prisoner rights, in part because their leaders were being locked up. This work helped them to understand that prisons are the final point of confrontation between the state and those who act against it. Indeed, this is precisely why prisoner struggles for human rights are components of the greater struggle for those rights.

As pointed out before, there are now over 2,000,000 people incarcerated in the United States. Prison construction and maintenance is often one of the larger elements of government budgets. This is despite the fact that crime has consistently gone down in the past decade. These facts make it clear that prisons are not so much about fighting crime as they are about controlling segments of the population. As austerity takes a greater hold on the US economy, one can be certain that more working and poor men and women will be sent to prison while the real thieves run the country further into the ground.

Besides being a detailed and inspiring account of a group of human rights activists, Nancy Kurshan's *Out of Control* is a useful resource for discussing the realities of prison in the twenty-first century United States. It is also the tale of a particular part of the movement opposed to that reality.

Albert Camus and the Liberal Dilemma

Algerian Chronicles—Albert Camus

Albert Camus is arguably one of the greatest writers of the twentieth century. His relatively short life is well chronicled and the fodder of multiple conversations in university literature classes. His novels and essays raise fundamental questions about life in a world where life can easily be seen to mean absolutely nothing. Like Jean Paul Sartre–another writer with whom Camus is often compared and contrasted–Camus' search for meaning in a world rendered meaningless strikes a chord in every human, especially those who do not seek easy answers. The conclusion these men reached was that it is up to us to provide our own meaning.

It has always been a curiosity, then, why Camus had such a difficult time understanding the desire of the Algerians to create a meaning to their lives that required overthrowing the French colonialists. His understanding that human freedom was perhaps the greatest quality humanity possessed seemed to stop short of recognizing the denial of that freedom under colonialism. This shortsightedness led Camus to justify situations in a manner that remind this reviewer of Rube Goldberg's inventions, only without the result desired. In other words, explanations full of loops and turns but without even the conclusive ending Goldberg's inventions achieved.

So, it was with just such a hope for clarification that I picked up Camus' recently published (in English) *Algerian Chronicles*. Perhaps these writing would reveal some clarity to his position not found previously. Unfortunately, I was disappointed. While Camus certainly goes further in explaining his position (or perhaps lack of a position would be a better phrasing) regarding the situation of the French vis-a-vis their occupation of Algeria, that position is no less muddleheaded than any explanation previously published.

This collection of writings includes a number of articles and essays Camus wrote for French journals. It also includes some rather extensive reporting on the situation of the colonized Algerians. These writings do much toward describing the plight of these people, but suffer from an inability to acknowledge, much less examine the root cause for their situation. After citing example after example of colonial neglect and abuse, Camus still fails to point the finger at the cause of these failings. My visceral reaction is simply, how can he not understand that these examples are not failings of colonialism, but exactly how colonialism works. The psychological underpinnings are fundamental to the dynamic, affecting both the colonized and the colonizer.

In what is best described as the liberal dilemma, by refusing to accept that history is as important as the present when examining colonial and imperial situations, Camus' writing consistently falls short in its explanation of why Algeria and France found themselves in conflict in the years of the Algerian liberation struggle. In the historical vacuum that Camus places himself in, he ends up accepting the facts of French colonialism and oppression as immutable. Furthermore, he seems to reject the idea that the Algerians should have any say in their own future unless it is on terms determined mostly by the French colonizers.

As always, Camus' writing shines. Reading these relatively short articles prove his ability to evoke emotion and make his argument eloquently. Unbeknownst at the time of their writing, Camus' writings about the French colonization of Algeria Camus are also chronicling its end. His personal laments regarding that demise represent the thinking of those who either cannot or will not acknowledge that the brutality and theft that all too often defines settler colonialism does not appear able to end without violence and tragedy.

Parallels to the situation of Algeria abound in modern history. One could easily argue that one of today's still existing examples of this dynamic is found in Palestine. The Palestinians are colonized in their own lands and their struggle to liberate those lands is often violent, as is the repression of that struggle. Most of the solutions presented are those created in Washington and Tel Aviv, much like many of the solutions to Algeria's situation were created in Paris. The idea that Palestinians deserve the right to determine the nature of their struggle is still not a popular one in imperial capitals. Neither was the idea that the Algerians (or the Vietnamese, to name another people struggling for their liberation) deserved that right in the time of their struggle.

A Human Rights Manifesto

A Human Rights Manifesto—Julie Wark

Julie Wark has written a manifesto for justice. Simply titled *A Human Rights Manifesto*, her book examines the UN Declaration of Human Rights and compares it to the current situation. In doing so, it is clear that we as a species have failed. While there is certainly plenty of blame to go around, from those activists who have resigned from the battle to those who have convinced themselves that the current political and economic systems are capable of remedying the daily violations of human rights, the bulk of the blame remains with the greatest violators of those rights. That means governments, their militaries and police officials, and their courts. The ultimate violator however, in every measurement Ms. Wark relates, is the current manifestation of the capitalist economy: neoliberalism.

This book destroys the myth that neoliberal capitalism is a positive force for humankind. It does so by merely stating the facts. Example after example of the cruelties and deprivations unleashed in the name of corporate and financial freedom leap from these pages. Thousands of children starving every day; forests, rivers and mountains ravaged, raped and destroyed by the machines plowing under our planet's future; wars undertaken and resistance destroyed to ensure the continued expansion until death of the capitalist system emanating from the world's financial capitals. The perversion of local and national food economies via corporate manipulation of production through the commodification of food and artificial GMOs to the withholding of fertilizers and food via sanctions, humanity's fundamental right to not starve is denied. Despite the ravages described in A Human Rights Manifesto, the author holds out an optimistic hope flickering in this litany of despair. That flicker emanates from that long-forgotten and ignored declaration.

It's been clear to many for a while that humanitarian interventions are usually something else entirely. How else could one explain the increase in death that often occurs after the supposedly humanitarian troops arrive with their automatic weapons, their fighter planes and attack helicopters? How else can one explain the fact that when the original military phase of such interventions are over, the foreign troops remain, imposing the will of their political and corporate commanders back home? How else does one explain that in so many of these interventions, the majority of the civilians residing in said countries still find their lives at risk? The nature of these interventions and their non-humanitarian results have led many to scoff whenever the words "human rights" appear as a motivation. This skepticism feeds into the invaders' dynamic quite helpfully, leaving their military power plays unchallenged in any meaningful way.

Ms. Wark's book reclaims human rights for those whom they were originally intended. That is, for all humanity, especially those whose existence is considered unnecessary by the Goldman Sachs of the world. Instead of defining these rights in a manner that considers the right to buy and sell to be more important than the right to eat, Wark's text is inspired by an understanding that human rights can only be human rights when they are applied to all of humanity, not just those of a certain nation, political or religious philosophy, and certainly not only to those with property and wealth.

Essentially anarchist in its analysis, The Human Rights Manifesto gives no government or economic system a free pass. Yet it is primarily a searing indictment of neoliberal capitalism.

Don Winslow is the author of several works of crime fiction. His novels are about people that travel in the smuggling of contraband, drugs and human. The laws of society rarely apply in Winslow's world. Instead, it is usually the individual who is most brutal and amoral that succeeds. When the force of justice does appear, usually in the form of a renegade cop or private investigator, that justice is without mercy. I mention Winslow because Wark quotes his novels in her book. The quotes she chooses are not laudatory. Instead, they compare the morality of those who run and profit from the neoliberal capitalist economy to those that operate in the murderous economy Mr. Winslow writes of so graphically in his novels. The difference, the use of these quotes seems to claim, is just a matter of scale.

Perhaps the most interesting discussion in this book is the one presented by Wark concerning language and its (mis)use and manipulation. She lambastes the misuse of words like justice and the phrase human rights. Not only has their meaning been manipulated, it has been rendered meaningless. If the words describing a phenomenon no longer have any absolute meaning, then the phenomena become whatever those in power decide. In this world, justice becomes revenge and war becomes humanitarian intervention.

When the original UN Declaration was signed in 1948, it combined economic and political rights. After the major capitalist nations balked at the two elements being linked, the declaration was split and those nations objecting did not sign the part dealing with economic rights, which included statements detailing the right of all humanity to form labor unions, earn a fair wage, have shelter, health care, food and education. Washington and its cohorts knew that including these in any declaration of human rights would make the world they hoped to help build–the world we live in today–pretty much impossible. After all, without the commodification of food, education, shelter and health care, how would the financial-corporate nexus control the world like they do now?

Julie Wark's book is a revolutionary tract. All it does is demand that the human rights claimed by the wealthiest and most powerful in our world be applied to everyone. It is a shame that such a demand has become a call to revolution. But, if that's what is demanded, then we would do well to begin.

2014-2018

From Stokely to Kwame

Stokely: A Life—Peniel E. Joseph

Peniel E. Joseph's newly published biography of Black liberation activist Stokely Carmichael not only takes its rightful place next to Taylor Branch's epic trilogy The King Years, but also to one of the most powerful autobiographies by any American: Stokely Carmichael's own Ready For Revolution. Although Ready for Revolution is more emotionally cathartic, what Joseph's book lacks in emotion he makes up in detail and research. Together, the two books add uncountable wealth to the story of Stokely Carmichael and US civil rights movement history.

Carmichael was a member of the Student Nonviolent Coordinating Committee (SNCC), an interracial student organization dedicated to ending legal apartheid in the United States and empowering African-Americans through voter registration, education and organization. Like the slightly older, slightly less radical Southern Christian Leadership Conference (SCLC) identified with Dr. Martin Luther King, Jr., most of SNCC's best known work took place in the United States' South. Young men and women lived, organized and marched through Delta towns in Mississippi and country hamlets in Alabama (along with much of the rest of the South), facing down virulent racists bearing guns, wearing hoods and police uniforms, and spewing hatred.

Carmichael joined SNCC while a college student at Washington DC's Howard University. Once on board, he never looked back. According to Joseph, Carmichael was a natural organizer and leader. His charismatic presence, easy interactions with all kinds of people and his natural intelligence were all ingredients of his persona that pushed him into the national spotlight by his early twenties. Often playing (consciously or not) the militant to Dr. King's assumed moderation, the two men and their organizations forged a new era in the struggle for Black freedom in the US.

Stokely: A Life details the personal relationship between King and Carmichael, drawing a portrait of a friendship behind the headlines that strengthened as the decade of the 1960s raged on. It was a relationship that broadened both men's understanding of history, politics and the human condition. As the book progresses, one sees King becoming not only more radical in his understanding of the US system of domination thanks in part to Carmichael's friendship; King's deeper understanding of humanity also seems to affect Carmichael. This relationship is but one of the threads running through this well-told biography.

Of course, that relationship was ended on April 4, 1968 when King was assassinated in Memphis, Tennessee. I recall seeing live television feed of Carmichael in Washington DC that night shouting something and waving a gun. I always wondered about that image. As it turns out, Joseph tells the reader, Carmichael had just taken that gun from a young Black man whose anger had exploded. He was part of a group of individuals walking through the DC ghettos with Carmichael and other radicals telling store owners to close. While most storekeepers heeded the request and Carmichael tried to keep angry citizens from breaking windows, those efforts were in vain. Washington, DC burned for seven days along with dozens of other US cities.

The incident is emblematic of the political/social rage of the time. It is even more descriptive of how the media portrayed radicals like Carmichael. All too often they ignored words and efforts of these organizers, choosing instead to quote them out of context and show footage without explanation. Of course, those images and quotes played into white people's fears and, at the same time, represented the racial fears of many news correspondents. Joseph's book does a fairly good job of providing the truth about several such instances surrounding Carmichael.

Stokely Carmichael is probably best known for his championing of the Black Power trend in the movement for Black freedom. Joseph's book frames most of Carmichael's work and writings with this in mind. He discusses, albeit briefly, the popularization of the slogan for the first time in Mississippi during a voter registration drive. It was Carmichael (as the newly elected president of SNCC) and his closest confidantes (among them Cleve Sellers) who unleashed the slogan, explaining that it wasn't anti-white but was an insistence that the only way Black people would achieve justice in the United States was by taking power, not by asking the racist system to give them some. The slogan struck fear in the hearts of white America–fear fanned by the media and politicians who feared the Black vote. It also gave African-Americans a new sense of pride and a certain sense that they had power; they merely needed to organize it.

Joseph relies on numerous interviews, FBI surveillance records, oral histories, books, newspapers and other media to tell his story. For the most part, this serves him well. However, as almost any researcher knows, all sources have their shortcomings. FBI records not only represent a certain bureaucratic and law enforcement take on their subject matter but also reflect the individual agent's own prejudices. Oral histories and interviews rely on memory and the interviewee's sense of importance. Mainstream media sources have their own agenda. Overall, Joseph blends the information from his sources with his own understanding of the history he is writing to create a rounded, political and personal portrait of a figure often misunderstood by historians. If there is one shortcoming to this text, it would be in Joseph's description of Black Panther activities and interactions with SNCC and Carmichael. The author tends to over-simplify the politics of the Black Panthers and dismiss their Marxism as dogmatic and superficial. In addition, in mentioning the murder of Black Panther Bobby Hutton by Oakland Police, Joseph regurgitates The New York Times version of the event–a version seemingly taken directly from a police press release that mischaracterizes the Panther's role in keeping the lid on riots in Oakland after King's murder. To say the least, that particular incident remains disputed at best.

Politically speaking, Peniel Joseph seems to understand and support Carmichael's Pan-Africanism, at least to a point. After Carmichael moved to Guinea and adopted Nkrumahism as his political philosophy, his anti-communist tendencies tempered. According to Joseph, so did Carmichael's radical democratic tendencies, which he replaced with Nkrumah's African socialism. Carmichael also changed his name to Kwame Toure. This political maturation is discussed in the text, but not necessarily in the context of Carmichael's previous understanding. Always a staunch anti-imperialist, but never a Marxist, Carmichael seemed to mix and match his political philosophies to create a stew that helped him understand the situation of his people and move them forward. If one were to place him in the context of the period, the best comparison would be the movement of non-aligned nations. This was an international movement of nations and national liberation movements opposed to US imperialism but not wishing to align themselves with the Soviet Union or its sphere of influence.

Stokely: A Life is a quality read. By highlighting the life of one of the US civil rights/black liberation most important organizers and thinkers, Peniel E. Joseph has done a great service to history and to the people Stokely fought for. Furthermore, Peniel's text has lifted Carmichael out of an obscurity he not only didn't deserve, but which also prevented a more complete understanding of a man who, with Malcom X and Martin Luther King, Jr., deserves to be recognized as one of the great leaders of one of the greatest grassroots movements for liberation in history: the Black freedom struggle in the United States.

The Evil That Was Phoenix

The Phoenix Program: America's Use of Terror in Vietnam—
Douglas Valentine

"Phoenix was far worse than the things attributed to it."
—Ed Murphy, former member of the Phoenix program.

There's a reason the CIA wanted to prevent the publication of Douglas Valentine's 1990 book, *The Phoenix Program: America's Use of Terror in Vietnam*. This masterwork is more than an exposé of the US pacification program in Vietnam the book is titled after. It is an indictment of a cynical and bloody plan to kill Vietnamese. In his book The Family Jewels, author John Prado wrote, "When a (CIA) Publications Review Board lawyer checked to see whether Phoenix was off-limits ..., he was advised to caution interviewees not to talk to Valentine." Valentine wrote in an email regarding the CIA's attempts to stifle his investigation: "There were other form of harassment as well, the kind all investigators of CIA war crimes are subjected to. The midnight calls threatening to kill me or burn my house down. My wife got in the habit of telling the callers to take a number and stand in line. We never took it seriously. Ironically, everything I was doing was legal, and I wasn't trying to hide anything....Many of the threats came from former Navy SEALs, who were angry about my portrayal of them as psychopathic killers on a murder spree. A group of former Phoenix advisors, who did not like characterizing them as war criminals for conducting Gestapo style operations against Vietnamese civilians, were also prone to threats and later, after the book came out, slanders on Amazon and elsewhere. This is the same "Swift Boat" clan that attacked John Kerrey during his presidential campaign.

However, times were slightly different then. Intelligence agencies, while powerful, were not as powerful as they are today, in part because of the popular revulsion at their modus operandi. So, one assumes, the Agency really could not prevent the book's publication. It has been out of print until now. Mark Crispin Miller, professor of media studies and a media critic, is now publishing it as the first of his Forbidden Bookshelf series; an endeavor involving reprinting hard-to-find books addressing the realities of the US social-political infrastructures from a critical (and mostly left) perspective.

The Phoenix program was the culmination of a number of counterinsurgency plans undertaken by the Central Intelligence Agency, the military and a few other related agencies. All of these plans, like Phoenix itself, were designed to infiltrate and destroy the infrastructure of the communist-led Vietnamese insurgency—or as it was known by most US residents—the Viet Cong. Valentine describes in specific detail a bureaucratic machinery of torture and deceit: a single-minded operation designed to sow distrust, uncertainty and death. The first several chapters in the book describe and dissect the agencies, programs and individuals involved in the counterintelligence precursors to the Phoenix Program. It is a tale of inter-agency competition and occasional cooperation, clashing egos in Vietnam and DC and differences of opinion between Vietnamese and US police and government agencies. The latter is perhaps best exemplified by the different meanings attributed to the Phoenix bird symbol. The Vietnamese word for Phoenix is Phuong Hoang, yet the graphic used by the Vietnamese represented hope, while the US symbol was a bird of prey holding missiles in its claws.

For those who don't know, Phoenix was a systemic attempt to find and kill Vietnamese fighting against the US and its designs. It did this through terror, torture, intelligence-gathering and the relocation (and murder) of the insurgency's civilian supporters. Even if one believes the worst of the US military and intelligence agencies in Vietnam, the facts on how Phoenix played out on the ground among the Vietnamese people remains difficult reading. Valentines journalistic "just the facts ma'am" approach does not hide anything. Nor is that his intention. By laying out the facts in the manner that Valentine does, the reader finds passages in this book where the recitation of those facts cause great sadness and anger. Perhaps the greatest such example of this occurs in the chapter Valentine calls "Modus Vivendi" where he summarizes the Vietnamese writer Truong Buu Diem's 1968 article in the liberal Catholic Vietnamese newspaper Tin Sang (Morning News). The article, which was titled, "The Truth About Phoenix," describes the violent and deadly effects of the program, questions its purpose, and calls it American revenge for Tet. The layers of hierarchy and bureaucracy constructed and maintained in order to facilitate this machine remind the reader of both General Motors and Nazi Germany's Reichssicherheitshauptamt (Reich Main Security Office.) Morality was not part of the equation. Although some military members assigned to Phoenix objected on moral grounds or because they were expected to violate the Geneva conventions, most of those who opposed their assignment did so on career grounds or because they resented being under CIA command.

Valentine ends the body of his text with a look at the US-sponsored warfare and counterinsurgency operations being waged in Central America in the 1980s (when his book was originally published.) If one extrapolates the essence and practices of the Phoenix Program to Washington's more recent wars—from Afghanistan to Iraq to the so-called Global War on Terror, it becomes clear that Phoenix remains a working template of how the US continues to conduct such operations. Furthermore, it is also a template occasionally used by Washington's clients overseas.

The Phoenix Program is an alternative history of the US war on the Vietnamese. It is closer to the truth than anything published by the military or intelligence establishment and gives lie to the ongoing efforts by various veteran and government historians to turn the US war into a noble effort—something that it never was. There is currently a campaign to commemorate the fiftieth anniversary of the US war in Vietnam. The campaign relies on a revisionist retelling of that adventure and attempts to relieve US forces (military and otherwise) responsibility for the death and destruction they caused. This is one more reason the republication of The Phoenix Program is therefore quite timely.

Seduced by Surveillance

Technocreep: The Surrender of Privacy and the Capitalization of Intimacy—Thomas P. Keenan

We live in a world overwhelmed with intrusive technological gadgets. Most of us have learned to live with this fact and many of us have even embraced it. The latter are those who have apps to close their garage door and check the lights at home while they wait for their plane in an airport a thousand miles away. They are also those who post everything they eat and do on social media apps that then store this information for eternity. The omnipresence of social media and the technology that makes it possible has created a serious ethical situation regarding the question of personal privacy. For agencies where ethics are nothing more than a minor hindrance–government intelligence agencies and organized crime for example–this technology is a godsend. What once required actual feet on the ground and snooping inside homes and other private property is now able to take place from an office cubicle with a laptop. When one considers the voluntary provision of too much information (or TMI as the popular acronym proclaims) that social media encourages, one can understand even better why the aforementioned agencies truly appreciate the new internet-related gadgetry.

Government agencies and criminal enterprises are not the only entities enjoying the new availability of personal information. Corporations are too. As most people know, every keystroke and touch screen touch is recorded by any number of internet robots, stored and then regurgitated as an advertisement. This creates occasionally humorous buying suggestions for the user and annoying advertisements that assume too much and transform every interaction into a commercial possibility. This is an ideal metaphor for the neoliberal capitalist world we live in; it is also a disturbing trivialization of our ever-more-trivial lives.

There is also an element of the entire internet snooping abilities that is, for the lack of a better word, just plain creepy. This element is one that internet security guru and University of Calgary professor Thomas P. Keenan addresses in his new book, *Technocreep: The Surrender of Privacy and the Capitalization of Intimacy*. It's clear from the title that the use of the word "creep" is a play on its multiple meanings. It is also clear that the book is about much more than just the potential creepiness of unwanted Facebook "friending" or inappropriate and offensive advertisements appearing in one's social media account. Indeed, the true focus of the book is the steady integration of this technology into not just our public lives, but also our intimate existence.

Furthermore, perhaps the most unpalatable aspect of this techno-creep is that it is done under the pretense that it is to the social media users' benefit, when in actuality its only purpose is to further atomize human existence; an atomization designed by and for a capitalism that demands greater and greater numbers of consumer units to satisfy its ravenous needs.

Keenan's approach utilizes anecdotes and facts. Some of the anec-dotes are humorous even as they uncloak one more invasive intention of the surveillance web. Others are not funny at all, evoking paranoia well beyond that which Winston Smith and Julia lived under in George Orwell's 1984. Technocreep is not a call to arms, nor is it a hacker's handbook. However, behind and beyond the seemingly never-ending description of tools designed to record the most intimate details of our lives and store them for corporate and governmental powers, Keenan hints that the only certain method to prevent total surveillance and domination is by outsmarting the corporate-owned geeks who create the code and devices being used to create this panopticon. In other words, anti-corporate/government hacking is legitimate self-defense. Keenan does not provide instructions on how to hack, but he does end his book with a list of tips on how one can make it more difficult for snoops to do their snooping.

If nothing else, Kennan has written a helpful description of what kind of surveillance is undertaken by corporations, governments, criminal enterprises and just plain creeps every second of every day. He presents that description with humor and a knowledge that comes from years in the industry. There is also a healthy mistrust of those who write the laws and how easily those laws are not only ignored, but irrelevant before their ink is dry thanks to the much quicker pace of technology. This book should be read by anyone who uses a smartphone, computer or other device connected to the internet. It won't make you feel better, but at least you'll know what you're up against.

Mr. Kurtz Comes to America

*An Indigenous People's History of the United States—Roxanne
Dunbar Ortiz*

Joseph Conrad is responsible for some of the best writing on imperialism's darker side in the English language. The jungles of Marlowe and Kurtz in his classic novel Heart of Darkness remain some of literature's ugliest manifestations of European hubris and white racism ever written. Conrad's characters are so well contrived they have become metaphors for the imperial economic and cultural system of domination that is championed by its kings and rulers as much as it is maligned by its victims and those opposed to its machinations. The sheer brutality of the rational yet insane Kurtz represents the reality of colonialism at its most murderous. Kurtz's statement at the end of the novel, "Exterminate all the brutes!" is the most succinct take on colonialism and imperialism's final solution to challenges from their subjects that exists.

Furthermore, that statement represents not only a solution for Kurtz and his real life inspirations and imitators; it also represents the history of European subjugation of the planet. This is why essayist Sven Lindquist used it for the title of his classic on the history of imperialist racism, Exterminate All the Brutes! Likewise, a new history of the United States from Roxanne Dunbar Ortiz, titled *An Indigenous People's History of the United States*, discusses and illuminates what may be the most obvious and complete expression of Kurtz's sentiment— the genocidal destruction of the indigenous peoples of North America. This genocide was close to total. Entire nations of people were killed off, their cultures denied, and their lands stolen. The physical methods undertaken in the course of this destruction gave new definition to the term brutality. The philosophical underpinnings of the centuries'

133

long endeavor provided a spiritual and epistemological rationale for the brutality.

Virtually all history has elements that are never pretty, never uplifting, and rarely mentioned by most historians. This book is one such history. The saga Dunbar Ortiz chronicles is one born in resistance to European and American colonialism and imperialism. From the struggles against the early British settlers in New England and Virginia to the final catastrophes at Sand Creek and Wounded Knee, Dunbar Ortiz never flinches from the truth. Because it is a history of the United States, and given the fact that the United States was created on land absconded from the people living on and cultivating the land when they arrived, it is also a history whose primary definition is that resistance. Early on, the comparison to the more modern settler states of South Africa and Israel is made. However, it remains clear that the land called the United States is the template for settler colonialism. This history makes it clear that this process is not only about land, it is also about the total erasure of those being replaced from human memory. Undertaking such a project involved a combination of murderous militarism, psychological manipulation and the creation of a myth that told the settlers any killing they undertook against the natives was blessed by God, no matter how cruel a form such killing took.

There were various colonial-settler warriors who took greater delight than others in the mass murder they perpetrated. Andrew "Old Hickory" Jackson and William Tecumseh Sherman were two such men. Jackson had no shame when it came to his racist attitudes towards Native Americans and Blacks. Indeed, his men fashioned reins from for their horses from the skin of Shawnees they had killed. Meanwhile, Sherman's reputation as the reigning master of total warfare against a population was only enhanced during the US counterinsurgency campaigns against Native Americans. His burning of Atlanta during the US Civil War remains as one of history's most brutal and bloody campaigns against a civilian population in the long and bloody history of warfare. Some of his final public statements quoted in this text prove his bloodlust never changed. As Dunbar Ortiz reminds the reader, the tactics of war undertaken by these men and the multitude of other US soldiers and militia men remain in use today in every military foray undertaken by Washington's troops and mercenaries.

Some stories cry out to be told. Often, the reason they have not been told is because those in power fear the particular truths of the tale.

The story told by Roxanne Dunbar Ortiz in An Indigenous People's History of the United States is one such story. It has been too long in telling. Dunbar Ortiz's writes her narrative with a measured rage that enlivens the history being told, challenging the reader to reconsider every other history ever written about the United States. Essential myths of American exceptionalism are destroyed in these pages while the truths of its bloody genesis and maintenance are categorically declaimed. Informed by Frantz Fanon and Tecumseh alike, Dunbar Ortiz has written a well-researched and important history of genocidal war and indigenous resistance. When it comes to the settler nation called the United States, there is very little virtue in what is written in these pages. This book takes its place in the library of those history texts that tell the history the rulers do not want told. That in itself is justification enough for its publication. Dunbar Ortiz's captivating and incisive writing only enhances that justification.

Making Liberation

Seizing Freedom: Slave Emancipation and Liberty for All—David Roediger

In 1863, the US Civil War was raging and Black men were finally being encouraged to join the fight. Abolitionist and freed slave Frederick Douglass published a broadside titled Men of Color, Call to Arms! Desiring to emphasize that only the slaves could free themselves from their bondage, Douglass borrowed the line, "Who would be free themselves must strike the blow" from Lord Byron's epic poem "Childe Harold's Pilgrimage."

In his new book titled *Seizing Freedom: Slave Emancipation and Liberty for All*, historian David Roediger discusses how enslaved Black America did "strike the blow" and in the process opened up the avenues for women and labor to begin to free themselves. Conversely, he also discusses the ongoing attempt to stifle movements for labor rights, Black and women's liberation after the emancipation of the slaves. This latter tale is one of repression by the economic and power elites that run the United States. It is also the story of organized terror gangs like the Klan and unorganized white mobs fighting and killing in their determination to defeat those gains toward liberation.

Roediger uses W.E.B. DuBois' classic text Black Reconstruction as a primary inspiration, while informing the text with text materials from the likes of Sojourner Truth and Elizabeth Cady Stanton; Karl Marx and Frederick Douglass and a myriad of contemporary historians from Hank Gutman to Eric Foner. Seizing Freedom is not so much a chronological history of the period covered as much as it is a penetrating examination of the ideas, individuals, movements and debates composing the movement to end US slavery forever. By providing the readers with this examination, Roediger makes clear and essential links to movements that came into existence largely because of the abolitionists.

There are moments in human history where everything seems possible. The period of revolution in Europe during the latter decades of the 18th century is one such period. So was the period after World War Two now known as the Sixties. Another historical moment that must be included is the one discussed in this book. Besides including the abolitionist period, Civil War and Reconstruction in the United States, the revolutions of 1848 in Europe are also part of those decades' weltanschauung. Roediger borrows a phrase from historians of the French revolution describing such moments as "revolutionary time." In short, to quote the author, it is a time "in which the pace of change and the possibility of freedom accelerated the very experience of time." Indeed, even if the times do not bring about a revolutionary overthrow of governments, the popular groundswell these times engender force governments to make very radical reforms. They are also usually followed by periods of reaction and disillusionment.

Seizing Freedom delves into both the revolutionary and post-revolutionary time periods as they reference the emancipatory movements of the mid-nineteenth century in the United States. The unity of the various elements involved in forcing the end of slavery prior to, during and immediately after the Civil War is juxtaposed with the exposure of differences based on race, class and gender in the movement as the forces of Southern reaction coalesced with the interests of northern liberals interested in maximizing profits. In a drama that has been repeated more than once since that time, the special interests based on gender, race and class of groups in the anti-slavery coalition turned those differences into fissures that could not be resolved. This provided the power elites an opening to regain control and forced the formerly liberation movements into election slogans and special interest groups. This marked the end of that particular revolutionary time.

Bob Dylan wrote in his memoir Chronicles: Volume I that the United States is still fighting the Civil War. This latest text by David Roediger assumes a similar understanding. It further enhances this understanding by examining the revolutionary effects of the emancipation of the slaves that that war was a crucial (if not the most crucial) part of. He tells the reader that it wasn't Abraham Lincoln who freed the slaves, but the slaves themselves who struck their own blow for liberation. It was the slaves who inspired and motivated a grand coalition of women, clergy, writers, laborers, businessmen, soldiers, farmers and others in a revolution that overturned the dominant understanding in the US that black men, women and children were, first and foremost, property. Another equally important aspect of this revolution was ridding the nation of the perception that African-Americans, even if they were free, had no rights that white men had to respect. It is telling that more than one hundred fifty years later, Black residents of the United States are still fighting for that respect.

Going Down to Highway 61, Again

On Highway 61: Music, Race and the Evolution of Cultural Freedom—Dennis McNally

US Highway 61 is the subject of a number of American songs. Blues pianist Roosevelt Sykes cut "Highway 61 Blues" in 1932. In 1933 Memphis bluesmen Jack Kelly and Will Batts recorded "Highway No. 61 Blues," and the Tupelo-born Sparks Brothers recorded "61 Highway" Other similarly titled recordings from that decade included "Highway 61" by Jesse James and "Highway 61 Blues" by Sampson Pittman. These songs and others were subsequently recorded by other bluesmen and women. Then, of course, there is the song titled "Highway 61 Revisited", that appears on the album Bringing It All Back Home by Bob Dylan. The road itself stretches from Minnesota's northlands all the way to the Gulf of Mexico, paralleling the mighty Mississippi River. Like the waterway itself, Highway 61 cuts through the US heartland, sharing its weathered surface with rich men and poor women, dark-skinned and light, descendants of slaves and slave-owners, soldiers and civilians, hoboes and RVs, wanderers and folks with a purpose; they enter and leave the road, appearing and disappearing into the fabric that is the North American heartland. Also like the Mississippi River, it is the source of memories and tall tales, some written and many more shared among friends and acquaintances made in a bar or by a campfire.

It is this latter tradition that author and cultural historian Dennis McNally explores in his latest work, titled *On Highway 61: Music, Race and the Evolution of Cultural Freedom.* Having already made his mark in the cultural realm with his comprehensive biography of Jack Kerouac (Desolate Angel: Jack Kerouac, The Beat Generation, And America) and the official biography of the musical and cultural traveling show called the Grateful Dead (What a Long Strange Trip It's Been), McNally adds to his credits, and our understanding of the United States, with this exploration of the intersection of culture, race, and the idea of freedom intrinsic to the American myth.

McNally begins the journey in New England, hundreds of miles from the Mississippi and his fabled road. This beginning is a philosophical one, founded in the thoughts of Henry David Thoreau. Specifically, his thoughts on one of the United States' most damning and unforgiving stains—the stain of African slavery. McNally succinctly ties together Thoreau's expression of the American ideal that places individual freedom at its core, the obvious contradiction such a philosophy comes up against in a slaveholding nation, and Thoreau's increasingly radical writings opposing the institution of slavery itself. This chapter ends with a brief look at Thoreau's essay titled "A Plea for John Brown;" a man who in Thoreau's estimation (and McNally's too, I venture) embodied the genuine freedom considered essential to the American settler myth. After all, Brown acted as a free man to free other men held in slavery by a nation unwilling to face one of its most fundamental failings.

Next, McNally takes the reader west to the Mississippi. To Hannibal, Missouri to be precise. He introduces the reader to the young Mark Twain (Samuel Clemens) and then to his masterwork; his tale of two outsiders on the Mississippi, one a lost boy named Huckleberry Finn and the other an escaped slave named Jim. The Adventures of Huckleberry Finn remains in the top echelons of literature composed in the United States. Nominally the story of these two people, their relationship, their hiding out from their pursuers and the people of the river, this novel is an abolitionist novel in a manner so intrinsic that aspect of its essence was (and is) missed by all too many of its detractors. For McNally, its publication in the late 19th century is the beginning of a neverending journey of discovery, denial, reconciliation and rejection for Americans white-skinned and Black. Like Huck and Jim's travels down the river, there is never any genuine certainty things will turn out well.

There are many sides to the story of the United States since the Civil War and Reconstruction. Almost all of them include tales underwritten with hate and filled with violence. Some of them are told in narratives of poetry and novels. Others are told in song. Those are the ones McNally is interested in; the songs of black men and women, of blues and jazz. Also, those moments when white-skinned America hears those songs and makes them their own. It is an essential fact of US culture since the Civil War that much of its musical tradition was (and is) born in its African-American communities. Over the next couple hundred pages of On Highway 61, McNally relates the dynamic of this coming together, complete with a multitude of songs, the artists, and the recordings. In his telling, the reader gets a history of jazz, the blues, and US race relations. Additionally, conventional myths like those of American exceptionalism and equality are exposed for the lies they are while some of the wounds they have caused are exposed. More than an indictment though, McNally's narrative is also a study of the never-ending struggle to obtain the equality and the freedom promised in that myth of American exceptionalism. It is also about the disappointment that ensues when the struggle fails, again.

McNally ties up his history by looking at a musician whose songs, performances and adult life provide an almost perfect synthesis of those that preceded him in his trade. That man is the one they call Bob Dylan. Robert Johnson and Son House; Bessie Smith and Elvis; Charlie Patton and Alan Lomax; Willie Dixon and Benny Goodman—and all that came between. Bob Dylan was born near the northern beginning of Highway 61 and left his home rolling on that asphalt. He learned the blues, hillbilly, jazz, and folk, mixed it up with poetry, politics and rock and roll and turned on the pop music world. McNally considers this and does his best to explain how Dylan pulled it off—mostly by being a bluesman. It had worked for his predecessors and by god, it worked for Dylan, too.

I finished reading On Highway 61 while riding a bus down Vermont's Route 7, a small US highway that goes through the towns and villages that populate the eastern shore of Lake Champlain. Like its grander cousins in the old (pre-interstate system) US highway system, Route 7 goes through the population centers it serves, unlike the interstates which pass them by. Sugar houses and falling-in farms are scattered along its shoulders; the bus stops in almost every town along its route, taking on passengers and letting others off, each of them with a story to tell. Route 66 goes from east to west and is a road filled with legend. US Route 1 goes from New England to Florida, finally ending in the tip of

Florida—tourists, retirees, immigrants and contraband have traveled its path for decades. None of these roads (or their similarly numbered cousins around the countryside) bears the weight of history like Highway 61. Like other roads, it is both metaphor and reality. Northward migrations of people and cultures and songs of love, despair, tragedy and joy are but a small part of this road's essence. Dennis McNally is but the latest guide to take the reader on its byways. The job he does is matched by few and his perspective is his alone. Indeed, McNally rocks, rolls, burns, cruises and kills it in this book, his pedal to the metal from beginning to end.

Love Letter From Paris

letter to jimmy (On the twentieth anniversary of your death)—
Alain Mabanckou

Racism is white people's problem. Unfortunately it is those who are not white-skinned that suffer most directly from this problem. Although the legacy of Western colonialism means that every people and every nation involved in said colonialism has something to answer for, no nation has as much to answer for as the United States. This is true for one very basic reason. That reason is the enslavement of Africans and their descendants; and the subsequent economic and legal structure put in place to ensure the continuation of much of the oppression and repression established during slavery's existence. Elements of this structure encompass everything from the denial of the vote to laws designed to restrict the Black vote; lynchings and the failure to prosecute the lynchers to police murders of African-Americans and the refusal to prosecute those police; the denial of education to the denial of funds for equal education; the de jure segregation of housing to the redlining of traditionally Black housing areas; ad infinitum.

So much of America (especially white America) does not understand what it's like to be harassed by the police almost every day just for acting like you believe you are free. They don't get what it means to have to be always wondering if the police are going to ask you for ID, insult you personally and racially, make you empty your pockets and throw you up against the wall. They don't really understand what it means to feel like you don't belong in the neighborhood you live in because the police (who usually come from a different town and often are of a different skin tone) stop you and fuck with you whenever they want. And they really don't understand what it means to know in your heart that those cops

143

could kill you, get away with it, and become TV stars in the process. The racist legacy of slavery is still too much a part of the American way..

Author James Baldwin, who wrote about life in the United States in the shadow of slavery better than almost anyone, once stated "I know what the world has done to my brother and how narrowly he has survived it. And I know, which is much worse, and this is the crime of which I accuse my country and my countrymen, and for which neither I nor time nor history will ever forgive them, that they have destroyed and are destroying hundreds of thousands of lives and do not know it and do not want to know it... But it is not permissible that the authors of devastation should also be innocent. It is the innocence which constitutes the crime."(The Fire Next Time)

Nothing proves this statement better than this fact: at this writing a Black man is killed about every 28 hours by police in the United States. Further proof of Baldwin's concern is the never-ending excuses provided by the police, courts and politicians and media spokespeople rationalizing law enforcement's practices. The fact that police are rarely if ever prosecuted lies in the very fact that the law guarantees their immunity. The fact that we accept those laws guarantees the persistence of these murders.

James Baldwin grew tired of the racism ingrained into life in the United States and moved to Paris. This provided him with a chance to see his native country even clearer. It also meant that his life in Europe would be different than that of his African expatriate cousins. This is one of the themes explored by author Alain Mabanckou in his recently released (in English) *letter to jimmy (On the twentieth anniversary of your death)*. Written in the form of a letter addressed to Baldwin, the text is a personal rumination on Baldwin's life and works. It is simultaneously compelling and profound in its approach.

Mabanckou begins by discussing James Baldwin's relationship with his stepfather David. It is this relationship, writes Mabanckou, that informs the stepson's relationship to the world and to the complicated web that comprises race relations in the United States. His anger and what James perceives as self-loathing taints the relationship between father and son, while also inspiring the son to look at the world in a different way. Mabanckou describes this phenomenon like this: "David

Baldwin is black, and does not realize that he is beautiful, you point out." It was the younger Baldwin's mission to bring the beauty of every human, especially those cast as ugly by the dominant culture, to the forefront of our consciousness.

James Baldwin was a gay man. For lack of a more descriptive term, this meant his alienation in the gaze of the white and straight culture that dominated his world was doubled. Mabanckou acknowledges this and, like many critics since, asks what this meant to Baldwin's worldview. I wonder what Baldwin's perspective might be if he were alive today—in a western world where, for many people, his homosexuality would be more acceptable than his Black skin.

In letter to jimmy, Mabanckou takes the reader on a walk through James Baldwin's life and writing. Although possibly more meaningful to the reader who knows at least some of Baldwin's books, the power of this text lies in Mabanckou's direct and personal style and his ability at making the reader an intimate in his epistle to Baldwin. The fact of the book's existence seems to indicate Baldwin's inspiration in Mabanckou's writing. Mabanckou even describes his tract as a "love letter" to the late author to whom the letter is addressed. Baldwin's writing always worked on a multitude of levels, emotionally and intellectually. In this wonderfully written tribute, Alain Mabanckou writing does so, too.

Rejecting Revisionist History

War and Revolution: Rethinking the Twentieth Century—
Domenic Losurdo

A popular understanding of history in today's world involves blaming the most radical revolutionaries of France in the late 18th century and Russia in 1917 for many of the modern ills. This trend is espoused in intellectual and popular culture and is the foundation on which much of modern politics is based. For the wealthy and the currently powerful, it is a self-serving and incredibly useful understanding. Hence, any popular attempts to alter this view are ruthlessly belittled and denied. It was exactly this that took place in the 1960s and the 1970s when colonized peoples, young people, workers and others reconsidered their role in history and took to the streets, forever changing the political/cultural landscape we live in.

In the years since, however, it is the historical understanding that serves the powerful that has been on the ascendant. Most commonly known among historians as revisionism, this understanding not only blames revolutionary forces for humanity's murderous excesses, it also urges a return to a semi-feudal situation that stratifies people in terms of class, race and gender, allowing different levels of economic and political freedom according to a hierarchy designed by those in power. In effect, it wishes to legally create the political world already being formed economically through neoliberalism.

Revisionism is a liberal approach to history. It equates the colonialism, racism and anti-Semitism of Nazism with the anti-colonial, anti-racist and liberationist foundations of communism. In doing so, it also ignores essential indisputable facts of western capitalist development. Foremost among these denials are the role the African slave trade

146

played in every European nation that was involved, its fundamental role (along with slavery itself) in the United States, and colonialism. By ignoring colonialism's essential role—and because of the racism inherent in the revisionist analysis—wars against colonized peoples are not even considered wars. In other words, unless Europeans are dying on a massive scale, there is no war. This is especially the case in those situations (for example, the massacre by German settlers of the Herero and Nama peoples in southern Africa or the US in Grenada, Panama and the first Gulf War) where the number of dead at the hands of the victor far outweighs the number of the victorious army's dead.

In the conduct of war, all governments involved are more alike than different, more genocidal than peace seeking, more authoritarian than rights protecting. Total war means total mobilization and imprisonment or even death to those who disagree. God forgive the soldier unwilling to participate: Losurdo writes of an Italian general during World War One who "carried out trench inspections with an execution squad in tow" to save time. The battle is the most important thing, after all. The unwilling cannon fodder had best be aware.

The end of the 1970s did not mean an end to the non-revisionist understanding of history made popular by the masses in the streets. It did, however, signal a renewed effort to stifle that particular strain. This was in line with the times. Thatcher and Reagan were presiding over neoliberal capitalism's opening salvos on the Keynesian economic state and re-arming their already powerful militaries. The Soviet Union was heading towards a demise fostered by political and economic miscalculation intensified by a war against its 1917 revolution that began before the revolution had the means to solidify. In the face of the neoliberal attack, socialist and social democratic governments in Europe were beginning to become their opposite, remaining socialist or social democrat in name only. Ever since then, the Left has been either fighting to regain a sense of possibility or signing up with the neoliberal offensive pretending it can still be leftist while embracing monopoly capitalism's most inhumane incarnation to date.

Domenic Losurdo is an Italian Marxist and philosopher. He is also one of today's most acute critics of liberalism. His latest work to be translated into English, *War and Revolution: Rethinking the Twentieth*

Century, is an intellectual rebuke to the revisionist historians masquerading as objective arbiters of the past when in reality their words serve finance capital and its ravaging of the planet. Losurdo rejects the West's portrayal of itself as civilized and humane in contrast to Russia and the East. Philosopher by philosopher, historian by historian, he dissects those western intellectuals' attempts to mythologize these lies cleverly and decisively. Losurdo takes the attempts by various revisionist historians to blame the Bolsheviks and French Jacobins for the history of terror and turns them on their head. Instead, he writes, It is the reactionary and liberal capitalist regimes whose policies of total war and forced removal of populations (the Native Americans and the Africans, most notably) which created the reaction of the revolutionary governments. In other words, it was not the revolutionary forces as represented by the Jacobins and the Bolsheviks who brought mass murder, ethnic cleansing and slavery into this world, but the governments against which they revolted. Furthermore, Losurdo includes the phenomenon of twentieth-century fascism in the western colonial tradition. In other words, Hitler's plans to colonize Eastern Europe were not outside of the West's previous colonialist endeavor. In fact, as Losurdo repeatedly mentions, Hitler admired the totality of the American settlers' eradication of the indigenous peoples whose land they stole and saw it as a model for his brand of fascism.

Losurdo argues that in the reactionary system there is no war but "racial" war. He cites the propaganda used by the capitalist nations to mobilize the citizens in their respective states, turning the twentieth century wars against communism into wars against foreign, "Asiatic," even Jewish ideologies. One finds a similar scenario in the twenty-first century where wars against nations with large Muslim populations have become "racialized" wars against the Muslim world itself. As Losurdo makes clear, this racialization has helped create a mindset allowing for what he calls "the rehabilitation of colonialism." In other words, the powers that be promote their self-serving idea that there are parts of the world—mostly non-white—that could benefit from being colonized by those powers. In what can only be described as an ironic instance, I heard this sentiment expressed by two African-American men in Greenwich Village's Washington Square Park on September 11, 2001 while the smoke from the burning Twin Towers scraped the nostrils and throats of every one present.

War and Revolution: Rethinking the Twentieth Century is a relentless document. It is dense and disconcerting. This is precisely why it should be considered one of the most important history books written since the events known as 9-11. After all, it was those events which took the revisionist project already underway since the late 1970s and put it into hyperdrive. By intention, there has not been a day of peace since. This fact is not an accident. That is the essence of Losurdo's text.

The Tragedy of Capitalism

Stop, Thief!: The Commons, Enclosures, and Resistance—Peter Linebaugh

In 1968, the article "The Tragedy of the Commons" was published in Science magazine. The author of the article, Garret Hardin, whom critic Beryl Crowe called a "psychologically brave, but professionally foolhardy soul" in his response to Hardin's piece the following year (also in Science), essentially argued that the commons could only be maintained in today's world if it was privatized. He based his argument on an understanding of humanity that was Malthusian in its approach and assumed that the "rational" human is essentially a selfish human. Historian Peter Linebaugh published an essay titled "Enclosures from the Bottom Up" in which he labels Hardin's argument "a brutal argument with an inhuman conclusion."

That essay is but one of several that appears in Linebaugh's 2014 book *Stop, Thief!: The Commons, Enclosures, and Resistance*. The collections of essays are, when considered as a whole, a history of the struggle over the commons, from medieval times up to today. That struggle is a struggle between the rich and the commoner, the corporation and worker, the state and the people. It is a struggle replete with tales of heroic resistance and murderous repression. It is also a struggle which has probably never been sharper than today. Linebaugh examines this history, mixing stories of Luddite resistance with critical analysis of Karl Marx's *Das Kapital*.

The book opens with a mention of the Occupy movement of 2011. Recalling that popular upsurge involving people collectively occupying space in cities across the globe (especially in the United States and Europe), Linebaugh suggests that the movement was a contradiction. The city, he writes, is a place of consumption, whereas the countryside is where food and other materials required for life are produced. It is in the latter where the commons have been historically maintained and fought over. Yet, the Occupy movement existed and flourished in urban spaces. He counters this perception by providing a history that shows the city to be originally the result of the enclosure of the commons. From this point on, *Stop Thief!* takes the reader on a ride through revolutions and reactions, colonialism and imperialism, Karl Marx and Tom Paine.

Over the course of that ride, the reader is presented with a reasoned and reasonable look at the phenomena that encroach on one's life and liberty. He first introduces these culprits in an essay titled "The City and the Commons: A Story for Our Times." The culprits are not only named by their mode of operation—land privatization, population control, criminalization of custom, and imprisonment—they are also named by those their parents gave them. This gang of four's names are Jeremy Bentham, Arthur Young, Thomas Malthus, and Patrick Colquhoun and their mark on history and humanity remains. It is the story of this reality that fills the rest of Linebaugh's text.

Summoning Marx's discussion of what the landowners called the "theft of wood" from the forests they had their armies enclose; Linebaugh begins a fascinating discussion of capitalist accumulation and its ongoing role in today's mechanics of neoliberalism. In his essay on the fictional hero Ned Ludd, the Luddites and Percy Bysshe Shelley, one is reminded that class suicide existed well before Amilcar Cabral or the Weather Underground. In later chapters that include discussions of the French revolution and the American War for Independence, Linebaugh challenges the official narrative and asks why the Native Americans and African slaves are not included. In one chapter, the resistance to the enclosure of the Otmoor commons in Oxfordshire is described. This enclosure involved the privatization of the moor and the exclusion of sheep and cattle from grazing there. Peasants resisted with force and creative takeovers of the lands.

Incorporating feminist thought and Marxism, the role played by the division of labor that occurred in the wake of the industrial revolution is examined. According to Linebaugh, when women were relegated to the home they were, in essence, being enclosed away from the commons. If they did work, their job was likely to be performing one small task as part of the creation of a whole product. This alienation from the final product is in itself an enclosing of the mind, spirit and even the person. Of course, this alienation was felt by men in the factory, too. In shutting down the relationship to the completed product, the human being is/was being cut off from the commons. Karl Marx expresses this aspect of modern labor more precisely than anyone before or since in his section on estranged labor in the Economic and Philosophical Manuscripts of 1844:

"What, then, constitutes the alienation of labor? First, the fact that labor is external to the worker, i.e., it does not belong to his intrinsic nature; that in his work, therefore, he does not affirm himself but denies himself, does not feel content but unhappy, does not develop freely his physical and mental energy but mortifies his body and ruins his mind. The worker therefore only feels himself outside his work, and in his work feels outside himself. He feels at home when he is not working, and when he is working he does not feel at home."

Like Marx, Linebaugh draws the connection between the privatization of property and the estrangement of labor; the enclosure of the commons/common good and the alienation of humans from their work and from each other. *Stop Thief!* is simultaneously a look at the history of this process through a series of essays discussing people and events important to it and a discussion of its meaning for the present. Linebaugh blends the tales of the common man and woman, the poet and artist, and the economist and political scientist into prose that is poetic in approach and a delight to digest. One cannot help but learn from the lessons herein.

Women, Girls, and the War on Terror

Separate and Dominate: Feminism and Racism After the War on Terror—Christine Delphy

Christine Delphy is a French feminist. She founded the journal *Nouvelles questions féministes* (*New Feminist Issues*) with Simone de Beauvoir in 1977 and is a key proponent of the branch of feminism known as material feminism. This type of feminism is one that utilizes a Marxian class analysis to inform the role of women in capitalist society. Instead of the lukewarm and individualist feminism prevalent in the United States (and present in other Western nations including France), this approach challenges the essentially biologist emphasis of the mainstream movement and makes class and race a fundamental part of its analysis of women's oppression and resistance.

In recent years, she has been an outspoken opponent of the racist laws against Arabs and Muslims in France, especially those that are aimed specifically at women and girls. Foremost among these laws are those forbidding girls to wear the hijab in France's public schools. Besides calling out these laws for the tools of oppression they are, Delphy has recently published a text that examines the language and structure of the US-led global war on terrorism, France's role as willing accomplice in most of its aspects, and the nature of the French republic's insistence on secularism, at least when it comes to the Muslim religion. In the course of these discussions, the nature of colonialism and its aftermath are also discussed. So are racism in France and the French power structure's continued treatment of "second and third generation" immigrants as something less than French citizens—mostly because of their heritage and skin tone.

To begin the book, which is titled Separate and Dominate: Feminism and Racism After the War on Terror, Delphy discusses the concept of the Other. The essential point of this discussion is one that not only goes to the root of the concept; it takes that root and cracks open the seed from which it came. The Other exists, writes Delphy, because of a total lack of reciprocity in regards to those that determine who the Other is. In other words, the Other exists solely and only because of its lack of power in relation to the part of those who dominate. In other words, the role of the Other cannot be turned around to create a situation where the dominant groups (the Ones) become the Other. This is because the very definition of what defines the Other is based in its subordination to the Ones. The Other can be based on race, gender, sexuality or class; it can be any combination of these, and it is always subordinate to the Ones, because it is the master groups that have created the definitions of race, class, gender and so on. The subversion of this matrix is the only way to ending it. Delphy underlines her argument by pointing out that our understanding of the Other is a purely Western invention and is part of the sociology of colonialism.

The shortest essay in this collection is titled "War without End." It was written after the US invaded Afghanistan and challenges the war's entire rationale. By attacking "terrorism," writes Delphy, Washington is providing itself with a rationale for never-ending war, since the war itself will create more of those fighters the West calls terrorists. This argument is well-worn by now; almost fourteen years after those first planes attacked the mountains populated by the Pashtun in 2001. Ina subsequent essay, the author discusses the rationale belatedly put forth by George Bush and company that the war on Afghanistan was for the liberation of the Afghan women. While Delphy notes that the liberation of women is always desirable, she pointedly argues that imperial war cannot achieve that goal. The discussion that ensues is a valuable and insightful look at the language of western empire in the twenty-first century and the contradictions of white feminism.

The book's final essay, titled "Anti-sexism or Anti –Racism" is an insightful and well-crafted discussion of every idea presented earlier in the text. By once again utilizing the battle in France over banning the wearing of the hijab as both a metaphor for more fundamental differences and as the crucial element in the debate it creates, Delphy rips apart the hypocrisy of French society—including the so-called Left—in its defense of the oppression of Arabs and Muslims in the name of secularism. Insisting essentially that this secularism relies on intolerance no different than that practiced by fundamentalist religion, she elucidates the need for a true feminism and radical critique that defies the structures of domination, not one that reinforces them. Certain to challenge her English-speaking readers as much as she challenges her readers in French, Christine Delphy's text is an important addition to the discussion around religion, racialism, and the aftermath of colonialism.

Spying on Black Writers: the FB Eye Blues

F. B. Eyes: How J. Edgar Hoover's Ghostreaders Framed African-American Literature—William J. Maxwell

"Got them blues, blues, blues
Them mean ol' FB Eye blues…"
　　—Richard Wright

The Federal Bureau of Investigation (FBI) is the oldest official national police force in the United States. Its focus has always been at least twofold: to investigate perceived threats to the existence of the US government and to go after criminals who commit certain crimes across state lines. The former focus has most often been turned towards the left side of the political spectrum, although recently that eye has turned a greater part of its view towards radical Islam. Like the leftist "threats" in the past, it seems from a daily reading of the news that many of these supposed threats are either paranoid fantasies of the Bureau and its agents or actually contrived by the Bureau itself. Another similarity is the lives these phantasms have destroyed.

One other consistent target of the FBI has been the non-white community in the United States. For the most part, at least until recently, this meant the African-American people. Indeed, the FBI is considered one of the most racist institutions in the US government since its inception. This was true in the case of its hiring practices and its approach to carrying out its mission. Any Black organization or individual standing up to racism was suspect; from the NAACP to Marcus Garvey and from Martin Luther King, Jr. to Black Panther Fred Hampton, fighting for equal rights and racial justice was automatically suspect.

The stories of FBI surveillance and harassment of Martin Luther King, Malcolm X, and numerous other civil rights and Black liberation activists are fairly well known. So is the racism of the long term director of the Bureau, J. Edgar Hoover. Less well known is the Bureau's harassment and surveillance of Black writers and other artists. That is the subject of the recently published book by William J. Maxwell titled *F. B. Eyes: How J. Edgar Hoover's Ghostreaders Framed African-American Literature.* The text was sourced primarily from FBI files the author Maxwell procured via Freedom of Information Act (FOIA) requests. He lists these requests and their results (whether he received any documents, how many pages and amount of redactions) in the book's appendix. The book also includes an excellent annotated index that in itself is quite a read for anyone interested in US government surveillance of its citizens.

Underlying Maxwell's text is the convincing notion that the control of African-Americans was central to the growth of the FBI and its presence in the popular imagination. It is the story of a megolomaniacal man (J. Edgar Hoover), his extreme nationalism/patriotism, racism, and ego. Naturally, it is also a history of Washington's ever-intensifying centralization of surveillance. Informed by Hoover's own racism and apparent doubts about his own heritage, Maxwell contends that this phobic obsession with Black America was as important as the Bureau's early focus on leftists and anarchists and its 1930s campaign against outlaws like John Dillinger and other so-called public enemies.

Like other histories detailing US racism and its continued existence after the Civil War and Reconstruction, FB Eyes relates the tale of the great boxer Jack Johnson and his persecution by racist law enforcement agencies around the United States. It was Johnson's flamboyant disregard for laws and customs forbidding interracial sexual relations and his ability to beat any white-skinned competitor (plus his tendency to brag loudly about it afterwards) that brought down the wrath pf white society and its enforcers. In fact, it was his bringing a white girlfriend with him across state lines that gave the FBI the opportunity to prosecute him under the Mann Act (this law was used to prosecute musician Chuck Berry many decades later.) Johnson was forced to flee the US, only returning after seven years in exile to serve a year in federal prison.

News stories announcing the existence of government surveillance have not surprised civil libertarians and left radicals for decades. When Edward Snowden exposed the scope of eavesdropping and other surveillance by the National Security Agency (NSA) in 2013, there was substantial outcry from the mainstream media, Congress, and many ordinary US residents, but for the aforementioned skeptics, Snowden's revelations only confirmed what the Left and civil libertarians already suspected. This was also the case in the 1970s when the Church hearings in the US Senate made official the information regarding COINTELPRO that was revealed in the FBI documents stolen from FBI offices in Media, PA by a group of heroic antiwar activists. Maxwell's book continues this tradition of exposing government surveillance, with a specific focus on FBI spying on African-American writers and poets. If nothing else, it is a comprehensive look at this aspect of FBI surveillance of US citizens. Complementarily, it is also a primer on some of the more influential African-American writers of the twentieth century.

The approach Maxwell takes in his book is somewhat unique, at least for studies of government surveillance. As the subtitle implies, FB Eyes (which is taken from a poem by one of Hoover's favorite subjects, Richard Wright), Maxwell suggests that the surveillance conducted by the FBI helped "frame" African-American literature from 1919 on. This "framing" occurred in a number of ways. Some of those methods included simplistic approaches such as threatening to cancel or not renew visas for writers living abroad unless they informed on their fellows who were Communist while other means were more sophisticated and included the creation of literary journals that published and reviewed some writers while ignoring others. Another tactic involved pressuring publishers to not publish writers the Bureau considered radical or revolutionary. This latter tactic was also used against the counterculture/New Left underground media during the 1960s and 1970s to great effect. Indeed, many of the FBI tactics of surveillance and harassment (black ops in today's parlance) that were used on the New Left and antiwar organizations of the 1960s and 1970s were first used against Black organizations and individuals earlier in the century. Tragically, the tactics used during COINTELPRO against African-American groups were generally considerably worse than those used against predominantly white organizations. As any student of the period knows, FBI operations against

African-Americans included murders, false charges and imprisonment, the destruction of personal and political relationships via lies and intimidation, to name just a few of the more popular tactics.

According to Maxwell, his reading of the FBI files he was able to procure reveals an FBI that seemed to understand the importance of culture as a means of social change. It was this understanding that inspired Hoover to set up the program discussed in this book. Although the motivation behind the FBI's relatively exhaustive study of Black literature was to stifle and subvert its liberatory possibilities, Maxwell writes that in doing so, the Bureau became one of "the most dedicated critics of African-American literature," at least during the time when Hoover was its director. Given the importance placed on literature and culture by Hoover and his agency–especially in relation to the US Black community–it was only natural that the Bureau would try to shape its content and direction. Although this attempt was occasionally successful, it seems fair to state that by the late 1960s, the predominant influence of the FBI on African-American literature (and culture in general) was in direct opposition to the FBI and its director.

Maxwell opens FB Eyes by describing a letter written by one of Hoover's top agents, William C. Sullivan. The letter, which was part of the COINTELPRO operation against Reverend Martin Luther King, Jr., was a fictionalized plea from a non-existent African-American upset with rumors about King's purported infidelities and ties to communism. "King, look into your heart..." it reads. "You know you are a complete fraud and a great liability to us Negroes...." (Maxwell, from the Introduction.) According to his memoirs, Sullivan perceived himself as an antiracist and FBI surveillance as a means of keeping the struggle for civil rights within the parameters of mainstream US politics. In order to achieve this task, Sullivan was willing to violate a good number of articles in the Bill of Rights. In fact, Maxwell describes Hoover actually reining Sullivan in some during Nixon's presidency when a plan designed by Tom Huston considered, among a multitude of other police state tactics, spying on every single US college student. (The plan as a whole was eventually rejected, in large part because Hoover saw it as an attempt to usurp his power. However, many individual elements of the plan were put in place.)

Sullivan was killed in a suspicious hunting accident in 1977, perhaps because he knew too much.

A common misconception of liberal US residents is that it is the political right wing that favors government surveillance and harassment of civil rights and other predominantly left-leaning groups and individuals. While it is true that some of the greatest violations of civil liberties occurred under the Republican Presidents Richard Nixon, George W. Bush and Ronald Reagan, anyone who has paid the least amount of attention knows that Barack Obama's administration is no slouch when it comes to such conduct. Much of the surveillance discussed in Maxwell's book began under the liberal Administration of Franklin Delano Roosevelt.

William Sullivan was but one purveyor of the belief that CONTELPRO was primarily designed to destroy the Klan and other groups in the white racist movement. While this may have been the intent of various liberals in the FBI involved in the project, the historical facts are that the New Left and Black liberation movements bore the brunt of COINTELPRO and the Klan never disappeared. In fact, the Klan's continued presence in the US white racist movement is testament to the untruths present in such a supposition. Given the historical truth that African-American radicals of every stripe were one of the primary targets of the FBI from its inception, the theory that the Bureau prioritized ending racism seems a bit far-fetched.

The League of Empire

The Guardians: The League of Nations and the Crisis of Empire—Susan Pedersen

World War One was the first round of the long war that defined the twentieth century (and perhaps the twenty-first). Although this century long conflict is conventionally thought of as a series of wars, anyone with a consistent anti-imperialist analysis can quite easily perceive it as one long war. Of course, World War One and World War Two were the largest and therefore bloodiest conflicts of this 100 year conflict. However, when one includes several other conflagrations–from the various colonialist battles on the African continent to the more recent US-led conflicts in the far East, the body count of the earth's most recent millennium is almost beyond comprehension. The first few years of our current century reveal how little things have changed in this regard.

Despite the myths we are fed about it being about freedom and democracy, when considering the First World War, it is easy to see it as a battle among colonial powers for supremacy. Likewise, the negotiations after the end of hostilities were merely a continuation of those battles, with the victorious powers forcing the losing nations to accept their terms for the division of the spoils. Simultaneously, however, was a desire by some men in the halls of power for a new institution whose purpose would be the peaceful resolution of rivalries like those that led to the war. It was from this desire that the League of Nations was created.

However, even in its creation, there was a fundamental understanding that the colonial powers would remain colonial powers. The colonized peoples would not be gaining nationhood any time soon under the League's rules. Indeed, if certain forces inside the League had their way, such nations would never have their independence. This is the subject of Susan Pedersen's recently published history of the League of Nations. An epic and incredibly researched work, the core thesis of *The Guardians: The League of Nations and the Crisis of Empire* seems to be that the League of Nations was both a challenge to the European colonial system and an attempt to continue that system. It was this contradiction that helped ensure the leagues demise. Nowhere was this clearer than in the establishment and maintenance of the mandates in certain regions of the globe.

The first page of The Guardians makes it clear the creation and administration of the mandates was grounded in a colonial mindset. These mandates, from the South Pacific to southern Africa and the Middle East, were the focus of much of the League's administration and were also the cause of many of its internal conflicts. As Pedersen describes the creation of the mandate system, the reader is introduced to an interesting mix of well-meaning internationalists, anti-slavery crusaders, and just plain old unreformed European colonialists. The result of this mix of philosophies, intentions, and ambition was the creation of what could best be termed a colonialists club informed by paternalist and supremacist ideologies and underlined with a desire to steal the wealth and labor of the subject peoples.

The rest of this magnificent history of the League of Nations mandate system relates the story of how, in practice, this mindset was even worse than it sounds. It manifested itself in massacres of local indigenous peoples bordering on genocide, the manipulation of local rivalries to benefit European capitals, aerial bombardment of civilians in the name of pacification, and the never-ending theft of resources from the colonized mandates. Informed by racist and supremacist philosophies developed by men with similar motives and a certain ignorance of the human race, the story told in these pages is a tale of collusion between colonial governments and their henchmen to maintain a dying colonial order.

Speaking of henchmen, the story of one particular mandate is one almost certainly familiar to every reader. That is, of course, the story of Palestine. Pedersen details the collusion between elements of the Zionist movement and the British government to prevent the possibility of a Palestinian nation in order to establish a future Jewish state instead.

The series of actions undertaken with this goal in mind not only helped lead to the ultimate failure of the mandate system, it also led to the current situation of occupation and conflict that exists today in the former mandate and throughout the Middle East. It is while reading this section especially that Pedersen's text reminds the reader of how much nothing has truly changed in the attitudes and practices of the western capitols' understanding of treatment of the rest of the world, especially as regards the nations and peoples of Asia Africa and the Middle East.

Despite the best intentions of some of the internationalists involved, the imperial governments made certain the league was structured to maintain and protect their interests. Naturally, those interests were in large part financial. Policies in both the remaining colonies and in the mandates were established to insure the colonial powers would reap the benefits at a rate much greater than any group in the subject nations. In what is now called free trade, the siphoning of resources from the latter group to the former combined with cheap (and sometimes forced) labor was part and parcel of the League's form of governance. Even when a formerly subject nation was granted a nominal form of independence, as in the case of Iraq, that independence was, in Pedersen's words, "safe for Empire."

Pedersen's voluminous text makes a few things quite clear. Among those is the fact that the League of Nations was intended to prevent wars between imperial nations over colonies, not to support struggles for national independence by colonized peoples. This was apparent in its structure, bylaws, and methods of governance. Ironically, Pedersen writes, its very existence paved the way for the success of those national liberation struggles in its attempt to prevent wars between colonial powers. Indeed, The Guardians is not just the history of an ill-fated attempt to rewrite the world order; it is also a history of how that order was rewritten in ways not foreseen by those powers that created the League. Furthermore, it is a description of how the machinations of the League of Nations foretold the century of bloodshed and struggle that followed.

Rosa Luxemburg–From Street Organizer to Street Name

Red Rosa—Kate Evans

The first time I heard the name Rosa Luxemburg was when I was in high school. I was standing in the Opernplatz in front of Frankfurt am Main's bombed-out Opernhaus listening to a speaker lambaste the US bombing of northern Vietnam and the mining of its harbors in May 1972. My understanding of the German language wasn't the best, but, if I listened closely (and stayed near one of my bilingual friends to translate those phrases I didn't quite catch) I made sense of most political speeches. As I looked around at the sea of red flags and thousands of mostly young Germans in military fatigue jackets and bellbottom jeans, I heard her name shouted from the podium. I don't recall the reference or much else from the speech because immediately afterwards, we began marching. It was a rather eventful protest, with the police opening their water cannons several times along the route and us marchers blocking streetcars and traffic in response; which naturally gave the police another opportunity to use their water cannons.

Luxemburg was not only one of the few women prominent in the socialist movement of the twentieth century. She remains one of its most inventive and radical theoreticians. Her works on imperialism, credit, the role of the strike, and imperial war are both relevant and prescient in their application of Marxist economic theory and capitalist war. Indeed, her discussion of credit under monopoly capitalism is essential reading for anyone who wants to understand why the capitalist economy crashed in 2007-2008 and why it will crash again. Her unrelenting opposition to imperial war and disgust with those who call themselves socialist yet support such wars is an inspiration to those of us who find ourselves in a similar situation today. Most importantly, her commitment to revolutionary struggle and a personal freedom unknown to most women of her time (and to many if not most women today) is an inspiration.

Her life is an inspiration in itself. That is the message one gathers while reading the recently released biography, *Red Rosa*. Composed as a graphic "novel"—what I still call a comic book—this work is a reasonably complete introduction to Luxemburg's life and works. It is also a historical overview of the times she lived and worked in. The excellent artwork is accompanied by a slightly fictionalized narrative (think poetic license) portraying this revolutionary's life, loves, fears and joys. The creator, Kate Evans, provides enough political and historical context to paint a narrative that shows Luxemburg to be a woman both of her time and ahead of her time. One discovers the trails she blazed in her personal life complemented those she forged in the world of revolutionary socialism. This was a time when women were not expected to take on the roles Luxemburg insisted on. The force of her thought and the relentlessness of her political being demanded that otherwise dismissive men both in opposition and solidarity consider her presence. The notes and commentary provided by Evans and her editor Paul Buhle are both a useful addition to the graphics and text and a means to an even fuller understanding of Luxemburg's life, thought and times.

On September 16, 1913 Luxemburg gave one of her most famous antiwar speeches in Frankfurt. In that speech she called on Germans to refuse to fight and was arrested for the speech's content. In the winter of 1914 she was sentenced to a year in prison. Riots against the sentence broke out in several cities across Germany. Nowadays, a road built in the 1990s named Rosa Luxemburg Landstrasse runs through part of Frankfurt am Main, apparently with little or no irony intended on the part of the authorities (to its credit, Frankfurt has been governed by a mostly left-leaning council for several decades.) Given the fact that Germany has sent troops to various regions under the NATO banner in recent years, I wonder how Luxemburg's antiwar sentiments would be received in 2015. Also, given that Luxemburg and her fellow revolutionary Karl Liebknecht were murdered by the predecessors of at least one of the political formations who named that street (the Sozialdemokratische Partei Deutschland -SPD), I also can't help wondering if she would reject what was certainly meant to be an honor.

Red Rosa is a wonderfully composed and lively book. The story it tells is compelling, inspirational and fundamentally human. Instructional in its politics and discussions of economics, Red Rosa is also at turns humorous, romantic, and emotional. The decision to write this work in the graphic novel form was a brilliant one; if there is a biography whose multiple dimensions requires more than words to tell it, Rosa Luxemburg's is such a biography.

Leningrad, Shostakovich and the Music of Transcendence

Symphony for the City of the Dead: Dmitri Shostakovich and the Siege of Leningrad—M.T. Anderson

Before I began writing this review I put Dmitri Shostakovitch's Seventh Symphony on my CD player. This symphony, known as the Leningrad Symphony, is the inspiration for a new and wonderful history by M. T. Anderson. As I write these words, the First Movement is approaching its end. The Nazi armies are beginning their ferocious attack on Leningrad and other parts of the Soviet Union in Hitler's Operation Barbarossa. The symphony's previous sounds of beauty are replaced by sounds of fear and threat; air raids and bombardments. The fear of Stalin's police is superseded by the Nazi assault and the fear and death it brings.

Dmitri Shostakovich is one of the greatest composers to have ever lived. His works are musical documents of the times he lived in and timeless works of beauty. From the bloodshed of two world wars, a revolution and counterrevolution, to the fear and brutality of Stalin's rule, his symphonies, suites and chamber compositions reflect and inform the events which make up that history. The Twentieth Century will be remembered for a multitude of things; among them are the scientific advances we take for granted and the great progress humanity made in improving our species health and prolonging our lives. Despite these positives, though, there is another much darker set of memories. Foremost among the latter are the two world wars. Both wars were ultimately fought for reasons of power and wealth, and both caused the death of tens of millions. There is nothing else in history that compares to these bloody exercises in death. Virtually every nation bears some responsibility for the carrion that rotted into the ground because of these wars and their aftermaths. Naturally, there are two or three nations who bear the bulk of that responsibility, just as there are others who bore the bulk of the casualties.

The Soviet Union was perhaps foremost among the latter. Millions died in its fight against the Nazi armies. More than a million of those died during the Nazi siege of the city of Leningrad–a siege that lasted 872 days. People ate paper and sawdust to survive. Some ate the dead, while a few even killed living humans and ate them. Corpses lay in the frozen streets after they fell dead from starvation and the unbearable cold of the Soviet winter. Thousands of residents were smuggled across a frozen lake out of the city during the winter, yet even then thousands died during their transport. Yet, when spring came, the citizens gathered their minimal strength and buried their dead. Some even planted flowers while many ate grass only because it was the only thing to eat. The story of this siege and the humans who survived it is one of humanity's greatest and most heroic tales ever.

The siege is the setting of M. T. Anderson's newest book, titled *Symphony for the City of the Dead: Dmitri Shostakovich and the Siege of Leningrad*. Anderson, who writes for the Young Adult market, is perhaps best known for his dystopian novel Feed and the Life of Octavio Nothing Duet, a pair of novels about an African slave in the period of the American colonists' war for independence with a contrary take on that war and its myths. Symphony for the City of the Dead is a non-fiction work. Part biography and part history, it is a sweeping look at the life of Dmitri Shostakovich, the rule of Stalin, and the fate of Leningrad under the Nazi siege.

Before one begins reading this book, it is essential to dismiss the classification of it as a book for young adults. Like Anderson's other works, this book transcends marketing classifications. It is a work that, in its majesty, defies expectations and creates new definitions. The composer is the center of the tale, but, like all of us, he is also a plaything (perhaps even a victim) of forces and circumstances much greater than him. Born into pre-revolutionary times and witness/participant in subsequent revolutions, the Shostakovich presented here is first and foremost a musician. Yet, he is also a patriot and a believer in the Soviet revolution. Many of his compositions are an attempt to reconcile these aspects of his intellectual being.

Anderson reflects these facets of Shostakovich are being in this biography. The reader can feel the triumph of the composer when his first symphony is performed in public the first time. They can also anticipate the fear that comes from living under the iron hand of a ruler whose actions are inconsistent and often brutal. The joy his children bring him and the hopes they represent are felt as clearly as the death present every day of the bloody war.

Symphony for the City of the Dead is also the biography of the Leningrad. Always Russia's city of the arts and music, it is also a city of revolution. Naturally, it buckles at the rule of a man like Stalin, but it keeps its figurative head high. It is this pride that helps its people survives the siege. Daunted and desperate, the spirit of Leningrad's residents is really the ultimate determinant of its survival. This is why the story of the siege is such a heroic tale. Anderson understands this and makes it the foundation of his history.

The final piece of this biographical triad is the story of the symphony itself. Titled the "Leningrad Symphony," it is Shostakovitch's Seventh. Shostakovich attacked the composition with vigor until he and his family were moved out of Leningrad with dozens of other artists. After leaving his city, he sunk into a depression and stopped composing. Anderson writes that Shostakovich told friends he could not write knowing how many people were dying in his city. Of course, he did eventually complete the work and performed it. Its first performance was broadcast over the radio. The reception was instantaneous and thunderous. Shostakovitch's symphony rallied his fellow citizens. Next was a performance in the city of Leningrad itself. It was a city slowly rising from the coma of the siege; musicians were hard to find and, when found, often too weak to play their instruments. Yet, the performance took place, after weeks of rehearsal. Meanwhile, the symphony's score had been put on microfilm and was being smuggled to the United States, where it would be transcribed onto staff sheets and sent to Arturo Toscanini, who ultimately performed it with the NBC Radio Orchestra to a national radio audience on July 19, 1942. This performance is legendary. Indeed, it is one of the most legendary radio broadcasts of the Twentieth Century. It would help turn the US Congress in favor of joining the Soviet government's armies to defeat the Nazis.

M. T. Anderson has written a marvel. Symphony for the City of the Dead is a singular and spectacular book. Although I found the politics occasionally too simplistic, this isn't really a book about politics. It is much more. It is a powerful and wonderfully told narrative about the sheer majesty of the human will and the power of music to not only transcend the depths of human suffering, but to go deep into that pit, struggle there, and deny the victory of those demons who would rule us with hatred, fear and brutality.

Anarchy in the USA

Unruly Equality: US Anarchism in the 20th Century—Andrew Cornell

From the beginning of *Unruly Equality: US Anarchism in the 20th Century*, Andrew Cornell situates US anarchism in the leftist milieu. The book begins with a look at the various anarchists and anarchist movements that existed before the Industrial Workers of the World (IWW); the reader is briefly introduced to early anarchist theoreticians Kropotkin and Bakunin and their split with Karl Marx and the communists at the First International. Naturally enough, it is somewhere in the discussion of these precursors to US anarchism and the popular success of the IWW that the reader is introduced to the two strains of anarchism that would define much of the movement in the Twentieth Century: the insurrectionists and the syndicalists. The former being those who consider individual or small group direct action to be the best way to move the struggle forward and the latter being those who believe organizing workers and others in a movement shaped around the destruction of the capitalist system and other authoritarian systems into the moment when the revolution erupts into the struggle ultimately creating the classless and anarchist organized society.

After the surge in anarchist participation in the workers' and antiwar movements in the early 1900s came repression. In a scenario never exactly replicated on the same scale, the United States Department of Justice under Attorney General Palmer (with the eager assistance of a rising police star named J. Edgar Hoover) carried out a series of raids, imprisonments and deportations against anarchists and their fellow travelers. The repercussions from these police actions would ripple through the rest of the century. In essence, the anarchist movement in the United States has yet to recover the numerical strength it had before this repression. Cornell argues, however, that despite the decimation of the movement, its influence continued to be felt in the arts and politics in a manner well beyond its numbers.

It is this facet that Cornell spends a fair amount of his book discussing. In doing so, Unruly Equality not only makes a convincing case for the influence of anarchist philosophy on the US pacifist movement, it also illuminates its role in several Avant garde movements in the creative arts. Cornell's stories of poets, writers, philosophers and activists mixing it up during the years of World War Two and the decade afterwards make this section of Unruly Equality uniquely interesting, both in terms of the text and the broader history of twentieth century United States. Furthermore, they describe a shift in the movement's focus that placed considerably more emphasis on the role of culture in movements of radical change. This transition was precipitated by creative artists now legendary in certain circles: poets Kenneth Rexroth, Robert Duncan and Philip Lamantia, actors and playwrights Julian Beck and Judith Malina foremost among them. In later years they would also include various poets tied to the Beat movement and certain African-Americans. Of course, the artists and poets were but one part of the anarchist milieu.

The transition from the fairly hardcore political movement in the early part of the century was succeeded by at least two decades of mass participation by working Americans in anarchist causes. Foremost among these causes was the struggle to save fellow anarchists Sacco and Vanzetti from execution by the state. This movement incorporated millions of people around the world and was enjoined by other leftist organizations, including the newly formed Communist Party. Simultaneously in the Soviet Union, anarchists were being persecuted by the state as the revolutionary government struggled with a military intervention from the capitalist states and internal struggle from its class enemies and those to its left opposed to the authoritarian turn it was taking. This led anarchists in Europe and the United States to distance themselves from communists and socialists (and place them on equal par to most capitalists on their enemies' list) while also raising money for their fellows being imprisoned in the Soviet Union.

These differences would ultimately contribute to a further shrinking in the numbers of US anarchists over the next decades. As the Great Depression hit the United States after the 1929 stock market crash, the Communist Party of the USA (CPUSA) was considerably more successful in organizing the suffering workers, including the increasing numbers of them who were out of work. Meanwhile, in Spain, the Spanish anarchists were fighting the fascists and the Stalinists. Elsewhere in Europe, Nazis and Italian fascists were consolidating their power. When the Second World War broke out, left and anarchist organizations around the world debated what position to take. Anarchists are by definition opposed to wars between governments. However, the nature of the fascist threat ultimately convinced many US anarchists to begrudgingly support the US war effort. Others chose to object to the draft and the war and were imprisoned for the duration of the war, mostly in detention camps set up specifically for that purpose. These men used this opportunity to, among other things; organize against racial segregation in the camp lunchrooms. Many of the connections made during these detentions would become even more important after the war when the men were once again on the outside. Underlying the transformations taking place in the US anarchist movement meant a shift away from its earlier focus on the working class. This was partially related to the changes in the US working class's fate after the New Deal, but it was also tied to anarchism's greater appeal to poets and artists. This trend would intensify over the years.

Then there is David Dellinger. One of the aforementioned war resisters, Dellinger would, along with A.J. Muste and J. Philip Randolph, be a major influence on the antiracist and antiwar movements of the 1950s and, especially, the 1960s. Cornell tells the story of these men during those decades, but more importantly, he describes the anarchist elements and influences of those movements and the roles these men played. Like the rest of this wondrous history, this section reveals new information and provides a new perspective on those most important struggles. In the postscript to the century, Cornell briefly discusses anarchism's continuing popularity with various subcultures in the United States and its presence in the Occupy movement of 2011.

Unruly Equality fills an important space in the library of United States history. More specifically, it furnishes us with an important addition to the anarchist histories already in existence. These histories, where they exist, seem to be mostly about individual groups, acts or individuals; there does not appear to be a survey like this one. Cornell's text is broad yet detailed in its sweep, incorporating agitators and artists, propagandists and poets, and organizers and bombers into a remarkable and compelling history. It brings together the political individual and the artist, poets and writers into a well-told history of a philosophy whose influence in the 20th century is only somewhat recognized, even among those of us who should know better. The writing is descriptive and accessible, with a story both fascinating and important in its scope.

Fire and Blood, Socialism or Barbarism

Fire and Blood: The European Civil War: 1914-1945—Enzo Traverso

I recently re-watched the German 1986 biographical fiction titled Rosa. It is a film about Rosa Luxemburg. The film itself is a bit more stylized than Luxemburg's life probably was and its politics are not nearly as radical as Luxemburg's were, but they do show her consistent anti-imperialism, her Marxism, and, on the personal level, the passion and intellectualism so obvious in her writings. I also recently finished the newly-published English translation of Enzo Traverso's exceptional study of World Wars One and Two, *Fire and Blood: The European Civil War: 1914-1945*. This combination was remarkably compatible in its analysis of the history of that period.

To begin with, both the book and the film (via Luxemburg's speeches and written words in the film) make the point that the colonialist period prior to World War One was not a period of peace and prosperity around the globe. It was, however, that for much of Europe. All the wars and such took place in other places in the world as colonial powers fought the native peoples (and occasionally each other through proxy and directly) for control of those colonies. The World Wars then, were called this only because of colonial hubris and arrogance which considered Europe as the "world," while simultaneously rendering the non-European world to a lesser even non-human category. Of course, the label given the rest of the world then was "non-civilized" and not non-human, but the implication was the same.

This text is not a history of dates, battles, leaders, and armies. Neither is it a political history detailing the debates between and within parties, legislatures and monarchies. It is something much broader and more fundamental. In this book Traverso examines the meaning of the cataclysmic and catastrophic changes wrought by the carnage and movements these wars wrought. He looks for those meanings in the art, the film, and even the philosophical writings of the time discussed. In doing so, he makes his case that the decades of and between the two world wars were schismatic in nature. Indeed, the conflict was the historical equivalent of a natural disaster on a global scale, as if the flood of Genesis were remade in poison gas, aerial bombardment, and apocalyptic politics. Or less, biblical but still religious, Traverso compares the effects of this European Civil War with the previous one we call The Thirty Years War.

In the nuanced and erudite discussion that makes up this reflection, Traverso invokes Nazi philosophers, Marxist ones and liberals. It his contention that the polarization made all too obvious by the carnage of World War One killed the remaining remnants of bourgeois liberalism; the very political philosophy that was birthed a century earlier during the years of French Revolution and American colonies war for independence after being conceived in the decades preceding those events. The pretense at tolerance maintained by the liberal political state was firstly applicable only to the colonizer nations and secondly attacked by the rightist yet revolutionary phenomenon called fascism. The intention and organizational approach of fascism was (and is) to polarize. The decades between the wars saw this approach take hold and met with an equal reaction from the Left.

This isn't to say, though, that Traverso repeats the liberal trope that wants us to see Leftist responses to fascist provocations as equivalent. Likewise, he refuses to concede that the revolutionary violence of the oppressed somehow denies the justness of their cause. He does, however, note that violence in the name of revolution tends to bring the most authoritarian elements of the revolution to the fore, if only because the military becomes the most capable defender of the revolution against its foes. Traverso remarks on the tendency of those in the liberal center (both right and left) who decry revolutionary violence yet defend or excuses the violence of the state, as if this latter violence had greater legitimacy. In essence, he writes, this period was one where public's perception of State violence as the only legitimate violence was successfully challenged. In its wake, new revolutionary states on both the Left and the Right were created. The rest of the century and most of the early twenty-first century involved a continuing rehash of this scenario.

One of the most interesting sections in Fire and Blood are the subsequent chapters titled "Imaginaries of Violence" and "The Critique of Weapons," wherein Traverso examines technology along with the manifestations of the war in art and culture. These years, writes Traverso, were years where much of art and culture left its traditional search for beauty and became the tools of the political. In other words, culture became propaganda, both in favor of the State and in opposition to it. Philosophical musings were utilized to justify an inhumanity never seen. Intellectual became soldiers in the service of the war and its masters. Technology made mass murder possible on a scale beyond any previous conception. Despite the attempts by historians to denote fascism and its authoritarian brutality as a rejection of the rationality symbolized by technology, Traverso tells the reader it was that rationality's predictable result.

Fire and Blood is more than a history of a catastrophe that began a hundred years ago. It is also a warning of a potential future. Traverso's discussions of the use of terror and violence, the migrations of millions because of war and politics, the industrialized nature of mass murder via military weaponry and desensitized soldiers and airmen, the manipulation of the popular will via culture and media; all of this describes the world we live in today. From drone operators killing humans thousands of miles away to award winning films and television shows celebrating torture and racializing crime and murder; from the state of war instituted in 2001 after the Twin Towers and Pentagon went up in flames to the cynical, brutal and often incomprehensible civil war/war by proxy especially in the Middle East; the killing fields of Traverso's exceptional history are a phenomenon that remains closer than one thinks. At the same time, the clues to preventing their repetition are inside this book, too. Even more valuable tools aimed at preventing a repetition of this apocalypse can be found in the writings and speeches of the revolutionary woman whose name began this review: Rosa Luxemburg. It was she who wrote in her pamphlet popularly known as The Junius Pamphlet: "Bourgeois society faces a dilemma; either a transition to Socialism, or a return to barbarism ... we face the choice: either the victory of imperialism and the decline of all culture, as in ancient Rome – annihilation, devastation, degeneration, a yawning graveyard; or the victory of Socialism..."

A Crisis With No Capitalist Way Out

Imperialism in the Twenty-First Century—John Smith

The world is in crisis. Capitalism, currently the only economic system in existence, is the cause of this crisis. It is a crisis that impoverishes millions more every year while enhancing the wealth of the rarefied few who conspire with politicians to make it so. It is a crisis that manifests itself in endless and meaningless wars. It is a crisis that dismantles schools, hospitals, roads, and other infrastructure in the name of private profit. Most ominously, it is a crisis which diminishes the health of the earth's ecosystem, undoing an already fragile environment in order to squeeze meaningless dollars from that which gives all earthly species life.

This is the premise of John Smith's newly-published work, titled *Imperialism in the Twenty-First Century.* It is an important, even crucial, work. Moving beyond and adding to classic Marxist understandings of imperialism, Smith destroys mainstream economic analyses that attempt to explain away the nature of the neoliberal capitalist crisis we exist in. By revitalizing the essential element of Marxist economics–the surplus value created by labor and its essential role in creating profit–Smith patiently examines the nature of the worldwide system of capitalism and its systemic and systematic exploitation of those who labor for its bosses. In doing so, he redefines how outsourcing actually works in the global neoliberal economy and, in the process, convincingly argues that the "developing" world should no longer be considered the periphery of the global economy, but the essential element of its continued ability to make profits and accumulate wealth.

This truth is grounded in the fact of the superexploitation that occurs in the nations that make up the "developing" world; a world located primarily in the southern hemisphere, but also in primarily non-white regions of the northern hemisphere, as well—in sweatshops and the euphemistically labeled Enterprise Zones of China, Mexico and other large manufacturing nations. Complementary, and almost as fundamental, to the new imperialism explicated in Smith's explanation are his discussions of how international loan and aid agencies like the World Bank and the International Monetary Fund (IMF) utilize economic theories that are not only beneficial to their overall strategy to keep wealth in the banks of the northern capitalist nations, but are also part of the growing problem of indebtedness and financial crisis. This is partially due to their outmoded understanding of outsourcing—an understanding that refuses to acknowledge that even though more and more of the world's production of goods and services is taking place in the developing world, the profits from this production are overwhelmingly going into the financial houses of the super capitalist nations in the north, specifically mostly to those in the United States and a couple nations in Europe.

In the process described by Smith regarding the new forms of outsourcing and its associated forms of labor exploitation, he discusses the nature of the outsourcing of the information industry, the destruction of local health care provision via IMF demands, and how so-called nonproductive workers can be exploited. Since I cannot explain this latter phenomenon more concisely than the author, let me just quote from the text:

"So long as workers are obliged to work for longer than the labor-time needed to produce their basket of consumption goods, they are exploited. This is independent of the specific way their labor is employed and of whether they are employed in production, circulation, or administration. For present purposes, we can assume that all these workers endure the (nationally prevailing) rate of exploitation in common with production labor." (63)

In the mid-1980s I lived and worked in a small town on the Olympic Peninsula in Washington State. The town had been founded by logging interests in the early part of the twentieth century and, after some battles between industry and the workers, had thrived for several decades prior to the 1980s. Workers made good wages for hard work, the corporation made big profits and the town had a decent school, a fair housing stock,

179

and supported a reasonably robust small-town economy. By 1985, this small town scenario had changed drastically. The recession that began in 1973 that was only exacerbated by the advent of neoliberal capitalism and the austerity politics of Jimmy Carter and Ronald Reagan ravaged that town. Most of the harvested timber was being towed offshore to an oceangoing non-union mill operation that cut the logs into boards. Meanwhile, the mill in town had gone from three plants running three shifts down to one plant that made pressed wood products and running two shifts. Over half of the mill workers had lost their jobs while the loggers—who were mostly independents—saw their prices drop and their stock decrease as clear-cutting took over the industry.

When I arrived, the only jobs in town were in the tourist industry (fishing, hunting and hiking), food service, the illicit marijuana cultivation trade, and one small plant on the edge of town that subsisted by getting outsourced work from the relatively new computer industry taking over the suburbs west of Seattle under the aegis of Bill Gates and Microsoft. This is where I got a job. The pay was abysmal at $2.85 an hour, the work was tedious, and the layoffs came about every three months. When there was work, we would often work sixty hours a week. Most of my co-workers were the wives of mill workers who had been permanently laid off. The wives took the jobs to supplement their laid-off partner's unemployment benefits. During the weeks I was laid off from the electronics plant, some friends paid me to take care of their marijuana plants. The only thing certain about the job security at the plant was its uncertainty. No matter what, though, the rent was still due and the kid had to be fed. So one did what one had to.

I mention this part of my biography to make a point about what I consider very human and important elements of the nature of contemporary imperialism described by Smith. The first is in regards to what is euphemistically termed flexibility in employment. As Smith describes it, this term is used to define several modern forms of labor, including but not limited to, subcontracting work like that of Uber drivers, temporary and/or part-time employment either directly through a firm or through an agency, and the cycle of work-then-layoff-then work ad infinitum I describe above. The intern and purpose of this type of employment sold to the modern worker as flexibility is to remove the negative effects of the increasingly volatile financial market from the industry and force the workers to bear the brunt of its ups and downs (mostly the downs.) In essence, this manipulation of labor has given the employers more leeway in their hiring by creating a surplus labor population that is global in nature, while also ensuring that market downturns are less likely to destroy the employers' capital.

In the later chapters of Imperialism in the Twenty-First Century, Smith discusses the crash of 2007-2008. In doing so, he reverses the commonly held (and the one pushed by mainstream economists) understanding of that episode. It was overproduction brought on by the super-exploitation of labor in the pursuit of greater wealth accumulation that caused the crash, writes Smith, not a shrinkage of credit which caused the financial industry to shrink, thereby lowering demand for goods and services (which resulted in overproduction after the fact.) In an explanation many will consider heresy, Smith tells the reader that the popular analysis of the crisis blames the symptoms of the crisis for the crisis, revealing not only a rather superficial understanding of how neoliberal capitalism works, but a rather foolhardy inability (or refusal) to acknowledge that the source of the apparent irrationality evidenced by the crash is built into the system of capitalism itself.

The book concludes by discussing the ongoing crisis and the system's eventual collapse. The stopgap measures that have kept capitalism going for as long as it has are ultimately unsustainable. This why we see crashes and peaks happening more frequently; it is also why we see more people living in shelters and their cars, not to mention the streets. It is why wars seem to never end and the ecological situation only worsens. It is the latter, writes Smith that will kill us all. He ends his text with a quote from Cuban revolutionary leader Raúl Valdés Vivó, who wrote "(this) is "un crisis sin salida del capitalismo," a crisis with no capitalist way out. The only way forward for humanity is to "begin the transition to a communist mode of production. . . . Either the peoples will destroy the imperialist power and establish their own or the end of history. It is not 'socialism or barbarism,' as Rosa Luxemburg said in 1918, but socialism or nothing."

Oakland, Hutton and Grant

No Doubt: The Murder(s) of Oscar Grant—Thandisizwe Chimurenga

"...how does one 'balance' a story about a lynching?"
— David Mindich, media critic

Every April 6th, I recall the memory of Bobby Hutton. Hutton was the first Black Panther member to be killed by police. The murder occurred during a confrontation between Oakland Police and two members of the Party—Bobby Hutton and Eldridge Cleaver. As in all killings by police, the initial reports of the murder blamed the victims and exonerated the police. However, given the growing popularity of the Party, the fact that Hutton's death took place two days after the assassination of Martin Luther King, Jr. in Memphis, Tennessee made some of those in power question the police narrative. Dozens of the nation's African-American neighborhoods were in open rebellion, with the military patrolling streets in tanks and other armored vehicles. To this day, the exact circumstances of the murder remain unclear.

Such is not the case, however, in another police murder of a young Black man in Oakland. That young man's name was Oscar Grant, Jr. Thanks in part to the advent of technology that gives any individual with a cellphone the ability to record live video, Grant's murder by BART police at Oakland's Fruitvale Station on his way home from celebrating New Year's in the early hours of 2009 was captured on such video. The killer was charged with manslaughter? Of course, there could have been a million videos of the murder and no police officer would have been charged if it had not been for those who protested the attempted cover-up by the judicial system. It was their public presence and radical insistence on some kind of justice that actually forced the District Attorney to bring charges against the police officer who pulled the trigger, Johann Mehserle.

This is the story told by journalist Thandisizwe Chimurenga in her 2014 book *No Doubt: The Murder(s) of Oscar Grant*. Utilizing the premise that Grant was murdered once by the police and then again by the media and Mehserle's defense team, Chimurenga dissects the police killing and the trial of the accused in a blistering and informed attack on the entire charade. As a journalist covering the trial, Chimurenga was witness to almost every piece of evidence and argument presented. Like the trials of too many subsequent murderers of young Blacks, the trial of Grant's murderer was turned into a trial of Grant himself. His character was attacked and his police record brought up, as if the fact that he was a victim of a racist justice system that targets individuals in his demographic somehow justified his murder. At the same time, previous instances of Mehserle's brutality against suspects were either minimized or not mentioned at all, as if they were not relevant to the manner in which he and his fellow officers treated Grant that New Year's Eve.

Portions of the trial are transcribed for the reader, with commentary from the author questioning the testimony's veracity and pointing out its contradictions. The decision by a local television station KTVU to air an interview of the accused killer is discussed in the light of the intensification of negative publicity concerning the murdered victim. Like the trial of the vigilante George Zimmerman in the murder of Trayvon Martin some three years later, the expressed fears of the killer that they were going to be attacked by humans described as superhuman thugs was considered in their defense, despite the obvious racism of such a portrayal, not to mention its untruth. In Grant's and most other cases, any potential threat by the victim was invalidated by the guns of the murderers.

Since the murder of Oscar Grant, hundreds of civilians (mostly non-white) have been killed by police in the United States. Most of the killers have not been charged and many have not even lost their jobs. When those that have had to pay for their murderous brutality were charged or dismissed, it was because of street protests (that were often violently attacked by the police). Indeed, the only reason Mehserle was charged in Oscar Grant's murder was because of such protests. Unfortunately, as the numbers show, neither the protests nor Mehserle's conviction made much difference in the way police interact with African-American and other non-white residents of the United States.

Thandisizwe Chimurenga quotes the media critic David Mindich who asked the question in his book Just the Facts: How "Objectivity" Came to Define American Journalism, "…how does one 'balance' a story about a lynching?" After all, that is exactly what Oscar Grant's murder was—a lynching. That is what so many murders of African-Americans by police are. In a system birthed in and maintained by the philosophy of control known as white supremacy, how can they be anything else? Even if the killers in uniform happen to be considered non-white themselves, their roles as police are fundamentally roles that cast them as enforcers of that system. This is the basis of No Doubt: The Murder(s) of Oscar Grant. It was also the basis of the Black Panther Party's program. Ultimately, it is also why both Bobby Hutton and Oscar Grant were murdered by the police.

Puerto Rico is a Colony, No Matter How Else You Dress it Up

War Against All Puerto Ricans: Revolution and Terror in America's Colony—Nelson A. Denis

The island called Puerto Rico is a colony of the United States. This fact means that the rights US citizens assume to be theirs do not necessarily apply to Puerto Ricans living on the island. The history of Puerto Rico since the United States military invaded it in 1898 makes this very clear. Whether one is taking a look at the economic relationship between the United States and Puerto Rico, the political relationship, or the military relationship, the blatant nature of the colonial relationship is foremost.

This becomes even clearer in Nelson A. Denis' 2015 history *War Against All Puerto Ricans: Revolution and Terror in America's Colony*. Partially a biography of the Nationalist leader and hero Pedro Albizu Campos and partially a history of the Puerto Rican nationalist movement in the early and mid-twentieth century, this text tells a story more people in the United States should know. The racism and just plain disregard for human lives described in Denis' narrative is a match for the very worst of humanity's inhumanity to other humans. The fact that it continues in Washington's current dealings with Puerto Rico is testament to the arrogance intrinsic to colonialism, no matter how it is dressed up.

In short, Puerto Rico is owned by Wall Street. Any investment or other input of money into the island's economy via investment in industry, agriculture or services is removed at a greater rate than it was put in. No matter what form this colonial approach takes and no matter what it is called, the fact is that the history of the people of Puerto Rico is one where their poverty only increases along with the debt. Because it is a colony and not a full-fledged independent nation (or a state), Washington controls much of Puerto Rico's political system. This has meant that the islands are not just home to large military bases; one island was used for bombing practice for decades. It has also meant that the minimum wage in Puerto Rico is not subject to the same restrictions. So, when the dominant industries want lower wages to make a profit, the wages have been dropped. Indeed, this possibility is part of Washington's current efforts to get Puerto Rico to repay the banks that own Congress and have bled the Puerto Rican nation over the past years via an economic development program set up for US industry and banking.

War Against All Puerto Ricans is a fascinating story of a movement and a man whose history has been intentionally left out of most history books. Instead of the truths told in these pages, what most US residents, including many of Puerto Rican ancestry, know about Puerto Rico is that it is an island with beautiful beaches and sugar cane. They do not know that it was invaded by US troops in 1898 toward the end of the Spanish-American War and has been occupied ever since. Nor do they know that its history since that invasion is one where most Puerto Ricans live at the mercy of corporate America, exist in poverty, and seen those country men and women who fight back killed by the US military and police forces acting in coordination with that military. They have not heard of the independentistas and the nationalists, nor do they know that many of those independence fighters have been in US prisons for decades.

Denis opens his book with a brief introduction to his family and his interest in Puerto Rico. From there the story moves quickly through a bit of Puerto Rican history, a description of the prison known as La Princesa—a prison condemned by the United Nations—where hundreds of nationalists were held after the insurrection he details at the end of the text. The book's tone is truly set in the chapter describing what is known as the Ponce Massacre. This murderous episode in Puerto Rican history took place on Palm Sunday 1937. Families had gathered in the town square for a celebration of the holiday and the independence movement. Police and military surrounded the crowd and fired their pistols, shotguns and machine guns. Thirteen minutes later, nineteen people lay dead and dozens more were wounded. The police lied to the press and said they had been fired upon first. Honest journalists decried the cover up and tried to get the news out to the world. The police cover up failed, but the world did not pay much attention.

Denis' utilizes a unique device to fill the middle part of his text. He introduces four men he considers crucial to the story he wishes to tell. The first is a man who would be a poet, an opium addict, a Nationalist and then a pawn of the FBI and US banks. Then there is the OSS agent, a filmmaker, the nationalist hero Pedro Albizu Campos and a barber who was so much more than just a barber. By providing biographies of these men, the author tells the history he set out to tell. It is a fascinating and engaging tale.

Denis writes these sentences towards the end of his book: "The story of Albizu Campos is the story of Puerto Rico. It is also the story of empire." Reading this book reminded this writer of all the lies told daily about Washington's overseas adventures today. It also makes clear that this is nothing new. War Against all Puerto Ricans is well-researched, quite readable, and essential to any reader interested in Puerto Rico, US history or the nature of colonialism. It is not a pretty tale, but it is one that must be told.

A Theory of Despair?

Grand Hotel Abyss—Stuart Jeffries

It's rare that a trend in philosophical thought actually applies Karl Marx's suggestion "Until now, the philosophers have only interpreted the world in various ways; the point, however, is to change it." In fact, it was the Institute for Social Research at the Goethe University in Frankfurt am Main that was arguably the first to do so. Indeed, this was the intention of those who founded the institute from its beginning. After establishing itself in a nondescript building in the Bockenheimer Warte section of Frankfurt in the 1920s, this group of Marxist intellectuals would go on to create one of the primary philosophical trends of the Twentieth century—critical theory.

Born in a despair that assumed a Marxist revolution had become impossible in the wake of consumerist capitalism, the Frankfurt school turned towards the role played by media and culture in manipulating the workers into becoming agents of consumption instead of agents of production. Theodore Adorno, Walter Benjamin, Herbert Marcuse and Erich Fromm are some of the best known names associated with the School. Their research would influence not only other Marxists, but also reach into the halls of academia, literature and advertising throughout the capitalist world. In addition, and perhaps more importantly, some of their analysis and theory would inform an entire wing of the Twentieth century Left, especially in the United States and Germany. Phrases like "repressive tolerance" and "dialectical enlightenment" became the New Left's equivalent to popular rock lyrics, while Frankfurt School member Herbert Marcuse became its version of a rock star.

Blending Freudian psychoanalytical theories and Marxist philosophy, the Frankfurt School created a synthesis that attempted to define the situation of modern humanity in a monopoly capitalist society. Ultimately, this synthesis resulted in a rather bleak vision that derived its pessimism partially from the intensifying fascist state that Germany was becoming. Yet, as a result of their continued critical observations, a realization developed in the school that so called democratic capitalism was equally repressive, except in a less crude manner. Indeed, this is the essence of the aforementioned phrase "repressive tolerance."

Recently, Verso Books published a fairly comprehensive critical biography of the Frankfurt School titled *Grand Hotel Abyss*. Authored by longtime Guardian columnist Stuart Jeffries, it is a valiant and worthwhile effort. In the text, Jeffries combines personal and group biography with a presentation and analysis of the group's most influential works and ideas. Lying underneath this web of biography and theory is the history of the twentieth century, the Left and the author's own perspective. The resulting work is a cogent and even absorbing narrative of an important group of thinkers, their thoughts and their influence.

In the course of the text, Jeffries reveals some interesting observations from the School with a distressing relevance to today's reality. Two that come immediately to mind are that fascism in Europe was a result of a series of pacts between the industrial bourgeoisie and the regime; the second was the philosophers' observation that massive aerial bombing undertaken by the United States and Britain over Germany during World War Two was pointless because it made it almost certain that the population being bombed would be able to do nothing but attempt to survive. This observation went against the military's supposition that such bombardment would anger those on the ground enough to resist their government and was ignored. In fact, if one listens to the rationales we are given today for massive bombing of another nation, they will find this rationale is still in the mix. In regards to the current situation, the School's depressing view that the proletariat will never achieve ideological maturity seems even truer today in a world not only where virtually everything is infantilized, but where such infantilism is considered a positive thing. One need only look at the 2016 presidential election in the United States for vivid and disturbing proof of this.

Jeffries' history is a combined discussion of the group as an entity, the individual members and the twentieth century. Mostly balanced, his prejudices show through mostly in his discussion of Marcuse's work on the methodology of modern capitalism titled One Dimensional Man. Indeed. Jeffries' criticism of that text reads like an attack on the 1960s movements and a defense of his lifestyle. However, if one remembers what Marcuse and his fellows theorized—that all of our needs and desires are ultimately creations of Wall Street and its advertising agencies—it is understandable why most folks would react somewhat negatively. After all, isn't one of our core Western values the idea that we are free individuals, even though most of that freedom is mostly about choosing different products that are essentially the same.

Warm San Francisco Nights

The Explosion of Deferred Dreams: Musical Renaissance and Social Revolution in San Francisco, 1965-1975—Mat Callahan

Mat Callahan's newest book, titled *The Explosion of Deferred Dreams: Musical Renaissance and Social Revolution in San Francisco, 1965-1975* is an impressive and exceptional work. Although the meaning of rock music and the counterculture is an oft-explored subject, Callahan brings a new and different perspective to the conversation. One thing in particular that makes this book unique is not necessarily its investigation of rock music and politics, but its definition of the music itself as revolutionary, not just its lyrics. In other words, it was the rock sound, especially that played by so-called psychedelic rock musicians from the San Francisco Bay Area, that were often more important than the lyrics. Why? Because those sounds liberated the body and the mind—the entire being. This liberation threatened the existing social order as much as any revolutionary lyrics or protests might. At the same time, they existed within limits that could eventually be made something other than revolutionary. This latter truth is part of any discussion of the meaning of the 1960s; naturally Callahan takes it on, too.

In 1975, I saw Callahan perform with the 1970s folk-rock duo Prairie Fire (Prairie Fire became a punk band later in the decade and worked with the Revolutionary Communist Party.) Afterwards he and his fellow band member led a discussion on the meaning of rock music in the revolutionary spirit of the mid-1970s. I recall the discussion as being a good one, although there were occasional short silences while the audience, which was made up of politicos and counterculture freaks, attempted to reconcile the contradictions between Bob Dylan's support for George Jackson and his blatantly apolitical music of the early 1970s.

191

What strikes me most about this memory is how much music actually mattered in the lives of both political and cultural revolutionaries then. This is the spirit this book is written. Indeed, Callahan draws on both his radical and musical pasts in The Explosion of Deferred Dreams.

From the Fillmore and Avalon dancehalls to the KMPX and KSAN radio waves, this grassroots revolution in music was created by the people in the streets and houses, not by producers and corporations. However, given that this occurred in the world's biggest and most powerful capitalist nation, it would not stand. Then again, perhaps it would not have stood in a lesser outpost of profiteering, either. The battle for the music and its genuine soul is another crucial element of this text, as well. Callahan discusses this throughout the book from a variety of angles—musician, promoters, media, audience and the record companies. In his discussions, he saves a special venom for the promoter Bill Graham and the Rolling Stone newspaper founded by the nowadays media mogul Jann Wenner. By pointing out Graham's intense pursuit of profits in spite of opposition from a more egalitarian community, he explains how Graham's almost innate understanding of the business (despite his lack of experience) both destroyed the ethos of community while simultaneously saving the financial asses of certain groups like the Grateful Dead. In discussing Rolling Stone's access to musicians, he also points out how the magazine became a shill for the industry, which ultimately helped force its more culturally radical competition out of business.

This book takes us deep into the nexus where art and politics collide and collude; specifically, the nexus where the music of the San Francisco Bay Area colluded to help inspire and inform a cultural revolution that changed minds and social realities. Written in the context of revolutionary culture—with Mao, Marcuse, Marx and Fanon as informants—The Explosion of Deferred Dreams brings Simone De Beauvoir, the Black Panthers, La Raza and the Students for a Democratic Society into the discussion, as well. The result is a radical left critique of culture under monopoly capitalism and a fun ride through the streets, parks and dance halls of 1960s-1970s San Francisco. The reader becomes an observer of community meetings and community squabbles over art and profit. They are also presented with an argument that describes the racial and

192

ethnic diversity of the Bay Area's counterculture scenes. This latter element is often ignored by most writers and, to be fair, the reality is that the counterculture was mostly a white-skinned phenomenon. However, if there was one geographical region where this was less so, it was the Bay Area. Rock bands did benefits for the Black Panthers and striking farmworkers and the people in the streets banded together across color lines to defend their culture, their public and private spaces, and the revolution against the cops, the mainstream media and establishment politicians.

Unfortunately, the power of money won out. The rock music audience became segmented along multiple lines, including race and gender; concerts were rarely ever free; and radical politics were repressed and removed. Yet, the suggestion of that liberation one feels when they hear certain songs—the ones that make you shake your hips or pump your fist—remains. It will never go away and one hopes it will continue to be discovered anew. Mat Callahan helps make sense of why this is so.

Striking in Reagan Time

Song of the Stubborn One Thousand: The Watsonville Canning Strike 1985-87—Peter Shapiro

The history of labor movements is an essential history. Without the stories and analysis of the organizing struggles of working people in the past, those of us who are workers today would find the task of organizing for fair wages and decent working conditions even more difficult than they already are. This fact is a primary reason the history of labor movements—of union organizing and strikes—is rarely taught to workers or their children. It is also a reason labor reporters no longer are found on the staff of mainstream media outlets and labor classes are few and far between in universities and colleges. Most importantly, and probably most detrimental to working people, the lack of knowledge concerning the historical and current struggles of working people for wages and dignity is a big reason right wing rulers like Governor Scott Walker in Wisconsin can destroy the unions of thousands of workers with the consent of thousands of others.

This dismal reality is why I am both cheered and compelled to champion labor histories when they are published. That task becomes considerably easier when the book in question is well-written, fast-paced, and inspiring. I just finished reading such a book—*Song of the Stubborn One Thousand: The Watsonville Canning Strike 1985-87*. This masterpiece of the genre is simultaneously an education in labor organizing in the multinational workplace and a stirring tale of struggle by some of US capitalism's most exploited workers. It is a story with many twists and turns and a determination and sense of justice. The publisher, Haymarket Books, is probably the best current publisher of labor history; with this book both Haymarket and the author Peter Shapiro have outdone themselves.

The strike began in 1985. Ronald Reagan was in his second term as president. His first term had made it clear that he hated unions and wanted to help bust as many of them as he could. In addition, the economy was well on its way to the stage that became known as globalization and workers everywhere were suffering the consequences. Jobs were being moved out of the country so their owners could squeeze more profit from the labor forces while simultaneously using the threat of such a move to demand concessions from the workers in the United States. Despite the odds against them, the mostly Latino, mostly female workers in the canneries in Watsonville decided to strike.

At the time, Watsonville's population was predominantly Spanish speaking. I remember hitching through the burg a year or two earlier and stopping for lunch at a cantina. I had done some day labor in the fields near the town before, but had only seen it from the back of a pickup as we drove back to Oakland after a day of work The food in the cantina was predominantly Mexican, the beer choices were Tecate and Modelo and the jukebox featured only two musical artists who were not singing in Spanish—The Doors and the Rolling Stones. It was like being in a town in Baja or on the Mexico-Texas border.

The town's council and landowners, however, were mostly Anglo/white. Like towns and cities throughout the US Southwest, they had arranged the political situation so they could dominate. The lack of Latino political power in Watsonville was another aspect of this strike. Perhaps the most important result of the workers' campaign was the realignment of political power so that non-Anglos representation in civil affairs was more representative than ever before. Of course, money still trumps everything else in a capitalist system.

Shapiro relates the intricacies of organizing and maintaining the strike, something made even more difficult given the situation within the Teamsters Union, who represented the cannery workers. In part because of how the international union was organized and in part because of the entrenched power of the man who had run the local for decades, conflicts arose inside the strikers' various committees and meetings. In addition, personal resentments, personality clashes and political differences occasionally challenged the unity any such endeavor requires. Underlying these currents was the fact that many of the strikers were women, whose insistence on inclusion was (and continues to be) a challenge to unions traditionally dominated by men. However, without the women there could be no strike. Song of the Stubborn One Thousand does a masterful job at weaving these lines of the narrative into a cohesive and elucidating tale of sacrifice and inspiration.

The tale of struggle told in this book is interesting enough to go gain the readership of labor history's typical audience of students, labor organizers and leftists. The vivid rapid-paced nature of Peter Shapiro's narrative could propel it beyond that audience. Not only does the text share the same environment of some of John Steinbeck's best novels, it even reads like one of them on occasion. In fact, Watsonville was actually the town Steinbeck set the novel In Dubious Battle in. Even though the Watsonville strike took place some fifty years later, some of the same types of characters can be found in both books: communists, distressed workers at the mercy of heartless owners, frustrated organizers and union members ready for sabotage and destruction, and, mostly, a group of committed workers fighting to make their lives better and achieve a broader social justice.

In a world where labor is exploited even more than it was in 1985, Song of the Stubborn One Thousand is a study guide, a lesson, and an inspiration for the working people of today. In a time when recent electoral results portend a working class divided at the behest of the rulers, the Watsonville canning strike of 1985 provides a hopeful and progressive alternative.

Islam: A Conversation on Paper

The Mosaic of Islam: A Conversation with Perry Anderson—
Perry Anderson & Suleiman Mourad

Islam has long been an enemy of certain sectors of the Christian and Jewish worlds. Despite its genesis in the same geographical region as the two other Abrahamic religions and the fact of its lineage going back to the same genealogical wellspring, the three monotheistic faiths have been repeatedly locked in battles over time. Or, perhaps it is precisely because of this shared lineage that the battle refuses to go away; like brothers fighting for their father's favor, the adherents of these faiths insist on fighting as if they have something to prove. Currently, this enmity defines the political and military policies of the world's most powerful nation. The most obvious results of this are the millions of refugees wandering the planet with few places to go and the wasted billions of dollars on war and weaponry. Another less obvious, but equally important effect is the fact that Islam is understood even less by those who have made that faith their enemy.

This is the circumstance those desiring an end to the atrocities of war and displacement find themselves in. Fear and hatred of a created other override any attempts based on a desire to understand, thereby providing those interested in manipulating that fear into more war an easy avenue. Simultaneously, those calling for understanding are dismissed as sympathizers and fifth columnists suckered into self-hatred. As Muslim extremists attack those they deem infidels (mostly other Muslims), certain power elites in the West plot ways to expand their imperial drive to expand their hegemony over the unruly regions from whence those extremists come. It doesn't matter that the primary targets of their plot usually have little to do with the aforementioned attackers; the lack of understanding about Islam plays into the power elites' hands, making all Muslims suspect—and all of them targets of the bombs, the missiles, the travel bans and the migrant roundups conducted by the forces of the Western powers.

Suleiman Mourad is a Muslim born in southern Lebanon. He is a religious scholar who has written and co-edited several texts on Islamic history and scholarship. He attended the American University in Beirut and studied under faculty from various persuasions within the multifaceted Islamic religion. He is currently a professor in the United States who teaches courses in history and religion. Sample course titles include The Islamic Tradition and Islamic Thought and the Challenge of Modernity, Jihad and the Qur'an. The Holy Land, The Making of Muhammad, and The Qur'an.

Perry Anderson is a British historian and writer. He currently teaches history and sociology at UCLA. A Marxist, Anderson was an editor of the British journal New Left Review from 1962 until 1982. His books include Passages From Antiquity to Feudalism (1974), A Zone of Engagement (1992) and most recently, American Foreign Policy and Its Thinkers (2015.) Mourad and Anderson recently published a book titled *The Mosaic of Islam: A Conversation with Perry Anderson*. It is a text with a grand mission: to introduce and inform non-Muslims of the history, and philosophical underpinnings and debates that make up the Islamic religion.

Despite its rather small size, the book manages to succeed in its task. Anderson asks questions of Mourad—questions most of those raised in the relatively secular world (albeit informed by Judaism and Christianity) of the west might ask of Mourad themselves. Mourad responds with information packed answers that situate the faith in the world of monotheism. The Mosaic of Islam is an excellent primer on the faith's beginnings and its spread throughout the world. It discusses the different strains of the religion and the development of those strains while simultaneously placing that development in a historical context that explains the political and economic forces that caused certain elements of Islam to dominate others. In terms of today's political situation vis-à-vis Islam and the world, the final chapter discussing the rise of Wahabbism and its roots in Saudi Arabia is objective, concise and much more informative than its relative brevity would suggest. Likewise, the history of the Sunni-Shia splits and the theological differences informing those divisions are discussed in a depth belied by the length of the discussion.

When I was a youngster, I lived in Peshawar in what was then West Pakistan. Like all the other military officers on the colonial outpost where my father was stationed, my parents hired a couple Pakistanis to do gardening and housework. The gardeners, who smoked a water pipe at lunchtime and usually prayed during the day, seemed more devout than the man who worked in the house. His name was Sharif and he spoke at least three languages: Pashtu, Urdu, and English. Although I was only ten years old (he was around nineteen), he treated me as if I were almost his equal. We conversed about a lot of subjects; cooking, the meaning of various English and Urdu words, the assassination of JFK, the war between India and Pakistan in the fall of 1965, and religion. Indeed, it was Sharif who first told me that Jesus was a Muslim prophet and that his mother Mary was the equivalent of a Muslim saint. This knowledge destroyed the story I had been told in Catholic school and church that Catholicism was the only true religion. Ever since that conversation with Sharif I understand the commonalities between Islam and Christianity as being much greater than the differences. Unfortunately, this view seems to currently be a minority one.

I wish one book could change this reality. Admittedly however, such a scenario is quite unlikely. Yet, this does not mean there is no point in reading The Mosaic of Islam. Indeed, the text's straightforward and plainspoken approach makes it the essential book to read about Islam, especially if one is only going to read one book on the subject. It patiently explains the religion in its extremes while emphasizing its basis in moderation and tolerance. If I were a preacher or priest, I would not only read this book myself (and keep it in plain view on my rectory shelf); I would also insist that all of my parishioners did the same.

One Hundred Years That Shook the World

October: The Story of the Russian Revolution—China Miéville

China Miéville is best known for his fiction. His novels weave intricate worlds of fantastic architecture, complex politics and intimate personal relationships into tales that combine intrigue and the mundane; the lofty and the subterranean; and fear and its opposite. The results of these efforts serve as metaphor for the current reality and as fictions sometimes too amazing to be believed. His latest work shares all of these phenomena that make Miéville's fiction so unique. However, the tale he tells in this work, titled *October: The Story of the Russian Revolution* is not fiction, but historical fact. This in itself makes it profoundly more breathtaking, and equally fantastic. It is a story of the year 1917 in revolutionary Russia.

As any student of Twentieth Century history knows, the year of the Russian revolution was one of those years that changed the course of human history. World War One—an imperialist quarrel that ended up being an incomprehensible exercise in human slaughter and a precursor to another even deadlier conflict—was in its final throes. Troops were dying, mutinying, and just walking away from the horror that was their war. Civilians young and old struggled to survive; some became angels of mercy while others turned into barely human monsters. In between these two extremes were the bulk of European and Russian humanity. The nobility, generals and the bourgeoisie in all nations involved in the conflict were angling on how to keep their positions, their lands and their wealth. Revolutionaries watched, waited and organized; they knew their moment was nigh.

Given its momentous place in human history, there are numerous histories of the Russian Revolution told from a multitude of viewpoints.

The three-volume set written by the Russian revolutionary Leon Trotsky is probably the most complete and certainly the most inspiring of all of these histories. It goes almost without saying that the revolution itself has been disparaged by capitalists and their cheerleaders ever since that first moment in February 1917 when the soviets took over in Petrograd. Even more damaging then the aspersions of the capitalist media though, was the counterrevolution launched against the revolutionary government and the subsequent machinations of that government which caused its mutation and ultimate dissolution barely eighty years later.

As I noted above, China Miéville just published a new history of the Russian Revolution's first year—1917. It is a fast-paced history that weaves in and out of the debates and discussions in the soviets, the various revolutionary and leftist political parties, the military and the provisional government. At the same time, the reader is presented with vignettes of actions in the streets, at the battle front, in the apartments where Lenin is hiding and conspiring with other Bolsheviks for the revolutionary overthrow of a provisional government leaning further and further to the right. As Miéville's story unfolds, the momentousness of the history being told reveals itself in a manner similar to a new wave film. The movements of individual revolutionaries, aristocrats, fearful but boisterous generals, wavering liberals, and angry worker and peasant masses play across the screen of the reader's mind with a passion and clarity that defies rhetoric as surely as the revolution defied the arrogant assumptions of the Tsar and his sycophants.

There are many who have claimed the legacy of the revolutions of 1917. There will be many more who will attempt to do so in the future. The reality though, is that that legacy is not a thing of the past, but is part of an ongoing struggle to define and change the human condition. The fact of its existence as history serves as both a lesson and an inspiration. Miéville's book serves both functions. Perhaps more importantly, it also serves as an introduction to the Russian revolution for those who might otherwise ignore it. This latter group probably includes many fans of Miéville's fiction; readers unaware of his socialist leanings and possibly apolitical in the extreme. October is short on analysis, which is not a critique of the text. Indeed, this is a work of historic journalism. It's as if John Reed, author of the classic piece of revolutionary journalism,

Ten Days That Shook the World, woke from a decades-long sleep to tell the story of 1917 once again. Although there is less personal detail, the sweep of Miéville's story is equal to Reed's in its breadth while matching it in passion. It is Reed's contention that the masses of workers, peasants and soldiers were at the front of the revolution. One hundred years later, Miéville's telling agrees.

Housing for People, Not for Profit

The Autonomous City: A History of Urban Squatting—Alexander Vasudevan

Anyone attempting to rent or buy a place to live in the past several years has noticed that costs just seem to keep on going up. Even after the crash of 2007-2008 that was fueled by manipulation of mortgage debt by some of the largest financial houses in the world caused a downturn in the real estate market, the fact remains that most houses cost more than they did ten years ago. As for rents, they just keep on rising. In some US cities, rents are so high that working people find themselves living in cars and shelters because they cannot afford to pay rent, even for a closet in an apartment. The reasons given for this situation by the mainstream media are many, but they all lead back to one root cause: financial speculation. In other words, property owners are being offered incredible sums of money for their properties, so they force the current tenants out and sell their property. The result is some rich people get richer and lots of humans have no place to live. This is why so many people live in tents in many US cities, especially in the southern and western parts of the country. While this phenomenon may seem to be fairly recent, the truth is that it has existed in varying degrees for decades. Alexander Vasudevan's new book *The Autonomous City: A History of Urban Squatting* is the most recent book to tell this history. It does a fine job.

The book begins its historical survey by discussing the film of a movement among Puerto Ricans living in squats in New York City in the 1970s. It ends with an examination of a more recent series of home occupations in that same city. In between, the reader is presented with a history and analysis of squatting movements from Copenhagen; this chapter discusses the beginnings of the world famous Christiana neighborhood which has recently been under serious attack from the state. From there he takes a look at Britain and the squatting scene in some of its cities. Then various building and house occupations that existed in 1970s Frankfurt am Main and Hamburg in what was then West Germany are discussed; it was these squats which both influenced the Autonomist movement and were influenced by it. Indeed, one of the primary aspects of these squats was the social centers most of them included. I spent a number of nights as a teenager living in Frankfurt in the early 1970s at one particular social center in Frankfurt's Westend listening to music, smoking hashish, and watching political theater. From western Germany, the author takes the reader to Amsterdam and Berlin—both sites of some of the longest lasting and most successful squats in the history this book covers. At the same time, the squats in those cities were the targets of some of the most brutal police and army assaults on the squatting movement ever seen in the west.

Without any aspersions to the rest of the book, it is the chapter on the Italian squatters' movement that this reviewer found the most interesting. Firmly situated in the independent left-anarchist workerist movement of the late 1960s and 1970s, the Italian movement was about much more than housing. It was a revolutionary movement that, together with factory occupations, university disruptions, alternative media and culture, pushed the establishment of Italy up against a wall and changed Italian society. The uncertain economy of Italian capitalism, combined with massive corruption and an official communist and socialist movement which was more part of the established order than in opposition to it, was the reason for the revolutionary upsurge in Italy. The creativity, determination, and marginalization of many of its young people were the reason its effects were so widespread and earthshaking.

What becomes very clear while reading this history is that housing in capitalist societies has very little to do with providing people shelter and plenty to do with exorbitant profiteering. In today's world this has been made even clearer in the wake of the 2007-2008 stock market crash brought on by the effects of housing speculation. In many cities and towns, rents are higher than before if one can find a place to rent. Tens of thousands are finding themselves homeless while speculators from high tech, Wall Street and the banking sector force longtime tenants out of their apartments and sell their properties at exorbitant prices. No one in power seems to care; rent control is not even discussed and tenants attempting to protest are often met with forceful evictions. Politicians of almost every stripe join in the frenzy of profiteering; rejecting any claims the more liberal ones among them may have once made regarding the right people have to shelter. Oftentimes, the reason for this turnabout is the fact that so many of these politicians have a financial stake in the current system of speculation and profiteering.

Besides the activist history and the economics of housing, the author also discusses the cultural reality of the squats he describes. Indeed, as mentioned above, many of the occupations in this book began as attempts by countercultural youth to create a cultural space. Besides this aspect, the meaning of squatting in western North America is examined in relation to its role in pushing out the indigenous peoples of those lands. Equally important to these discussions is Vasudevan's commentary on the roles played by feminist squatters in squats where young men often dominated the conversation and the building. This latter dynamic is one left untouched by most other texts that have written about the squatting phenomenon.

The Autonomous City is a detailed and sympathetic history of squatting movements in Europe and the United States. In addition, it is a discussion of its meaning in the ever fluctuating meanings of urban living. Part academic treatise and part action-packed history, Vasudevan's text provides the reader with a nuanced look at the nature and meaning of the housing crisis in the capitalist West and the solutions housing occupations can provide. In doing so, he brings in the political, cultural and historical meanings behind the squatters and the communities they occupy and create. This is an essential book for anyone interested in the meaning of housing in modern society. It is also a sort of a guidebook for those tired of waiting for the economic and political systems of their respective nations to resolve the crisis that exists in almost every urban zone and who are willing to take matters into their own collective hands.

Eve of Destruction...Or Revolution?

Creating an Ecological Society: Toward a Revolutionary Transformation—Fred Magdoff & Chris Williams

"In order to replace capitalism with an ecological society we need a revolution." That modest sentence is how Fred Magdoff and Chris Williams, the authors of *Creating an Ecological Society: Toward a Revolutionary Transformation,* begin the last chapter of their new book. Although the chapter is the end of the book, it is also an opening to a new direction, a new movement. It is also the essence of the entire text. Capitalism is the reason our biosphere is collapsing and the only way humanity and the rest of earth's species can survive is by ending capitalism. Given that capitalism and those who profit most from it have proven time and time again that not only are they unwilling to give up the rapacious economy that is destroying earth, but that they even refuse to admit that it is that system which is the cause, the only solution is revolution.

This text is written by two environmental activists (and teachers) with credentials that more than back up the science they explain in this book. Indeed, it is their understanding of the science involved when discussing the ecological crisis we face that has helped inform their Marxist politics. Both Magdoff, author most recently of What Every Environmentalist Needs to Know About Capitalism (with John Bellamy Foster) and a Plant and Soil scientist who taught for decades at the University of Vermont, and Williams, who teaches secondary school and wrote Ecology and Socialism: Solutions to Capitalist Ecological Crisis, patiently present empirical and anecdotal evidence to shore up their argument that the ever-intensifying pursuit of profit that capitalism needs to survive is a death knell for the planet. That is, unless there is radical change that ends that pursuit.

But what about human nature? Aren't we wired to compete and control? Don't we want to have a lot of material goods? Just as they take on other questions that would seem to prevent the revolution so urgently needed, the authors answer these questions about human nature with data and patience. In essence, they convincingly argue that empathy and cooperation are not only other aspects of human nature, but are historically greater than the desire to compete and dominate. Specifically, Magdoff and Williams argue it is the human tendency to cooperate which has helped humanity to survive over the millennia; this is clear in how tasks were divided before capitalism came into being and in how even today, humans work together in times of disaster. Continuing this explanation, it is pointed out that capitalism encourages competition, consumption and individualism because that is what makes capitalism thrive. In turn, this is why those aspects of human nature seem to be the only ones.

Each chapter of the text opens with a quote. Many of those quotes are from Friedrich Engels and emphasize the fact that humanity is not above nor separate from nature but a part of it. Once one accepts this consciousness, argue Magdoff and Williams, the idea that what happens to the plants and animals in our world matters as much as what happens to humans becomes considerably easier. If we accept this consciousness, then the need for a society that sustains that life–an ecological society–becomes not just apparent, but necessary.

As I write this, F-16 fighter jets from a local Air National Guard base are flying over my residence, practicing bombing runs like they do so many days here in northern Vermont. The ungodly noise they make is but the least of their faults. Being built for nothing but war, these planes represent in more ways than one can count exactly what the authors of Creating an Ecological Society are writing about–a dependence on fossil fuels sold for profit and controlled by war and the threat of war. Each plane costs millions of dollars and runs on very expensive fossil fuel extracts. Besides the pollutants these training runs leave in the air above my house, the death and environmental destruction they wreak upon those in countries the flight crews are sent to attack is immeasurable and not easily reversible. As Magdoff and Williams point out numerous times in their text, the US military is not only the world's biggest consumer of fossil fuels, it is also one of the world's largest polluters. I mention this to emphasize the point that any true environmental movement must by necessity also be an antiwar and anti-imperialist movement. Creating an Ecological Society also makes it clear that this movement must by nature be anti-racist and anti-sexist. After all, it is often women and people of color who are among the most affected by the environmental damage of capitalism.

This book is a serious examination of the ever more serious problem humanity is facing while it destroys the biosphere. It is also a convincing argument for a socialist solution to that problem. While providing a detailed and understandable analysis of the science that proves the ecological crisis we find ourselves in, Creating an Ecological Society also breaks down the essentially suicidal nature of the political economy of capitalism. The authors make it clear that the time for apathy is over, as is the pretense that the cure for capitalism's deadly excesses can be found in capitalism itself. While reforms undertaken with the understanding that they are a potential beginning of a livable world and not the solution can help us continue, the message inside these covers is that humanity cannot survive if it allows those whose existence is determined by pursuing profit to determine our future–if we want that future to be a livable one for all species, including homo sapiens.

Gregor Samsa's Twentieth Century Blues: Marc Estrin's Roach Novel

Kafka's Roach: The Life and Times of Gregor Samsa—Marc Estrin

In the aftermath of any nuclear apocalypse, the story goes that cockroaches will be one of the few species to mutate and survive. If this is true, then one could reasonably argue that the transformation from human to cockroach of Franz Kafka's character Gregor Samsa, in his story story "The Metamorphosis" was an evolutionary step forward.

The underlying context of Marc Estrin's novel *Kafka's Roach: The Life and Times of Gregor Samsa* is the relationship of the Other to a world where its inhabitants reject, ignore and even murder those it considers different. To emphasize this, Estrin's Samsa is both a cockroach and Jewish; both of them the subject of revulsion in many circles. Set in the Twentieth Century, the story of the man-become-cockroach is as much a story of despair as it is a story of hope. The question the reader is left with when Estrin is through with his tale though is whether or not hope and the actions of well-meaning people are enough to overcome the misery and murder other humans willingly inflict on humanity and its environs.

Estrin composed this novel around the turn of the current century. The towers of the World Trade Center were in hospice when he started and some kind of apocalypse seemed possible by the time the first version was published. I remember reading through various drafts, eagerly awaiting the next chapter he would deliver when I stopped by his house. In 2002, after numerous revisions with his editor, a version of the tale was published by an imprint of Penguin titled Insect Dreams: The Half-Life of Gregor Samsa. This version checked in at just under five hundred pages. The version under review here is what I like to call the director's cut. It checks in at just under eight hundred pages. What this means for the reader is that the transitions in Mr. Samsa's life and in the writing itself are smoother. To continue the film metaphor, the transitions in Insect Dreams were similar to the film-editing style known as "jump-cut," whereas the transitions in Kafka's Roach are considerably smoother and much less jarring. Simultaneously, the extended text allows for the author to expound (a la novelists like Tom Robbins) on ideas that one presumes are dear to his heart.

The story begins in the immediate aftermath of the transformation described in Kafka's brief yet earth-changing tale. In the original story, Samsa the roach is discarded in a rubbish pile. In Estrin's opening, Mr. Samsa is secretly removed from this residence and transferred to the equivalent of a circus freak show owned and managed by a man who is a bit of a freak himself—a certain Herr Hoffnung. Like certain other names in the novel, Hoffnung's moniker is specific and intentional. The English translation of hoffnung is hope. Herr Hoffnung's character epitomizes that part of the faith, hope, and charity triad taught to Christians every-where. A victim of the rapid aging disease called Werner's syndrome, Hoffnung surrounds himself with other freaks of human nature and provides the whole bunch of them with employment and a community, thereby rescuing them from a life of ostracism and depression. It is here where the reader is first introduced to Estrin's dissertation on Otherness in human society. This band of freaks has formed its own society in the midst (or is it on the outskirts) of so-called conventional society and are on most accounts happier for their endeavor.

Samsa becomes an intellectual celebrity of sorts, reading scientific texts, then Rilke and finally the then-popular book The Decline of the West by historian and Prussian nationalist Oswald Spengler. This last book would be adopted by the Nazis and Italian fascists as rationale for their rule, despite the fact that their interpretation was both ego-centric and an incorrect interpretation of Spengler's timeline, which actually states that his so-called time of the Caesars would not begin until the year 2000. As the Nazis begin their rise to power and the Jews of Germany begin to understand that they are the Nazis' primary inter-nal target for destruction, Estrin's Samsa flies away to the United States where he has become something of a celebrity thanks to a fluke and the nature of popular culture.

This is when Samsa's adventure truly takes off. This is also the beginning of the reader's winding journey through Twentieth Century history as told through the compound eyes of a roach as interpreted by the author Estrin. From his humble beginnings as an elevator operator in Manhattan to his stint in Charles Ives' New Jersey insurance company where he "invents" the science of risk assessment to the Franklin Delano Roosevelt household as an advisor to the president, Gregor Samsa seems to be living a textbook version of the American Dream. Then he is sent to Los Alamos, New Mexico to work on the creation of the atomic bomb. It is here where he meets the narrator of Estrin's novel. It is also in Los Alamos where Samsa faces his ultimate existential crisis. The development of the weapon not only appalls him, it also fascinates him. Like so many others, the implicit power given to the humans working on the bomb and of course in the bomb itself, makes Samsa question his involvement and the nature of his humanity (but then again, he is a roach.) In response, he resolves to make a political and poetic statement regarding its existence and its ability to end all life. Except perhaps, the cockroach.

Colonialism Never Gives Anything Away for Nothing

Inside the Battle of Algiers: Memoir of a Woman Freedom Fighter—Zohra Drif

Frantz Fanon made this observation in his classic text on revolutionary struggles for national liberation: "National liberation, national renaissance, the restoration of nationhood to the people, commonwealth: whatever may be the headings used or the new formulas introduced, decolonization is always a violent phenomenon." Like childbirth, it is simultaneously the creation of a new relationship and the creation of a new human. No longer is the oppressor, the colonizer, alone in their supremacy. Indeed, it is now the oppressed, the colonized who has demanded an equality. Of course, to the colonizer unwilling to release their power, this demand is not only impossible to fulfill, it must be put down with all possible means.

It is this understanding of the struggle against colonialism (and its successor imperialism) that forms the essence of Algerian freedom fighter Zohra Drif's memoir, *Inside the Battle of Algiers: Memoir of a Woman Freedom Fighter*. A bestseller in Algeria and France, this recently translated history stands with texts like George Jackson's Soledad Brother and Frederick Douglass' Narrative of the Life of Frederick Douglass in terms of its honesty and desire for justice. In addition to being the personal history of a revolutionary Algerian patriot, Drif's memoir is also a study of the tightrope women in movements like Algeria's Frente Liberacion National (FLN) must sometimes walk, given the nature of patriarchal societies and the armed struggle.

Although Inside the Battle of Algiers is informed by Fanon and the international struggle against European colonialism of the Twentieth century, it is first and foremost a narrative of the day to day events of a cell of dedicated revolutionaries. Zohra Drif begins her tale by describing her childhood. An intelligent student, Drif's education was encouraged by her family—especially her father—and was ultimately the means by which she made it to Algiers. Her awareness of the growing struggle for Algerian independence began when she was quite young and by the time she went to the equivalent of high school, Drif was a supporter of the most militant wing of the independence movement. Indeed, when they weren't studying, she and a good friend spent much of their first couple years in Algiers attending political meetings and hoping to be introduced to members of the underground.

When they finally did make a connection and gained the trust of their cell, the two young women were given their first assignment. This involved delivering weekly stipends to families of those fighters who were in the country training, in prison or dead. These tasks not only provided an essential service to the struggle's fighters and their families, they also helped Drif and her comrade gain a familiarity of the Casbah, a city within the city of Algiers. It is the Casbah that is the oldest part of the metropolis and was the heart and soul of the era of the revolution Drif and her comrades took part in. It was also the Casbah that was sealed off by the military and police authorities, much like the Israelis have done in Gaza and US forces did in Vietnam and Iraq. The scenario she describes is one of increasingly brutal police and military repression amidst a growing sense of the inevitability of the independence struggle's ultimate success. The reader is introduced to a number of Drif's comrades and confidantes as she describes her growing involvement.

That involvement included setting bombs. In her descriptions of these operations, Drif carefully describes the reconnaissance undertaken, developing of disguises and the actual carrying out of the operations. It is a narrative that brings to the forefront the issues of violence in the pursuit of freedom and justice while keeping the engaged reader on the edge of their seat, wondering if the freedom fighters will pull off their action without being killed or caught. In between these escapades, the reader is provided a glimpse into the day-to-day lives of those who decide to commit their lives to armed struggle. In essence, these details describe a growing camaraderie that compares to that of a family. There is a sense of a genuine love amongst the fighters and those that provide safe houses and cover for them. As the campaign of bombings and other attacks intensifies, however, those familial-like bonds are tested, with some members of the underground forces caving to the oppressor. To their credit, most members of the revolutionary forces did not cave either to bribery, threats or torture. Also to their credit is that those who did succumb to torture were not branded as traitors (like those who bend to bribery), but as victims of the same oppressor who had colonized the Algerian people for decades with dehumanization, violence and torture.

Although relatively light on political discussion, Inside the Battle of Algiers presents the reader with enough history and political discussion to provide the understanding necessary to appreciate the political struggle the FLN was engaged in. For this reader, the crucial political statement in the book is one spoken to Drif by her cell leader after she expresses impatience over a decision to cancel an operation she was involved in and had been preparing to undertake. "However you must remember that you are not—that none of us are—ordinary soldiers in a conventional army.... Never lose sight of what we are: political activists whom the colonial regime's arrogance has forced us to become fighters in a war of national liberation....we will oblige France to meet us on a different battlefield: the political one, where it can never win." In other words, the very asymmetry of the war demands that the national liberation struggle be primarily a political one. As it would in Vietnam, this approach turned out to be the correct one in Algeria, too. Also important are her discussions of the role of women in such a struggle; how far does one push for one's freedom as a woman in the context of fighting to free one's people? How does one address the psychology of patriarchy without alienating the masses?

Zohra Drif's Inside the Battle of Algiers is an emotionally riveting historical adventure that is both exhilarating and breathtaking. It is also an intellectually provocative study of a once-common form of political struggle that combined Marxist and nationalist thought in order to free the colonies from their yoke. Intensely personal, it is proof that a popular struggle must be of the people and by the people in order for it to succeed. Like Gillo Pontecorvo's masterpiece film The Battle of Algiers, Drif's memoir is a powerful and unforgettable work.

The Vietnamese War: a Different Take

Hanoi's War: An International History of the War for Peace in Vietnam—Lien-Hang T. Nguyen

Fifty years ago the southern Vietnamese revolutionary forces together with regular army units of the northern Vietnamese military launched a military offensive against the forces of the southern Vietnamese and US militaries. This offensive, known as the TET offensive because it took place during the TET holiday, involved hundreds of thousands of fighters on both sides and resulted in thousands of casualties. Residents of the United States, many of whom had relatives in their nation's military, watched as the US Embassy in Saigon (now Ho Chi Minh City) came under attack. Meanwhile, closer to the imaginary line on the 17th parallel that divided northern Vietnam from southern Vietnam, a battle raged in the town of Khe Sanh. US and southern Vietnamese forces (ARVN) would finally declare victory, blow up their base and leave in early July of 1968.

The intention of the anti-imperialist forces in this offensive was to spark a popular uprising amongst the civilian population of southern Vietnam. Communist political cadre had been educating and organizing among the Vietnamese south of the seventeenth parallel since well before the independence forces defeated the French colonial military at Dien Bien Phu. Although there was no popular uprising in 1968, the effect of the revolutionary forces offensive in the United States was one that ultimately turned the US population against the war. In other words, it was the beginning of the end to the popular belief among Americans that a US/ARVN military victory was possible. Indeed, within three months, President Lyndon Johnson had declared he would not run for re-election and instituted a halt to the bombing by US warplanes. Unfortunately, US

215

involvement would continue at a murderous pace for five more years. After the departure of most US forces by 1973, US aid to its client regime in Saigon continued until that regime's surrender in May 1975.

The paragraphs above summarize a common understanding of the US war against the Vietnamese. This understanding tends to diminish the primary actors in the war: the Vietnamese people. This in turn, has rendered the history of the war incomplete. Although various individuals who fought against the US military and its Vietnamese accomplices have written personal histories—General Giap probably foremost among them—to my knowledge here has been no history written in English that attempts objectivity and a Vietnamese perspective. In addition, there has been no such history written where the author had access to previously classified archives of the Hanoi government. The 2017 publication of *Hanoi's War: An International History of the War for Peace in Vietnam* should change this.

Lien-Hang T. Nguyen, the author of this new work, is a professor of history. She was born in Vietnam in 1974. Her parents left the country in 1975. Her interest seems to be inspired both by her personal history and the desire to present the Vietnamese "war for peace" in terms that re-define the role of the Vietnamese; transforming them into a people intent on determining their own fate, not merely as a people fighting an aggressor whose presence in the country is perceived by so many as a foreign policy "mistake." Like any history, this one is not complete. It is however a detailed look at the complexities in the Vietnamese revolutionary effort and its utilization of military, public relations and diplomacy in the long struggle to achieve its goal of independence.

Crucial to Nguyen's telling is what might be considered a sort of revisionism. This is most obvious in her conclusion that it was two men whose roles were the most important in the Vietnamese war against Washington and Saigon. Despite what could be considered the common understanding, the reader discovers their names were not Giap or Ho Chi Minh, but Le Duan and Le Duc Tho. For those who remember (and those who have studied this period of history) the name Le Duc Tho is probably familiar. After all, he was awarded (along with Henry Kissinger) the 1973 Nobel Peace Prize for his work in the Paris negotiations for peace in Vietnam. He also refused the prize because the war continued, in large part because the US refused to uphold parts of the agreement. Le Duan, however, is less known to the western reader. He was born in southern Vietnam and rose to the top of the Vietnamese Communist Party, becoming General Secretary in 1960.

According to author Nguyen, it was Le Duan and Le Duc Tho who insisted that the primary goal of the party and the Vietnamese after the Geneva Accords of 1954 should be the liberation of the South. This conflicted with those who considered the primary objective should be the industrialization of the northern part of the country while waging a protracted guerrilla war in the south. It was this debate that underlined many of the twists and turns in the Vietnamese conduct of the war, especially before the US began its escalation in 1965. After that turn of events, Nguyen argues that the debates became less about industrialization in the north and more about various military strategies.

This is not an overtly anti-imperialist history. Nor is it the opposite of one. It is a comprehensive look at the methods used by the Hanoi government to keep forging ahead in its goal of reunifying Vietnam. In relating her history, the author provides a detailed look at how Hanoi used its military, its diplomatic corps and international public opinion to win the Vietnamese struggle for independence. Although she occasionally diminishes certain aspects of the bloodthirsty and genocidal campaign Washington carried on against Vietnam and the rest of Indochina, her focus on the Hanoi government and individuals within it give the reader a much needed perspective that puts the Vietnamese role front and center. It is a text that avoids the US hubris common in most English language histories of the war. There is a familiar truism that history is written by the victors. This has not been the case in most English language histories of what Nguyen calls the Vietnamese war for peace. Hanoi's War could well be the first.

The Geography of Marxism

The Ways of the World—David Harvey

David Harvey is a geographer and a Marxist. A collection of his works titled *The Ways of the World* was recently published in paperback. A collection pulled from his writing and lectures, the works are insightful, both in their approach to the world and the manner in which he combines geography and Marxism. Geography is more than just places on the planet and their representation on a map. It is also an examination of how humans and their interactions with the earth and with each other affect the planet's ecology, climate and future. Buildings, roads, resource extraction, industry and population are but a few of the factors that go into the study of modern geography. The economy of capitalism influences them all. Therefore, a Marxist analysis provides a critical look at the nature of the influence capitalism plays. It is quite often not very pretty. However, once one accepts the approach, many things that made little sense before become clearer.

That is the beauty of Marxism. It clarifies phenomena that was once confusing, sometimes plain nonsensical, often inhuman, and always obfuscated. When David Harvey is providing the analysis, his explanations are straightforward and clear. Of course, his word is not the final one, but what he adds to any debate on economics, politics and the world we live in almost always provokes conversation. Not always polite, mind you, but always thought-provoking. Ideally, those conversations and debates create a new synthesis from which a better understanding of our situation can evolve. One such essay in this book is titled "The New Imperialism." Harvey's similarly titled book and this essay have instigated a necessary and useful discussion regarding the nature of imperialism in the twenty-first century. Likewise, his essay on the shift from what he

218

terms managerialism to entrepreneurialism in the administration of capitalist cities enables progressive and Left grassroots organizations with an understanding that can help fight the bankers' and developers' plans for urban United States.

Capitalism is constantly re-inventing itself. This is a basic message of this text, especially when considered in its entirety. Harvey mentions a fundamental rule of capitalism: it must maintain a minimum rate of growth of three per cent. He argues that it will do whatever it takes to maintain that rate. As he describes it, "capitalism is littered with technologies which were tried and did not work, utopian schemes for the promotion of new social relations (like the Icarian communes in the nineteenth century USA, the Israeli kibbutzim in the 1950s or today's "green communes") only to be either co-opted or abandoned in the face of a dominant capitalist logic." (314) With this cancerous approach to economics, capitalism destroys the planet. Yet, it continues to expand. This is one of the most important messages of this book. It is why capitalism itself must be defeated if we are to survive. There is no other path.

Perhaps the most interesting (and certainly the most poetic) essay in the book is titled "Monument and Myth." It is a history of the Basilica de Sacré-Coeur in Paris. It is also a history of workers' resistance and rebellion in that fair city. This means it is also a history of the royalist and reactionary resistance to that resistance. Woven seamlessly throughout this discussion of French history is an examination of the meaning of buildings and statuary—an examination quite relevant to the current battle over monuments to slavery and the Confederacy in states across the US South (and similar debates elsewhere around monuments to the genocide of Native Americans and its champions.) The idea that history is not subjective is given a serious blow in this piece.

Likewise, the idea that capitalism and its need to expand does not affect the environment we live in is given a serious blow in this text. In other words, human economics (not humane economics) do affect the environment. Harvey's scholasticism and insight combine to create a unified argument for radical change in the capitalist nations, especially the United States. Although it is little more than an introduction to his work, David Harvey's The Ways of the World can easily be classified as one of the more important expositions of contemporary Marxist thought.

Ideology of Self-Righteousness

A Short History of Western Ideology–Rolf Petri

Rolf Petri begins his introduction to his new book *A Short History of Western Ideology* by quoting Samuel Huntington from his too-often-quoted essay titled "The Clash of Civilizations." The essence of that essay was simple: the future of history will be the struggle between different earthly civilizations. More to the point, the likely conflict would be between Islamic civilizations and western ones informed by Christianity and Judaism. Instead of coexistence, it was to be the role of the west to enforce their doctrine of "human rights," even if that meant violating human rights in the process. This coming (current?) struggle between civilizations nee cultures would replace the struggle that had defined history to this point. In other words, the struggle between nation states and ideologies was done. Capitalist liberalism had won, defeating collectivist notions of governance resoundingly. Some theorists, like Huntington's onetime student Francis Fukuyama had even stated that history as struggle between ideologies was over.

After this introduction, Petri spends the rest of his text refuting Huntington's speculative declaration. He does so by dissecting western ideology, in the process making it clear that not only is ideology not dead, it is alive and well. Indeed, a western ideology whose fundament is in the idea that the individual is its center is more pervasive than ever. In large part this is due to the supremacy of capitalist economics in the modern world; a supremacy that has essentially put the profits of a few ahead of the rights of the many. In what seems to be a contradiction, this latter reality is not only supported and encouraged by those reaping the profits, but apparently by a majority of those whose growing debt is expanding those profits. In other words, the masses popularly labeled the 99% during the Occupy movement of 2011.

Petri's discussion of the nature and history of western ideology discusses the writings of philosophers and historians from Locke to Hobbes, and from Adam Smith to Marx and Engels. In the process, the reader is exposed to a critical and often innovative interpretation of these writers' works; their commonalities and their differences. As Petri implies, his use of this spectrum of texts illustrates the basis all of them have in the ideology he considers in the text. In addition to this discourse on the essential nature of the ideas expounded by the philosophers and historians Petri examines, the writing here considers the differences found in their approaches. Those differences continue to this day, but it seems clear that the Lockean principle that conditions all rights on the rights of property has won the battle.

On the afternoon of September 11, 2001 I found myself in Greenwich Village's Washington Square Park. A smoky haze from the morning's destruction a few blocks south hung in the air. The smell reminded me of a restaurant fire. My friend and I were two of maybe a thousand people in the park. Some were singing and playing musical instruments. Others were trying to contact family or friends. Some were smoking weed and drinking beer. The air was abuzz with hundreds of conversations. The one nearest me was between three men. After a few minutes, one offered me a hit from the joint they were smoking. I accepted his offer and listened while they discussed the burning towers and what to do with terrorists. Their consensus was simple: the US and other western nations should colonize the places terrorists came from and teach them how to be "civilized." To say the least, this consensus startled me, especially given that the men were all African-American and their ancestors had been the subject of one of western civilization's worst attempts to civilize a people.

I mention this conversation to illustrate Petri's contention that the wars launched by western powers are not led by elites whose consciousness is different from the majority of the populations in those western nations. For the most part, the elites are not just manipulating a humanitarian impulse to profit from killing for resources and markets. No, like the men in that conversation in the park, the populations in western nations believe it is their duty to civilize the world. This duty is not taken lightly and explains why liberals and conservatives alike support wars for empire. This is not a cynical misuse of humanitarian impulses but a genuine belief their wars are humanitarian. It stems from the Christian impulse to save heathen souls; an impulse that continues to exist in even the most secular societies. Indeed, this is one of Petri's fundamental arguments in this text. In other words, the merciless slaughter of indigenous peoples in the colonies, Muslims in the Holy Lands, and dark-skinned peoples in Africa and Asia is rationalized, even championed, in the name of the progress of the human race—its body and its soul.

According to Petri's work, there is no western population in history that is immune from this missionary zeal. Religious or secular, the armies of western ideology together with their soft weaponry of capital and propaganda are convinced their way of life is better than any other. Given this, too many of its champions have taken it on themselves to spread that way of life on populations willing and unwilling around the globe. Behind it all stands the economics of capitalism—a ravenous beast that devours human souls and redefines the world according to its appetites. A Short History of Western Ideology ends with a warning. "But I dare to make one prediction," writes Petri. "If we persevere in our self-righteousness over history, and in the presumption that we know better and 'line up' against evil better than others do, we will make everything worse."

Culture and Politics, Culture and Capitalism

Culture and Politics: The Selected Writings of Christopher Caudwell

Culture is a mutable phenomenon. Still, its constant motion in a society tends to maintain certain fundamental aspects which, when examined, represent the economics and organizational basis of that society. Although most cultural critiques one finds in today's media and classrooms rarely mention the economic basis of modern culture and accept the idea that it is something that naturally depends on its commercialization, a deeper economic reality exists. This fact, while acknowledged in a general way by some Marxists, tends to get pushed aside by most people on the left. Indeed, cultural critics are rarely found in most leftist media. There are a few worthy attempts to remedy this lack of left cultural criticism (Red Wedge being one of the more consistent such entities in the US), but, as anyone attending a leftist conference can tell you, there's just not much talk about the role and meaning of culture on the Left.

Monthly Review Press recently published a small collection of selected writings by the British poet and critic Christopher Caudwell. The texts, written in the 1920s and 1930s, discuss the nexus of culture and economics with an emphasis on poetry and its transition from a collective experience of oral recitation to the modern understanding of poetry as a mostly private matter between the poet and their world. Caudwell, who was a poet and a novelist, died fighting in the Spanish Civil War. One can only speculate as to what he would have observed and written if he had lived into the world that evolved after World War Two.

Titled *Culture and Politics: The Selected Writings of Christopher Caudwell*, the book itself contains selections from three of Caudwell's texts: Studies in a Dying Culture, Illusion and Reality, and Heredity and Development. Chosen and introduced by David Margolies, editor of the cultural journal Red Letters, the sections of these three books published here reveal a coherent and convincing argument on the nature of bourgeois culture and its role in capitalist society. At the same time, Caudwell's writing raises questions regarding the nature of history in both its making and its telling.

Margolies opens the text with Caudwell's consideration of the writer D.H. Lawrence. In this piece, Caudwell immediately challenges the conventional notion of freedom. In essence, he argues that freedom is not found by isolating one from society, but by humanity's very nature as a social creature. In other words, it is human interaction and cooperation with each other that provides the potential for the truest form of individual freedom. Capitalism and the culture of the class it upholds—the bourgeoisie—replaces the relationship between humans with a relationship between people and things. It is through the exchange of these things for money that prevents humans from realizing their full potential as individuals and as humans. Why? Because one becomes defined by their relationship to those things, those commodities; one either is a laborer whose labor is exploited to make those things or one is the one who exploits said labor. One becomes defined by their relationship to the means of production. There is no such thing as free choice in modern civilization, writes Caudwell, because the class structure prevents it. Not only does this structure limit one's choices, it actually eliminates certain choices altogether. A perfect example of this latter case is the person who wants to be a poet. Since there is no genuine way for most people thinking of such a future to make a living, this option is rejected. After all, one prefers a warm place to sleep and food on the table and that requires an income, something that is not a guarantee for the poet. This observation remains true to this day, despite the considerable changes in the nature of production and the nature of labor. Indeed, it is probably even truer.

Caudwell argues that the ideal of a return to nature is essentially a surrender to the reality of capitalism. Although there is an appeal in the idea of returning to a simpler time when human industry was based more on common lands and shared goals, the romanticization of such ideals in the modern world can easily pave the way to fascism. In order to accomplish such a goal would require a retreat from the consciousness humanity has achieved. This conundrum is not a solution, but a surrender to the forces that make true freedom difficult, thereby leaving the social sphere open to subjugation by those who prefer their capitalism with fascist accouterments.

This book is much more than a critique of Lawrence and other writers. It is a fascinating analysis of the history of poetry and, in turn, the nature of song. In addition, it is a Marxist take on the economics of culture, the role played by art and literature in human society, and the nature of the bourgeoisie. Caudwell moves seamlessly from the specific to the universal, strengthening his argument with each sentence placed on the page. After reading this collection, I was left with a desire to read more works by Caudwell and a newfound understanding of the English poets Milton and Pope.

We live in an ugly time. The forces of reaction conspire with capital to subjugate all of humanity in the name of freedom. Their task is monumental, but so is their effort. Just as they control the means of production, so do they control the means of creating culture. The sophistication required by Caudwell to make his argument regarding the nature and role of culture in capitalist society is barely needed in this period of decay. The nature of art is that it both reflects and encourages that decay in a manner insidious and otherwise. Most are none the wiser. The product being sold as culture leaves much to be desired. So, indeed, does the civilization from which it is derived.

Getting Pushed Off the Capitalist Cliff

Overripe Capitalism: American Capitalism and the Crisis of Democracy—Alan Nasser

The statement, "If democracy is indispensable, capitalism must be dispensable" appears on page two of Alan Nasser's recently published study of US capitalism, *Overripe Capitalism: American Capitalism and the Crisis of Democracy*. He continues by telling the reader that without popular, leftist and militant working class resistance, the likely future for the United States is not democracy, but fascism. Indeed, as Nasser and many others have stated, the current (Trump) regime in Washington is a very clear testament to this possibility. Although many of Trump's opponents on the left argue amongst themselves if his regime is fascist, some of his right wing supporters cheer and salute him as if he is. Another point Nasser makes early on in his text is that the only thing that can prevent the US from becoming a fascist nation is the aforementioned working class resistance.

Nasser's text is an economic and political history of the United States that begins in the latter part of the nineteenth century. In narrating this history, Nasser does not separate the economic establishment from the nation's political structure. Instead, each page provides greater proof of the intricate and intimate relationship between the two. It is the author's contention that capitalism as an economic system is neither moral or immoral. Instead, it is without morals of any kind. Like the algorithms Wall Street whiz kids create, capitalism does not know right from wrong. However, those who apply those algorithms do. Likewise, argues Nasser, the politicians and administrators in Washington, DC know right from wrong. When they vote to increase social spending, these men and women are making a choice to use some of capitalism's profits to help those left behind in the pursuit of those profits. When the politicians and administrators decide to remove so-called safety net spending, they are choosing to let the people affected by that spending suffer. In other words, they are making a moral choice no matter what decision they make.

Of course, there are other machinations and motives at play in these decisions. For example, the pursuit of profit has blinded stronger men than Donald Trump. It is also true that that pursuit has created an economy that does not fill the needs of all the people. Instead, it creates unneeded products and uses marketing to convince folks that such products are needed. As part of this mechanism, the act of buying and owning certain products creates artificial needs and desires. This understanding, perhaps stated best by Herbert Marcuse in his book One Dimensional Man, is an operative and fundamental part of contemporary human society.

It wasn't always so. Overripe Capitalism divides the history it provides into two essential sections. The first includes the decades of the late nineteenth century up to and including World War One. This period is defined economically by corporate and financial growth and monopolization. Most profits at this time were reinvested in machinery and factories in order to increase production. These years were marked by ever increasing exploitation of labor and a subsequent intensification of labor rebellion. Like always, corporate owners, their investors and upper management were determined to squeeze as much labor for the fewest pennies in order to increase their profit.

The second essential period according to Nasser began in the 1920s. This period is marked by

a turn from the economy's growth being dependent on increasing production to it being dependent on the population's ability to consume at greater and greater levels. It was this scenario that gave birth to the myth of the Roaring Twenties. As Nasser makes clear, at the time there were more people buying more things that were not staples, especially automobiles. However, this consumption was not being fueled by increased wages for workers, but by an expansion of credit and unregulated stock manipulation. That credit would be the cause of the 1929 crash and subsequent Great Depression. The years that followed were marked by capitalists' continued attempts to rein in the government for its own purposes despite the despair and abject poverty that had been created. In reaction, communists and other leftist formations organized across the country, helping to create a popular and militant movement defending workers and in opposition to the capitalists and their government. From this set of circumstances came the years of FDR's administration.

In discussing these years Nasser emphasizes, like most left-leaning analysts, the role FDR played in saving capitalism. Likewise, he discusses the nature of the programs instituted during his time in office and the built in compromises with Wall Street many of them contained. Most interesting, however, is his discussion of Keynesianism and how it is misunderstood by most economists right to left. As has been stated elsewhere, Overripe Capitalism notes that what saved US capitalism in the mid-twentieth century was the US military's entry into World War Two and the war time production that entailed..

Nasser's narrative continues, bringing the reader up to the current time. The years of economic growth and prosperity following World War Two are discussed, including the fact that those years were mostly prosperous for white-skinned citizens. During this part of the narrative, it becomes clear that what Nasser terms the Golden Years were not meant to last. The collapse began under Nixon and the Democratic party became openly complicit when Jimmy Carter was elected to the White House. The dawning and eventual supremacy of neoliberalism is chronicled in its cancerous ignominy for most of the rest of the text. Also present is a discussion of the role technology plays in making the working class even more irrelevant than it already is. In other words, the reason for replacing humans in McDonalds with robots isn't efficiency, as much as it is part of capital's desire to eliminate the unknown quantity human workers represent.

From Wall Street to the police state repression of the economically irrelevant; from the neofascist rallies of the alt-right to the white supremacists in the White House; from the stock market surges to the shrinking value of the US worker's paycheck, the reasons for our dystopian present are convincingly presented and discussed in this masterwork by Mr. Nasser. As he writes: "the current capitalist command of the American State is the result of repeated efforts, since the early days of the republic, by the capitalist class to gain control of the State. Economic elites have long understood that the hegemony of the capitalist class is possible only if the business class has full command of the State...." As he also makes clear: "No economic crisis, however severe, could spell "the end of capitalism." Only a politically educated working class, actively organized, could bring about a transition to a post-capitalist future." The alternative is almost certainly an authoritarian future that makes any dystopian fiction seem gentle by comparison.

2019-2023

Palestine: The History of a People

Palestine: A Four Thousand Year History—Nur Masalha

The world recently concluded a religious season when millions of people celebrate the birth of Palestine's most famous son. It is also the season when the fact of Palestine is further denied; denied both by some of those who worship him and by some of those who deny his divinity. While it is not the intention of this review to discuss matters of religious belief, the truth is that the history of Palestine and its people is wrapped up in religious beliefs. Those beliefs are used by many factions to both prove and deny Palestine as a historical reality. Over time, the discussion regarding that history has been dominated by those who pretend that Palestine was a land without a people. It is these same forces that use this denial to justify the continuing expansion of their occupation of Palestinian lands.

Without an acknowledged history, whole nations and peoples can be erased from human memory. Most invaders understand this dynamic and all too often determine that the best way to keep lands they have taken is to erase the history of those who lived there when they invaded. All too often, this erasure of the indigenous history and culture is accompanied by mass murder. The most egregious examples of this latter manifestation most often involve Europeans committing genocide in the Americas and Africa. In the case of Palestine, the mass murder was on a lesser scale, but the wholesale removal of the inhabitants of Palestine by Zionist/European colonizers in what is known as the Nakba was nearly complete.

Recently, Zed Books Press published what is perhaps the most comprehensive and complete history of the Palestinian people to date. Titled *Palestine: A Four Thousand Year History*, the text traces the Palestinian people and their culture from pre-biblical times to the modern day.

Author Nur Masalha has composed a narrative befitting a people whose future is ultimately crucial to the world's. Describing most historical narratives about nations as myths based on religions and folk tales, Masalha rejects this approach and takes the reader through a detailed examination of trade, governance, and various inhabitants' personal documents. In doing so he describes a history of a people and a place that began long before more traditional histories of either Palestine or Israel start. The result is a history based in verifiable data and unadorned by romantic notions of nationalism and religious mythology.

Furthermore, Palestine: A Four Thousand Year History challenges and broadens most conventional narratives that primarily highlight the role of the elites in recent Palestinian history. In other words, the text brings the role of the villagers, farmers and everyday working folk into the discussion. In a general way, this means it is a people's history.

The author begins his text with a discussion of the peoples in the region historically called Palestine. It is a description based on archaeological finds and interpretations that places different peoples coming together in what ultimate describes the historic beginnings of the Palestinians. Originally a polytheistic people, over time the Palestinians were (after the early polytheistic phase of prehistory), first predominantly Christian, then Muslim. Palestinian Christianity was part of the Byzantine rite and, like most churches under the eastern synod, fairly independent. It was during this predominantly Christian period that much of what we consider Palestine was politically organized and structured.

Naturally, the role of religion is important throughout the history delineated in this text. However, this is not unlike histories of much of the world. It is apparent from the reading that the wars waged over the lands that are Palestine have been sold to those invaders and occupiers as religious wars, even if they were primarily about land and conquest. This remains the case even as the text finally reaches the twentieth century and the actions of the Zionist movement to settle the land known as Palestine and remake it into Israel. When discussing this part of history, author Masalha portrays the role played by the Zionist movement not so much as a unique movement but as part of the ongoing European colonization of Palestine (and the world). In describing this, Masalha enumerates the multiple ways the Zionist occupation involved numerous British government and private endeavors –including cartographers, military members and diplomats—in their endeavor to erase Palestinian history and culture.

Palestine: A Four Thousand Year History is the most comprehensive English language history of Palestine to date. This book is a painstakingly researched and well-documented deconstruction of the myths too many Zionists and their western apologists have convinced the world to be factual history. In this careful reconstruction of Palestinian cultural and economic history on the land historically known as Palestine, Nur Masalha has provided a resounding renunciation of the modern Western understanding of Palestinian history. His work undertakes a tremendous and important task and succeeds—four thousand years of history cannot be denied. This book is an important work in its own right. In the politics of the times, it also becomes an important tool in the struggle of the Palestinian people.

Twenty-First Century Indian Wars

Our History is the Future—Nick Estes

The American war against its indigenous people is incessant, intermi-
nable and indefensible. From the Pequot Wars blessed by the English
Puritan John Winthrop to the present day destruction of native culture
and community in the name of resource extraction, there are very few
episodes in human history more bloody, brutal and relentless. The recent
attempts by indigenous Americans to defend their lands and culture
against the rapacious designs of the energy industry in Canada and the
United States exist as blatant reminders of this history. When members
of various indigenous nations represented their peoples (along with
allies) in the Idle No More protests that began in Canada in 2014, the
response from the authorities was swift, occasionally brutal, and mostly
dismissive of the native people's claims and demands. A very similar
scenario played out in the US Midwest during the direct actions against
the DAPL pipeline at Standing Rock.

Nick Estes, author of *Our History is the Future*, makes this very
clear. Given the history of indigenous peoples treatment at the hands
of the European invaders and their descendants, Estes' book title takes
on a double meaning. The history of genocide is as much a potential
future for the Native Americans as is the history of their resistance a
hopeful response to the genocidal legacy. A member of the Lower Brule
Sioux Tribe and co-founder of The Red Nation, Estes participated in the
Standing Rock resistance. It is within the resistance at Standing Rock
that Estes bookends his history of indigenous history in North America,
especially the land known as the United States.

Although the text focuses on the story of the Oceti Sakowin people,
the history told within these pages is the history of most indigenous

people in the United States. A combination of bloodshed, treaties made and usually broken, settlers with their own tales of hardship and woe, and a government whose philosophy is best expressed in its use of the gun, the bulldozer, and the dollar bills offered as compensation, this history is more than just history. It is the essence of the capitalist nation whose capitol is in Washington, DC and whose reach extends into space. It is to the beneit of all of us opposed to this monolith that the resistance of the indigenous peoples continues to not only exist, but to provide an example.

Our History is the Future opens with a description of the encampment at Standing Rock in 2017. Estes discusses the genesis of the movement to oppose the pipeline, the politics of the pipeline in the Dakotas and within the movement against it, and the machinations of the State and its armed forces aimed at disrupting and destroying the resistance movement. Woven neatly into this descriptive endeavor is a discussion that combines a Marxist analysis with a philosophy as old as the stories, prophecies and myths of the Lakota nations. Perhaps the best description of what I mean can be found when Estes writes after summarizing a myth where the black snake serves as a metaphor for the Missouri River, his people's historic lifeblood: "For the Oceti Sakowin, prophecies like the Black Snake are revolutionary theory...."

That river is not only the lifeblood of the Oceti Sakowin and other tribes, it is a central focus of the battle between the colonizers and the indigenous peoples. If the water can be taken away, destroyed or poisoned, its life giving properties for the native peoples will no longer be there to sustain them. It was this understanding that was part of the decision in the mid-twentieth century to flood the region for hydropower and destroy the riverbed where the tribe had been pushed to after the Indian wars of the previous decades. It is this same understanding which informed the decision by the corporate and military officials to move the pipeline away from the white-dominated city of Bismarck, North Dakota and run it through Standing Rock.

Estes' book is a vital history of the United States. It is a history told from a point of view that champions resistance and explores its meaning, specifically as it applies to the indigenous people of the land. From the Ghost Dance to the 1973 Wounded Knee occupation to the internationalism of the United Nations Indigenous Peoples Conference, Our History is the the Future is both a celebration and a warning. The hope and solidarity that has propelled the resistance historicized in these pages remains a genuine and viable reality in a world that seems locked in a struggle that could well determine its destruction or its salvation.

Israel-The Largest US Aircraft Carrier in the World

Israel: A Beachhead in the Middle East—Stephen Gowans

The Israeli government does not control the foreign policy of the United States. However, the two regimes have formed an alliance seemingly overseen by forces of darkness that is designed to keep the rest of the Middle East in check. The basic intention of that alliance is to control access to the massive reserves of oil in the region. This is the essential argument of Stephen Gowans' newest book, *Israel: A Beachhead in the Middle East*. It is a necessary and forceful rebuke of those on the left and right who insist that the US government is controlled by Zionists instead of a scenario closer to the opposite.. In writing the text, Gowans provides a reasoned argument against those who—for religious and/or political reasons—propagate what is an essentially anti-Semitic argument concerning the nature of the Washington-Tel Aviv alliance.

The book begins with a brief history of the Zionist movement; its beginnings in Britain in the late nineteenth century, its support from apocalyptic Christians, its essentially colonialist ideology and subsequent support by members of the British government. The Balfour Declaration is briefly discussed, as is its eventual realization as an endorsement of the Zionist colonial project in Palestine. Simultaneous to this discussion, Gowans relates a history of the Arab nations in the region that is both anticolonial and critical in nature. He highlights the governments who sided with the colonialists and those who opposed it, including the Nasser government in Egypt and the short-lived Mossadegh government in Iran. Woven into this discussion is the changing nature of the various imperial relationships, especially the growing power of the United States in the region as the power of the earlier colonial regimes of Britain and France subsided in the wake of World War Two. The fact is that the United

States was the victor in the inter-imperial rivalry that war was about. Its only competition was the Soviet Union, which was overwhelmed with internal and external issues that made their opposition relatively muted, despite the propaganda from Washington that pretended otherwise.

The history told here is fairly up to the moment. It is a story of lies and propaganda, power plays and bloody war. The constant thread in this narrative is the never-ending attempt to neutralize and destroy any and all attempts by the Arab and Muslim inhabitants of the Middle East to assert their right to live free of imperial intervention. From Nasser to Saddam Hussein, Mossadegh to Mahmoud Ahmadinejad, the Palestine Liberation Organization to Hamas, Gowans reminds the reader that the common link between these and every other organized resistance to US and Israeli attempts to dominate the region is their determination to rule themselves. In many of these cases, the other less fortunate link is the failure to achieve that goal because of US and Israeli intervention in their affairs.

The final chapter of the book, titled "Diversion," can be summed up best using Gowans own words. "It is not Israel that has made the Middle East a region of unremitting war; it is the mutual hostility of US investor interests and those of local forces of independence that have turned the region into a zone of unceasing conflict. These two forces are fighting over who will benefit from West Asia's petroleum resources—the local population, or the investors in New York." (206) His argument includes remarks from various US military leaders and Israeli cabinet members (active and retired), all of whom emphasize Israel's role as Washington's imperial beachhead in the Middle East and West Asia. An interesting anecdote provided in the text is that the approximately four billion dollars in military aid Washington gives Tel Aviv every year is about the same it would cost the Pentagon to have an aircraft strike force there year-round. In other words, the Israeli military presence is, in the minds of strategic planners in DC, worth funding given the forward role it plays in US designs on the region.

There are those who will dismiss Gowans' argument, despite its rationality, and continue to accept the trope that Israel controls Washington. Others will focus on his portrayal of the Ba'athist governments of Syria and Saddam Hussein's Iraq, consequently missing the point of his argument—that these regimes played significant historical roles in the resistance to US economic and political intervention in the region; roles that cost Saddam Hussein his life and put Syrian President Assad's nation under military and economic attack for over ten years now. Even if one holds either of these prejudices, reading this book is worth the time. It might change your mind. It certainly will give it something to consider.

A Battle for Existence

This Land: How Cowboys, Capitalism, and Corruption are Ruining the American West –Christopher Ketcham

They are landscapes my mind escapes to regularly. The painted canyons in eastern Montana and the Zion region of Utah. Forests of huge conifers in the mountains of the Pacific Northwest and northern California. The incredible arid desolation of Utah west of Salt Lake City and the deserts of Nevada. Sagebrushed plains in the Southwest. I spent many hours standing by the side of roads observing these and other landscapes in the western United States. Occasionally, I saw an elk herd in the distance or giant raptors flying above me. Once, I ended up covered in some kind of flying insects when I sat down either on or close to their nests in the Colorado heat south of Colorado Springs. Lizards often played on rocks nearby and I remained ever wary of snakes in crevices and shadows. There were a couple summers when I left the road and hiked into the mountains of Theodore Roosevelt National Forest near Boulder, CO. Just me, a sleeping bag and backpack with a little food, a collapsible fishing pole, some whiskey and some weed. Years have passed since those adventures.

Author Christopher Ketcham opens his book *This Land: How Cowboys, Capitalism, and Corruption are Ruining the American West* with a similar reminiscence. In the book's second chapter, he gets specific. He is in the Escalante region of the Grand Staircase-Escalante National Monument. The year is recent. The Trump administration has made clear its intention to shrink the monument's acreage in favor of private interests. This time it's cattlemen who consider the land to be theirs to destroy. All in the name of cowboy culture and rancher's profits. Fittingly, the tale turns to the story of Clive and Ammon Bundy. These

241

were the men who led the takeover of public lands in defense of their right to graze without paying a cent and then, after getting away with that, staged an armed takeover of the Malheur Wildlife Refuge in Oregon. As Ketcham describes the events, he also provides the history behind these actions. In short, the Bundy dramas were part of an ongoing battle over who should control those lands legally considered to belong to all US citizens.

Ketcham does not stop with the Bundys and their ilk–men who are actually bit players in the ongoing war between private interests and the public good. As his text moves forward, Ketcham casts his scrutinizing pen on the role played by the Bureau of Land Management, the Wildlife Services and the Department of the Interior—to name just a few of the government agencies involved—in the selloff of the lands. The story he tells is one of species threatened and species destroyed. It is also one that involves death threats and loss of employment to employees of those agencies who act as if their job is to protect the wild. It is a story that involves other powerful institutions in a conspiracy mired in greed and hubris: the Mormon church, the energy industry, agribusiness, and both political parties.

While it is clear that Ketcham's purpose in writing this book is to bring attention to the abuse of the wilderness and to name those most responsible for its abuse, it is also apparent that he has an appreciation, indeed, a love, for the lands and animals he describes. His prose when describing these aspects moves beyond the merely factual and into the poetic. So do his profiles of the women and men fighting the behemoth intent on destruction. Conversely, his anger at those who pretend to be friends of the forests, grasslands and the animals who live there is specific, biting and without regret. Indeed, his discussion of those organizations and individuals who call themselves "green" while they work with industry in destroying the wilderness for the profits of the cattle and extraction interests includes some of his harshest words. Likewise, he spares nothing when discussing the Obama administration, which gave away more wilderness to those interests than the Bush administration preceding it. In the final pages, Ketcham makes it clear: if you want to save the environment, you must oppose capitalism. There is no other way.

Relentless, well written and informed, This Land: How Cowboys,

Capitalism, and Corruption are Ruining the American West is an angry masterpiece. It eloquently describes an ecosystem disintegrating because of greed, ignorance, and the arrogance of humans. The heroes include the wolves, the grizzlies, the bison and the ravens, trying to survive against a conspiracy that only capitalism and a compliant and compromised civil authority could create.

At the end of the day, Ketcham's text not only channeled my anger at those whose profits depend on intentionally destroying the environment, it also reminded me of the rapturous and synchronous beauty that so desperately requires us to battle for its existence.

Calling the Kettle White: Ishmael Reed Unbound

Why No Confederate Statues in Mexico—Ishmael Reed

Ishmael Reed is one of America's greatest writers. His fiction is both comic and surreal. His body of work reveals cultural and historical truths while keeping an insightful eye at the situation we currently exist in. Over the course of time, he has angered colleagues and critics, been championed and ignored by the mainstream media, written plays, novels and essays, and run a couple journals and a publishing company. His fictional works satirize US history while his essays attack it head-on. They have celebrated African and African-American culture and stripped the hypocrisy from white America's presentation of that culture.

More pointedly, Reed's novels, plays and essays reveal how mainstream (popular and academic) authors, critics, and journalists perpetuate the racist history and mythology that underpins so much of what residents of the United States believe about themselves and their nation. Obviously, those revelations are often not pretty. His most recent fictional work is a play titled The Haunting of Lin-Manuel Miranda. It is a work which shreds the myths and outright lies the popular play by Miranda titled Hamilton is based on. In classic Reed fashion, The Haunting of Lin-Manuel Miranda pointedly rejects the idea Miranda's work rests on–that Alexander Hamilton and other founders of the United States were not just against slavery but were in favor of abolishing it; indeed, that they were abolitionists. Reed's play has been attacked by mainstream critics and money-changers who not only hear the cash registers ringing with the sale of every ticket to Hamilton, but who are also convinced that Miranda's use of non-white actors to play the roles of the slavers in his play is somehow revolutionary. As Reed points out in his newly released collection of essays titled *Why No Confederate Statues in*

Mexico, the reality of the play is much closer to the understood racism of a minstrel show than something revolutionary. In his discussion of this misrepresentation, Reed does express the fact that part of the reason for the play's lies are the lies about US history every school child is told repeatedly throughout their education. Foremost among them, obviously, is the lie that the founders of the United States were fighting for human freedom.

Reed's new book, which is a collection of writings (mostly essays) published over the past decade or so, continues Reed's critique of bourgeois feminism and its racism—sometimes deceptive and other times as obvious as the nose on one's face. Like others who have written on the subject, Reed's basis for his argument is the all too common portrayal of the Black male as a rapist and hoodlum by so many of this type of feminist. Although Reed provides the actors and even Lin-Manuel some leeway by acknowledging that they may be repeating the white rulers' version of history in the play Hamilton, he does not excuse the feminists who perpetrate the racist "Black male rapist" myth. It is understood that they should know better by now—and they should. His approach to this and the other subjects he writes about in the text subject is both combative and contemplative. It is an approach that demands the reader might have to move beyond their initial reaction to listen to his consideration of the topic at hand.

One of the most interesting essays in Why No Confederate Statues in Mexico is titled "Leroi Jones/Amiri Baraka and Me." It is simultaneously a brief history of the late 1950s-1960s Black Arts Movement and its demise and a short biography of the Black poet/playwright/activist Amiri Baraka. In his telling, Reed puts the story of Baraka and himself inside the context of the cultural nationalism of Black America in the 1960s and afterward. Baraka's journey that began with his involvement with the Beats is considerately chronicled in these relatively few pages. Other essays touch on jazz music and the attempt by some critics to whitewash its legacy, and the popularity of Reed's works overseas, especially in China.

Reed saves some of his most piercing criticism for the end of the book. In an essay discussing Barack Obama's August 2013 speech where Obama echoed white conservatives (and Patrick Moynihan) and attacked African-American men for their supposed failings as fathers, Reed destroys Obama's claims and wonders why he would side with conservatives whose understanding of Black people comes from Bell Curve author Charles Murray. After all, Reed reminds the reader, it's the Black people who will always remember Obama fondly, not the white racists he seems to want to please in that speech. That essay is followed by an examination of the racism of Donald Trump and his supporters—a phenomenon encouraged and propagated by the US media establishment since time immemorial. Ending the book with a fantasy of being a fly on New York Times liberal columnist Nicholas Kristof's wall is Ishmael Reed's coup de grace.

This book is cynical, critical, hopeful and incendiary. A worthy introduction to one of the sharper pens in the last seventy years, this collection of essays reveals the swift sword that is Reed's rapier wit and comedic talent. Why No Confederate Statues in Mexico continues his unique perspective on history, culture and politics in the USA.

The Essence of War

My Lai: Vietnam, 1968, and the Descent into Darkness—Howard Jones

Many US teenage boys in the late 1960s and early 1970s grew up wondering if they would end up in the jungles of Vietnam when they reached draft age. Some could hardly wait to go fight in their idealized version of honor and glory. Some knew by the time they were sixteen that they would do whatever they could to avoid going. The rest of us were somewhere in the middle. Although I leaned towards running away to Canada or Sweden, I included myself among the uncertain. If there was one instance that convinced me I was going to avoid military service no matter what, it was the exposure of the massacre in MyLai. I had recently attended my first antiwar protest in the suburban town I lived in between Washington, DC and Baltimore and was devouring all the antiwar literature I could find. Most of it came from a friend's older brother who was volunteering for the Vietnam Moratorium Committee and attended the nearby University of Maryland at College Park.

The literature provided arguments against the war and discussed how the US could end its involvement. I remember these arguments as intellectually appealing. However, it was the news articles accompanied by grotesque photos of dead babies that caused such moral revulsion I knew I could never participate in the war in any way. As it turned out, the disclosure of the massacre would convince many more of my fellow Americans that the war was wrong and needed to end.

As the months turned into years after the publication of the massacre, other revelations of various impact appeared in the media. Like the first news of MyLai, there were those who either rejected these revelations as lies, tried to diminish their importance or worked even harder to bury them deeper than where certain reporters had originally found them. Fortunately, the damage had been done. The US war on the Vietnamese ended ignominiously for the US in 1975.

Despite its importance, it was not until 2017 that an authoritative text about the incident and the attempted cover-up of it was finally published. Titled *My Lai: Vietnam, 1968, and the Descent into Darkness* and authored by historian Howard Jones, the work is a masterpiece. Jones utilizes virtually every document available about the massacre and includes information and anecdotes from interviews of individuals present at the scene and involved in the eventual trial. His descriptions of the murders by the US troops are detailed and horrifying, even sickening. Likewise, his reportage of the coverup and the bureaucratic gymnastics that are part and parcel of military life expresses the frustration of both those NCOs and officers trying to cover up the massacre and those journalists and military investigators trying to get to the bottom of the incident. The second half of the book, which covers the trial of William Calley—who was the only military man convicted of murder in the incident—reads like a well-made television courtroom drama. The only real conclusion one can take from this incredibly detailed and objective history is that what happened at MyLai in March 1968 was a war crime and that many of those involved in the crime and its coverup got away with murder.

A phenomenon I have observed over the years of watching and protesting US wars in other lands is the refusal of most US civilians to accept that the young men (and now women) they send into foreign lands to kill and destroy will commit war crimes. Although many of these same individuals will be quick to point out vicious killings and torture by the enemy of the time, they reject any suggestions that US troops are capable of the same acts. Or, more reprehensibly, they excuse them in the name of a twisted exceptionalism that paints US lives as somehow better than any others. As Jones made clear, this was certainly the predominant opinion in the months after the MyLai massacre was revealed in the press. Those reporters and editors who wrote and published the stories received death threats by the dozens. The military officers involved in the prosecution of William Calley were forced to watch their backs, too. Politicians supporting the war set up hearings designed to paint Calley as a hero and those soldiers who reported him to the brass as traitors.

I am someone who does not believe the massacre of close to five hundred women, children, old men and babies was an anomalous incident in the US war on the Vietnamese. Nor do I think Vietnam was the last place such crimes were committed by US military members. I remain grateful for the various reporters who uncovered the story of the massacre and the editors who published those stories and the photos taken by military photographers at the scene. If this hadn't happened, myself and perhaps many other young Americans might not have protested and resisted the US war effort. I have nothing but respect for those troops who attempted to stop the murders and consider those officers who pushed for a trial of Calley and wanted to go further up the chain of command to be men of honor. Howard Jones' text not only cements their stories for posterity, it also makes it clear that a soldier's nationality does not preclude their ability to commit mass murder or excuse them if they do.

The Blues Had a White Baby and His Name was Michael Bloomfield

Guitar King: Michael Bloomfield's Life in the Blues—David Dann

Michael Bloomfield began playing in Chicago blues clubs while still in high school. By 1968 he was considered one of the best guitarists in the world along with Jimi Hendrix and Eric Clapton. By that time, Bloomfield had joined and left the Paul Butterfield Blues Band, played on Bob Dylan's masterpiece album Highway 61 Revisited and formed the genre busting group The Electric Flag. Like so many other musicians, especially of his generation, he had also developed a taste for opiates and the relief they provide.

Michael Bloomfield died in 1981 on Valentine's Day. Although the autopsy report was somewhat contradictory, he probably overdosed on fentanyl (sold mistakenly as China White heroin), which had recently made an appearance in the San Francisco streets. I was never a user of opiates, but friends of mine were. They talked about a new monster high that was like heroin but much more powerful. The only reason I was personally familiar with fentanyl was because a friend had almost died from it earlier after buying some in Washington, DC. Bloomfield was supposedly cleaning up his act, but like most users, he wasn't done completely with narcotics. Unfortunately, he went back one too many times.

I had seen Bloomfield play in different venues since moving to the Bay Area and was always impressed. Sometimes his shows were so good I was left without words, only the ecstasy that otherworldly guitar virtuosity can create. Other times, they were just damn good blues/rock performances. The musicians backing him varied, depending on Bloomfield's current emotional and economic situation. According to a new biography by writer David Dann, titled *Guitar King: Michael*

Bloomfield's Life in the Blues, that situation was quite fluid, especially in his later years. As noted above, Bloomfield first came to national notice as a member of the Paul Butterfield Blues Band and then as a guitarist on Bob Dylan's album Highway 61 Revisited. Before that, he had been playing in Chicago blues clubs and taverns. Often, he was asked to sit in with some of the greatest names in the business—Muddy Waters and Howlin' Wolf were just two such musicians. Bloomfield's talent was a known factor to record company people in New York and by the time he was nineteen, he had a contract with Epic Records. Biographer Dann chronicles Bloomfield's rise and growing fame, intertwining his tale with his subject's issues with his family and schools. The son of a wealthy businessman with a nice house in the Chicago suburbs, Bloomfield's understanding of the blues was not from his upbringing like so many of his mentors and heroes.

Dann's biography is more than a chronicle of Bloomfield's life. It is also an ongoing discussion of his approach to the blues, his battles with bipolar disorder and substances he took to combat the disorder, and a unique look at the cultural mixtape that was the period called the Sixties. Dann deftly weaves the travels and travails of Bloomfield and his guitar into tales of free love and hippie ghettoes, LSD adventures and mishaps, racial strife and harmony, and the youth-led protest against the US war on the Vietnamese. It's a fascinating travelogue through the times steeped in blues and rock music and musicians. The context is the music of the Black ghetto and rock palaces like the Fillmore West. While reading the book, I was reminded more than once of a song by the blues guitarist Muddy Waters that includes the lyrics "Well you know the blues got pregnant/And they named the baby Rock & Roll...." Michael Bloomfield was one of those who was present at the birth, if not the conception.

Without diminishing Dann's stellar work in putting Bloomfield's role in music and culture on the written page in vivid detail, it is important to emphasize that Guitar King is much more than a biography of his life. It is also a discussion of his approach to the music he mastered. Dann not only discusses the intricacies of the recording sessions of the recordings Bloomfield was part of, he dissects Bloomfield's playing, detailing chord changes, note shifts and bends, key changes and tempo alterations. In doing this, the reader can almost hear the music in their head. Furthermore, these descriptions enable anyone who listens the performance being discussed in the text the ability to see what they are hearing and, if they so desire, attempt to replicate the Bloomfield style—a musical lesson in its own right.

Michael Bloomfield's life was both tragic and jubilant. He played guitar with a swagger and confidence that belied his insecurities. In his playing he opened up possibilities that might never have been conceived without him. Those who ended up being considered greater than Bloomfield—Eric Clapton and Jimi Hendrix, for example—acknowledged their debt to his revolutionary approach and his master musicianship. David Dann's book Guitar King is voluminous in size—as befits a man whose contribution to modern music is greater than history has ever acknowledged. Drawing from his deep research and numerous interviews, it is clear that Dann put tremendous effort into this book. It is a biography that puts Bloomfield back into his rightful place on the roster of rock and blues greats. The result is a tremendous and magnificent work.

Tempestuous Noise

Shakespeare's Tempest and Capitalism: The Storm of History—
Helen Scott

I first became aware of William Shakespeare's play The Tempest in Junior High. Our English class was reading Romeo and Juliet and each student was assigned to read another Shakespeare work of our own choosing. I chose King Lear, mostly because I felt an affinity with Lear's youngest daughter Cordelia. Later in my life I would also find an affinity with Falstaff—at least his preference for certain beverages. A girl who sat next to me in English class chose The Tempest. The general perception in our class was that this play was a fairy tale complete with a king, a prince, a princess, a whimsical spirit and a bad guy. The year was 1967. Little did we know that in the world outside our suburban class-room all of those characters and the play itself were being reconsidered and radically redefined.

One of the last dramas written by Shakespeare, The Tempest came into being when the European world was undergoing one of its many metamorphoses. The economic system that would become capital-ism was in its birth throes and the world of feudalism's monarchies and bloodlines was receding. As part of these changes, the commons were being privatized and industrial labor was slowly intensifying and expanding its grip over the peasantry and lower urban classes. Science and rationalism was replacing the Church, its faith and its mysticism. A new class, which would become known as the bourgeoisie was on the not-too-distant horizon. A rapidly approaching future would herald the great bourgeois revolutions that would reorder the world in ways ultimately foretold in this drama of Shakespeare's, but unforeseen at the time of its writing. As time moved forward into the twentieth and then the twenty-first century, this drama of Shakespeare's would be reconsidered. In time, it would be considered one of his most important works.

This reevaluation reflected the changes wrought by capitalism, its advances and its intrusions. To put it simply (perhaps too simply), the African Caliban, whose origins as the illegitimate son of a Black witch had so often cast him as villain, was recast as a revolutionary representative of the colonized—the people sold into slavery, forced to work their stolen homeland and die like so many insects. Prospero, the banished king whose magic allowed him to regain his throne and ensure his daughter's future was newly perceived as the colonizer and enslaver of not only Caliban, but of the spirit Ariel, too. All that was once right-side up was now upside down. In other interpretations more favorable to capitalism, it is Prospero—whose power is based in his book-learning and knowledge—that is the revolutionary.

It is these newer understandings of the drama on Prospero's island (or is it Caliban's?) that University of Vermont literature professor Helen Scott examines in her recent text *Shakespeare's Tempest and Capitalism: The Storm of History.* Relying on Walter Benjamin's remark in his Theses on the Concept of History that history is "a series of catastrophes" and informed by her socialism (Scott edited and wrote the introduction to a 2007 collection of Rosa Luxemburg's essays and is one of the editors working on a complete collection of her works), Scott invites the reader on a journey that sails through the turbulent history of the capitalist era. She characterizes the play as being poly-dimensional and ripe with contradictions, like the world it was written in. This is but one reason, Scott argues, why its popularity in times of historical crisis exists.

Scott's text examines The Tempest both as a dark study of power and as an illuminating discussion of the possibilities of resistance and ultimately liberation. It's a drama full of dualities like the world it exists in. Consequently, so are the multiple interpretations. Scott's critical journey incorporates poets, writers, critics and filmmakers from Edwin Markham to Sylvia Plath, WH Auden to John Fowles, HD to Derek Jarman, Aimé Cesaire and Silvia Federici, among others. Innumerable performances of the play are invoked in her contemplation of the changing meanings of The Tempest and the relationship between those meanings and the social conflicts of past, present and in the future. Likewise, the reader learns of creative works in other genres—novels, film, and poetry, even music—that add complexities to this drama my literature class once perceived as a playful bit of fun.

Ms. Scott has written a fascinating and lively take on a fascinating drama that involves history, revolution and reaction. An approachable text even for those not versed in Shakespeare, Scott's argues that The Tempest is a work which both reveals and in retrospect critiques capitalism: its revolutionary changes to human existence and its counterrevolutionary actions against those who would move humanity beyond it. She truly knows her subject, having read, viewed, analyzed and considered multiple renditions of Shakespeare's tale. As a result, Shakespeare's Tempest and Capitalism is considerably more than a history of the play, as performed, rewritten, critiqued and referred to. It is also a history of British, and ultimately Western capitalism, colonialism and imperialism and the resistance to its predation and degradations.

Manifesting Radical Feminism

Burn it Down! Feminist Manifestos for the Revolution—ed.
Breanne Fahs

Webster's defines a manifesto as "a written statement declaring publicly the intentions, motives, or views of its issuer." In her recently published book *Burn it Down! Feminist Manifestos for the Revolution*, editor Breanne Fahs notes that although the manifesto form began with nobles and kings who used them to tell their subjects how things were, the form has become associated with the Left and the street, so to speak. They are urgent, strident and occasionally nihilistic; contradictory and rabble-rousing. The best known of all manifestos is probably the one written by Karl Marx and Friedrich Engels—The Communist Manifesto. In this reviewer's mind, that work is one of the most powerful and concise pieces of text every published. Its purpose is clear in the first paragraph. The rationale it presents is as flawless and simple as an elementary school math problem. That pamphlet is the ultimate template for the form we call the manifesto.

On the other hand, the word feminism has no clear template, no text that exemplifies its essential meaning. To the modern liberal, feminism means, among other things, the right of women to compete equally in the capitalist economy she exists in. This same woman—whose bourgeois reality is assumed in the fact she is even competing—also means she has the right to choose who she sleeps with and whether or not she will have children. According to this definition, her destiny is as wide open as men in her position believe theirs is. The modern right winger accepts a similar definition. This means that they understand women are in competition with men. That understanding usually results in two main behaviors. One is filled with resentment which results in attempts to

256

restrict women to their home and their children. The other is also tinged with resentment but accepts that certain women are of use to the power structure in roles allowed them by the male power structure. Both of these positions never accept that women are as capable as men assume themselves to be.

Burn it Down! Is about another kind of feminism. It is a feminism that rejects capitalism and its sexist core. It is also a feminism that transcends the conventional and assumes nothing is as it was before. The manifestos range in time from Sojourner Truth's "I Am as Strong as Any Man" published in 1851 to the 2018 Susan Stenson tract titled "Occupy Menstruation." From Valerie Solanos 1967 SCUM Manifesto to Bikini Kill's Riot Grrl Manifesto of 1991. However, the bulk of the entries are from the period known historically as the second wave of feminism, which ran from the mid-1960s through the 1970s. It is that period which brought issues of race and non-heterosexuality into a discussion which to that point had been one focused mostly on the lives of white-skinned bourgeois western women. The numerous manifestos, poems, and rants from that period in this book address each and every one of these permutations from a multitude of vantage points—every single one of them radical and some revolutionary. This latter aspect can be attributed to the spawning grounds for this second wave of feminism—the New Left and the counterculture. While both of these movements were certainly male-dominated and heterosexist, it was the first stirrings of liberation and the consequent frustrations they provided to women that caused them to take a closer look at their situation.

As I read this text, bouncing from one manifesto to the other, I was struck by at least two phenomena. One thing that struck me was how familiar I was with many of the texts. I would argue that this familiarity is proof of the influence they had on those of us in the aforementioned movements (especially the Left). The other phenomena that hit me was how little some things have changed. Women are still fighting for equal pay and the right to choose their own destinies. Non-white immigrant women are still near the bottom of the economic and social order in the United States. Most Black women are right there with them. And most white middle-class women are still seeing their fight for equality as one that involves them competing with white men for the right to exploit and oppress those whose class and skin tone they do not share.

There are newer expressions of feminism printed in this text, too. Like the earlier manifestos, they are radical; anti-capitalist, anti-gender discrimination, and calling for a new social and sexual order. Also like the earlier submissions, some focus on capitalism and its well-documented shortcomings while others point their pen at sexuality and its meanings in the twenty-first century. This text is important historically and as a handbook for understanding and organizing today. Fahs has put together a collection that runs from the immediate and practical to the futuristic and abstract. In doing so, she reminds us that radical feminism is both utopian vision and practical argument.

Jackson State Shootings, 1970

Steeped in the Blood of Racism: Black Power, Law and Order, and the 1970 Shootings at Jackson State College—Nancy K. Bristow

It's hard to explain the situation in May 1970. I was in ninth grade at a junior high school administered by the US Department of Defense for what are known as dependents in military jargon. In plain English, they are family members of those in the military. Even from that seemingly remote environment, the events taking place in the mother country affected us—high school walkouts, GIs refusing to work, junior high students wearing black armbands and demanding an assembly, German students and workers marching on the IG Farben building where at least three US military commands were headquartered. We were not immune from the strikes, protests and battles raging across the United States in the wake of the US invasion of Cambodia on April 30, 1970. Given my experience thousands of miles away from the United States, I still can only imagine the considerably more intense climate there.

After the invasion was announced, students took to the streets around the United States and elsewhere in the world. A committee of organizers of national protests to free Black Panthers Bobby Seale and Ericka Huggins on trumped-up charges in New Haven immediately called for and began organizing a national student strike. Protests escalated across the nation. On May 4th, 1970, troops opened fire on protesters at Kent State University. Four students were killed and at least thirteen others were wounded. Police and troops fired live ammunition on other campuses, but none had the horrendous results as those thirteen seconds of gunfire in Ohio. Naturally, the protests grew exponentially until eventually, most US campuses had witnessed some action against the US war against the people of Southeast Asia and young people in the United States.

Often lost in the retelling of this historical moment are two other massacres by law enforcement. The first, which took place in Augusta, GA. On May 11th. It was during an uprising against a racist police force and city government that men attached to the Augusta Police Department, Richmond County Sheriff's Department, Georgia National Guard, and the Georgia State Patrol opened fire on African-American protesters killing six (four unarmed) civilians and wounding more than eighty. A few days later, On May 14th, members of the Mississippi Highway Patrol and the Jackson, Mississippi police force fired hundreds of shots at students hanging around the Jackson State campus, killing two people and wounding several more. All of those shot were Black.

It is the skin tone of those killed in Augusta and Jackson that provides a large part of the reason those murders did not get the headlines the murders of the Kent State students did. As any critical observer of US history knows (even if they won't admit it), killing African Americans is not an aberration of policy. Indeed, in most cases it is policy. The statistics detailing police murders of African Americans prove this to this day. Of course, if that's not convincing enough, there is the entire history of the nation.

In her new book, *Steeped in the Blood of Racism: Black Power, Law and Order, and the 1970 Shootings at Jackson State College*, author Nancy K. Bristow utilizes that history as the basis for her examination of the Jackson State massacre. It is her contention that it was more than anger at the US invasion of Cambodia and the Kent State shootings that inspired some students at Jackson State to gather and protest; it was also more than the constant harassment of those students by police. By presenting a history of the college, its legacy as a public and historically Black college, and its ongoing struggle with white racist politicians in Mississippi as an institution, Bristow provides the reader with a scenario familiar to most Black Mississippians even today. When expanded into the greater political and cultural context present in the 1960s throughout not just the US South but the entire nation, it becomes evident that the murders of students at Jackson State were a logical escalation of events forced onto the dead and wounded by the racist legacy of the United States. Hence the title Steeped in the Blood of Racism.

If one were to divide the text into smaller portions, the most obvious divisions would be the history of Jackson State and its place in Mississippi history, a recounting of the people and events of the week the murders took place, a discussion of the local and national media coverage of the events, and the subsequent presentation of the Jackson State killings in the historical retelling. Throughout each section the stain of white supremacy conscious and otherwise leaks into the story being told. Any discussion that left this out would not only be dishonest, but an insult to the truth that made the massacre not only a possibility, but a fact.

When Bristow describes the night of the murders, the Mississippi darkness comes alive, the hint of another steamy summer is present in the cooling air of the night even as the sirens and police ranks beat and chase young men and women through the campus and the streets. As she describes the final moments before law enforcement kneel en masse, turn and fire their variety of weapons at a women's dormitory and the students hanging around it, this reader's breath stopped even though I remember envisioning the maneuver the first time I read the news in the Stars & Stripes newspaper that day in May 1970.

Steeped in the Blood of Racism is a harsh reminder of the essential nature of the country that is the United States. As Bristow makes clear in her closing pages where she discusses the legacy of the murders and the nature of today's USA; where Black men and women are still shot by police for no discernible reason other than fear and the hate that fear produces, that history is not only in the past. She also makes it clear—in addition to what the news states daily—that the white supremacist society that informs the fear and subsequent violence continues its hateful legacy. Bristow's erudite and evocative text on the Jackson State massacre is an important and essential addition to the library of books on the 1960s and 1970s in the United States.

Kidnapping Kids: As American as the Fourth of July

Taking Children: A History of American Terror—Laura Briggs

It's been two hundred forty-four years since the declaration of independence was sent by horseback to the peasants, city dwellers and plantation owners in the colonies on North America's eastern coast. Britain's subjects across the ocean took up their cry. "Damn the English and their East Indies Tea Company and damn their taxes, too." The colonists' determination to take the mountains, valleys, swamps and beaches from the British crown was now a war. A war between white skinned folks over lands robbed from humans considered savages with no right to anything, not even their children.

Although Africans stolen from their homes were enslaved in both the northern and southern colonies, it's clear from history that the southern slavers who signed on to the declaration did so primarily to keep their slaves. Forever. The humans they worked and traded were more than labor. They were also accumulated wealth and investment property. The latter was especially true if one owned "good breeding stock" capable of producing lots of offspring. A mortgage could be had by a slaver with such collateral. The children birthed by these women rarely got to watch their children age. Instead, they were taken from their mothers and sold to another slaver or slave owning institution.

Today, families hoping to gain asylum, work or safety flee the lands to the US south. Escaping societies broken by US funded wars, unfair and exploitative trade agreements, corruption and bloodshed stemming from the racist war on drugs, these families languish separately and together in camps and detention facilities across the United States. The facilities are part of a policy of punishment founded in a denial of the families' humanity. As Laura Briggs makes very clear in her book *Taking*

Children: A History of American Terror, the policy is a bipartisan policy, its basic tenet of using children as chips in a negotiation where the State holds most the odds.

As the title states, Briggs' text is a history of officially sanctioned kidnapping in the new world. Although focused primarily on the United States, she does discuss the Argentinian children stolen by the ultra-right regime in that country during the 1970s and early 1980s. Many of those children were taken after their leftist parents were killed or imprisoned. In a similar, but less documented, manner, many indigenous families had their children stolen by the authoritarian regimes governing Guatemala. These are the children who became known as los desaparecidos.

Without missing a beat, Taking Children brings the reader back to the US and its decades long policy of kidnapping native American children and forcing them to attend schools set up by the military and different Christian churches. The point of said schools was to destroy indigenous culture and replace it with a rather extreme Christian capitalist ideology. Given that this was done in the name of Christianity, there was little outcry from any US citizens. Indeed, it was considered to be the white person's Christian duty as surely as killing those indigenous who resisted was. This is why many native children were adopted by white folks without the birth mother's knowledge. The fact that First Nations people continue to be treated as heathens and savages by too many elements of the state says a lot about the deep-rootedness of an Indian-hating ideology. As Briggs points out, the removal of native peoples from their lands is often related to the desire to extract resources from those lands. Obviously, that is more than just a coincidence.

If ripping infants from their mothers is considered an effective way to discourage asylum seekers from entering the US, many US citizens say let them rip. It's clear from the news coverage of the immigration patrols that there always seems to be enough uniformed sadists willing to carry out such deeds. When asked how they can participate in such an endeavor, those with something of a heart seem to always respond with the line made famous by Nazis in Nuremburg: "I was just following orders." Those who delight in ripping infants from their mother's arms or forcing young children to sleep on concrete and testify by themselves as to why they should be allowed in the US say little, but enjoy it the most. Beyond the emotional element lies something more insidious, and even more brutal. It is a philosophy based in white supremacist and imperial ideology, which in turn stems from and strengthens the essence of capitalism. That is, how can one extract wealth from this person? If there is no way to do so, then this person is expendable. Let them rot in the poverty capitalism has created. The ultimate outcome of such a mindset is extermination, but that would require taking responsibility for the deaths and misery these policies create. Instead, it is easier to cast those considered expendable to the wayside and let the market take the blame for the death almost certain to occur.

Taking Children is an incisive history of kidnapping as American policy. The author has composed a litany of historical moments of child snatching that would shame Leopold and Loeb. Furthermore, author Briggs connects these into a seamless tale of torment, torture and arrogance; a description of US history if there ever was one. It is a history that demands a reckoning. I, for one, hope to be alive when the time of reckoning comes.

Is a Feminist City Potentially a Humane City?

Feminist City: Claiming Space in a Man-Made World—Leslie Kern

The world we live in is a world built primarily through a male lens. This can be seen in film and on television, in politics and academia. The reasons for this are many, but boil down to one essential fact: the existence of patriarchy. It's true that in recent times, various aspects of male domination of the public sphere have been modified in reaction to the demands of women and the necessities of the marketplace. However, the patriarchal structure is still quite intact. Like white supremacy, it continues to distort and diminish the possibilities of the human experience.

Beyond the obvious masculine perspectives of the phenomena mentioned above are those unnoticed elements of our existence that accentuate the male gaze. Perhaps the least noticed of these is the masculine framework of urban life. It is at its most obvious when a cluster of sexual assaults on women take place in an urban area or the police are engaged in pursuing a serial rapist. Women and girls are warned not to travel alone, not to travel at night, and preferably to stay at home. They are further encouraged not to dress provocatively or drink alcohol. Right now, you might be thinking that these warnings are not sexist in any way but are just common sense. In other words, women and girls are told they must live in fear. Indeed, this is the case even when there is not a highly publicized sexual assault case. However, what these situations ignore is the social function of fear that geographer Leslie Kern describes in her book *Feminist City: Claiming Space in a Man-Made World*.

Kern's text follows in the tradition of urbanist Mike Davis and his discussions of how architecture enhances control of marginalized city dwellers and British Israeli architect Eyal Weizman's discussions of Israeli architecture and its purpose in controlling Palestinians. She looks beyond the three dimensional elements of urban construction and delves into the reasons cities are built the way they are. Although she touches briefly on the economics of capitalism in urban areas—with a special focus on gentrification—her incorporation of the role women play in gentrification is what makes her analysis interestingly unique. Given her life as an academic with a middle-class lifestyle and white skin, her perspective is representative of her class and position. At the same time, her political understanding that her desires and hopes are not necessarily the same as those of women of color, immigrant women, lesbians and trans women, sex workers and working-class women entails that she remind the reader of this. Indeed, when writing about gentrification, Kern discusses how highly secure condo buildings in formerly "rough" neighborhoods are advertised with women like her in mind. Given that these are often the first indicators of a neighborhood beginning gentrification, she notes that white women become the equivalent of settlers encroaching on native lands. Tangentially, she discusses how the tendency among some women to demand more police in these and other urban neighborhoods ignores the brutal reality of police harassment and surveillance of Black, immigrant and poor districts.

This is a small but provocative book. It is both an introduction to feminist geography and to modern feminism, with its multiple meanings and numerous contradictions. Kern does not provide many answers but raises many questions. In a world where the male gaze is so often the only gaze considered; so much so most people don't even think of it as being gendered in any way, Feminist City is revelatory. It is a look at urban worlds (especially those of the west) through the eyes of a woman. In other words, the female gaze.

If we accept Kern's text as a discussion of the modern neoliberal capitalist city through a feminist/women's lens, the selections in Black Rose's Social Ecology and the Right to the City is an expansion of that discussion. The context here is the political philosophy known as social ecology–an anarchism informed by Marxist thought and developed by Murray Bookchin and like-minded thinkers and activists. The other thinker referred to in some of the other essays is the French philosopher Henri Lefebvre, whose tract The Right to the City expanded the Marxian revolutionary class beyond workplace walls out to those who live in and democratize the city in defiance of the industrialists and financiers determined to make the metropolis just another point of profit for them.

Where Kern wonders how to create the feminist city as a humane space managed and designed by all those who live there, especially those who aren't wealthy and primarily interested in property as investment, this text presents efforts by city dwellers to establish such a space. In other words, it is necessary for the discussion about a future democratic, feminist city into the streets. Kern understands this, but seems unsure how to make it so. Most of the writers in this book either are already acting towards this goal or have some grassroots ideas how we might bring it about.

Amongst the essays discussing the nature of the metropolis in late stage capitalism and the need to wrest urban spaces back from the profiteers and financial predators are pieces describing recent and ongoing actions attempting exactly that. One article describes the politics and the practice involved in liberating and maintaining privatized space in Greek cities. These spaces are now public gardens and encampments; protest spaces and shelters. Another piece looks at squatting in Brazil and Spain. Still others refer to the attempts led by Kurds in Rojava to create the municipalities envisioned by those who call themselves social ecologists. Exhilarating with hope yet tempered by reality, the urban vision explored in this sharply edited collection is not out of reach. Like Kern's feminist exploration of the city, it is a response to the dystopian vision presented by our current trajectory—a trajectory driven by greed, militarized policing and greater poverty.

I currently work in Burlington, VT. It is a small city which is also the largest city in Vermont. The downtown area has been overly-privatized in the last couple decades. Large retail corporations have come and gone according to the whims of the marketplace defined by Wall Street. In other words, most of the stores and many of the restaurants are not committed to the people who live, work or vacation in Burlington, but to corporate and financial entities owned, sold and resold by hedge funds and large financial houses. The most recent example of this phenomenon is an endeavor that involved tearing down one shopping mall that was to be replaced by another. After one of the two corporate investors pulled out, the other investor (Brookfield) has yet to begin construction. A huge hole exists where the mall once was. The taxpayer monies (21 million dollars) provided to the investors are sitting somewhere if they haven't been spent. The reason for this situation is simple: Brookfield wants to do whatever it wants to with the property, despite ongoing lawsuits and protests by residents opposed to the plan. In recent weeks, an underground murmuring is circulating that suggests the city and/or its residents reject the capitalist venture and reinvent the space in a way that would keep the space and any money it ultimately produced in the area. Ideas like a year-round farmer's market, cooperatively-owned shops and restaurants, parkland and a place for the increasing numbers of houseless people to rest, clean up, eat and get day work are quietly gelling.

There's a refrain that tells us women's rights are human rights. When it comes to the nature of the modern metropolis, it seems fair to say that a feminist city is a humane city. It's a city that respects its residents no matter what their income, skin color, gender/gender preference, ethnicity or religion. It's a city where everyone who wants shelter has shelter; a city where safety does not mean police with guns and belligerent attitudes; a city that encourages compassion. In other words, a city where the most marginalized among us are considered the equal of the most privileged. It's a vision worth pursuing.

Based in Empire

The United States of War—David Vine

I spent much of my childhood on US military bases. From San Antonio, Texas to Fairbanks, Alaska and from Peshawar, Pakistan to Frankfurt am Main, Germany, my life was surrounded by military uniforms, ID cards, and walls. In his new book, *The United States of War*, author David Vine describes one aspect of these bases as attempts to create little suburbia for US soldiers and their families overseas. This was certainly the case in Pakistan. The houses were little three-bedroom ranches. There was a swimming pool and a golf course. There was also a grocery store (called the commissary) and a Post Exchange, where everything from blue jeans to shaving kits to record albums were available to purchase at reduced prices. The closed-circuit radio and television station played the latest Top 40 hits and showed popular US television shows. When I was in high school, living in Germany and going to a school on a military post, the cheap records at the Post Exchange were the best possible deal; I bought a good amount of my rock and roll at $2.50 a disc.

It was when I was reading Rudyard Kipling's novel Kim that I first began to understand that US military bases were more than just pieces of real estate granted by the host country to ensure that nation's security. Even though I had not begun questioning the US military when I was ten and reading Kipling, I did realize then that the US base was just a different version of the colonial outposts of the British Raj, from which the novel's protagonist came. No matter how interesting and enjoyable my life was because of my father's assignments, this was an essential truth I could not ignore.

This is the foundation of David Vine's newest book, *The United States of War: A Global History of America's Endless Conflicts, from Columbus to the Islamic State.* While expanding on his previous work, titled Base Nation, Vine provides a comprehensive history of Washington's quest for empire. Conceiving military outposts as actual colonial usurpations of other nations' land, Vine argues that not only do these bases assist the US military in its wars, but their presence across the globe makes war more likely and all too often the preferred means to accomplish the goals of Washington and Wall Street. This fact, when combined with the mammoth amount of monies spent to arm the United States, spy on humans around the globe, and defend markets and other resources abroad, puts the generals in the Pentagon at the helm of US foreign policy. That prominence is rarely good for any nation and never good for one that claims to be a democracy. After all, generals rarely answer to anyone and, when they do, they usually end up having the upper hand.

From the US Army outposts set up on the frontier in support of white settlers determined to take indigenous lands to the so-called lily-pond bases scattered around the globe in support of the US empire, author Vine has composed a catalog of destruction and mass murder. Not only were these bases essential to the expansion of said empire, they remain essential to its existence. Indeed, it is the author's contention that no anti-war movement can be successful unless and until one of its demands is the closure of all overseas bases. Furthermore, each base is in and of itself an extension of the United States, where for the most part its laws take precedence over that of the nation the land is actually located on.

From the first slaughter of the indigenous peoples in the first years by Puritan colonizers in North America to the ongoing special forces missions around the world, military outposts have been key to that history. Just like the US interstate highway system was built after World War Two to facilitate moving military equipment around the country, so is the global military base system designed to facilitate moving weaponry and troops around the world. In The United States of War, David Vine makes a powerful argument that demanding the closure of US military bases overseas is an essential and important part of ending us wars of empire. His text also makes clear that convincing people of this is not as simple as it appears. This is true because of their role in maintaining the US empire, but also because of the profits involved in the building, maintaining and servicing of those bases.

The United States of War is a unique history text. Convincing in its portrayal of US military bases as both the outposts of empire and the remote supplier to the troops whose mission is to maintain and expand that empire, the timeline the author constructs is one that argues the US has always been an imperial nation—and not by some accident or circumstance of history. The intention of the empire builders is as clear as the numbers of humans slaughtered in their pursuit of that empire; from the shores of the Massachusetts colony to the jungles of Vietnam, from the halls of the Navy Yard to the shores of Tripoli.

Ginsberg's America: an American Poet Describes an Uncertain Nation

The Fall of America: Journals 1965-1971—Allen Ginsberg

Allen Ginsberg was a rolling stone. He seemed determined to gather no moss. From 1965 through 1971, he traveled the world. Mostly, though, he traveled the United States. Sometime during those journeys (presumably near the beginning of the time period), Bob Dylan bought him a tape recorder. It had to be a reel-to-reel since cassettes did not exist on the market then. Ginsberg spoke into the microphone of that machine, recording what he saw and what he thought. Somewhere along the way, the fragments of what is termed auto-poesy were transcribed. Some of its finer iterations became Ginsberg's prize winning 1973 poetry collection titled The Fall of America: poems of these states.

This year, the University of Minnesota Press releases the journals from which that book was derived. Titled *The Fall of America: Journals 1965-1971*, the text is the third in a trilogy. Parts one and two described Ginsberg's early European travels and some of his Latin American travels. Even more than the previous volumes, this particular text is, at its core, a human cry in a wilderness of products and profits whose byproducts are poisonous and pervasive. Ginsberg's hikes in the mountains and along the beach, even his farm in upstate New York are reminders of what the planet could still be.

The Fall of America Journals begins with a description of a trek Ginsberg made with fellow poet Gary Snyder. They are hiking the wild beauty of the mountains of the US West—the Cascades, to be exact. The book finishes up a few hundred miles to the east in another mountain range and another trek to the multiple forms of beauty those ranges hold. In the pages between the mountain ranges exists what is essentially a very long poem, an epic if you will. Parts of this poem are rough as the rock one finds above the alpine line; others feature finished works flowing freely as a mountain stream. There are dreams and memories of two of his friends who died during that time —Neal Cassady and Jack Kerouac; there are also celebrations and complaints about those friends he still lived and traveled with. There are visits with other poets—most interestingly Ezra Pound who more or less acknowledges his flirtation with anti-semitism and fascism was not lunacy but stupidity. At times deeply personal and occasionally sexually explicit, the auto-poesy, the written notes and the various drafts of poems which would later appear in the aforementioned Fall of America and/or in Ginsberg's Collected Poems describe a nation at war with the people of Indochina and itself. Ginsberg was not necessarily a political person but he, like so many others in the Sixties (and now, it seems) were compelled by the transgressions he observed to become political. The war in Southeast Asia never retreats from these pages. Instead, its weary bloodshed and hateful presence increases, occupying more lines of Ginsberg's poetry in a manner similar to how it took over much of the world's consciousness during those years these poems were composed. It's present when he writes the incantation to raise the Pentagon at the October 1967 antiwar March on the Pentagon. It's present in his poem describing the battles in Chicago's Grant Park during the 1968 Democratic Convention; a convention marked by a Democratic Party willing to destroy itself to keep fighting the war and those who ever more aggressively opposed it. The war in Southeast Asia is also present as Ginsberg spends time at his farm in upstate New York—a place he bought for himself and his friends to get away from the madness consuming so much.

The title of the poetry collection is not meant to suggest Ginsberg wished the fall of America. It is more of an observation than a desire; more of a regret than a hope. I shared a joint with Ginsberg in 1980. Ken Kesey and Peter Orlovsky also inhaled. So did a friend of mine. I wanted the fall of America. We were in Boulder. The Grateful Dead were in town. Dozens of writers were gathered at a Naropa Institute commemoration of the publication of Jack Kerouac's novel On the Road. In the six years since the poetry collection was published, the actual fall of America was still considered an uncertainty and a possibility. Despite the nonsense coming from the Reagan for President campaign and its sycophantic media, it was not morning in America. Instead, it was something much closer to never-ending darkness. Most citizens were mistaking the sunset for a sunrise and the deteriorating nation for a city on a hill. Ronald Reagan was a worthy huckster for the scam being pulled. Genial of face and as mean hearted as the slaver smiling while he whipped his over-worked slaves, Reagan's patent medicine of trite lies and false masculinity would keep him in the White House for eight long years.

Fall of America Journals is a book that describes America's beauty and its bloodshed; its glories and its shame. It is a history, a road journal, a poetic odyssey with islands of magic, mountains of snow, psychedelic elixirs inducing visions. And dreams. An odyssey and an omnibus, these journals are a work meant to live on a nearby shelf, to be opened if in need of inspiration or assurance. It serves as a road atlas in a universe with multiple dimensions and numerous points of entry. Allen Ginsberg is not Virgil, but a narrator on the winding journey his words illuminate. His odyssey is not a journey driven by a desire to get back to home and hearth, but he tells it as well as Homer told us his.

Capitalism, Borders and the Damage They Do

Build Bridges, Not Walls: A Journey to a World Without Borders—Todd Miller

A Different Kind of War: Uneasy Encounters in Mexico and Central America—J. Malcolm Garcia

Todd Miller writes about modern empire and borders. His works tell of a US border security apparatus that extends into other nations around the world and provides various immigration police agencies in the United States to operate anywhere they please inside US borders. His descriptions of the surveillance technology and its uses are simultaneously fascinating from a scientific point of view and terrifying in their potential. The reports he includes about the human side of border and immigration policing is just frightening. The inference I have drawn from his descriptions is that even if an agent of the immigration or border police is inclined to act humanely when it comes to dealing with migrants, the very structure and mindset of the agencies makes such acts subject to discipline from above. The conclusion is a simple one—open borders to people, not just business.

Build Bridges, Not Walls: A Journey to a World Without Borders, is a new book from Miller. In it he utilizes his understanding of the US border regimes to inform a collection of encounters with those affected by that infrastructure. This includes border patrol agents, border abolitionists, academics and most importantly, migrants themselves. The reader meets Miller as he drives in the Sonora Desert about twenty miles from the US-Mexico border. He sees a man on the side of the road hoping for a ride. Although Miller gives the man a ride, taking him to a shelter run by a group established to assist immigrants without question, he acknowledges his hesitancy in doing so. The reason

275

for Miller's hesitation is the fear he could get stopped by law enforcement and charged with a felony for helping an undocumented migrant. The reader is barely five pages in when the question which propels this text becomes obvious: "what happens to our collective humanity when the impulse to help another is criminalized?"

The answers to this are hinted at throughout this slender book. Many of them are manifestations of something I would call evil; the evil of intention and the banality of bureaucratic evil. Sometimes the two find a home in one individual—a sadistic guard in a private immigration detention camp. Most of the time, however, it is an evil defined by its lack of passion or personal delight. It is the uniformed official doing their job or the bureaucrat issuing citations on their keyboard. Or it is the egocentric and sycophantic politician voting yes on laws that criminalize kindness and demonize children. It is this evil which informs the actions of a society with little self-reflection and an outsized sense of entitlement. It is a society so removed from its kinder impulses that locking up battered and abused people because their papers are not in order is justified by almost all those in control.

The humans J. Malcolm Garcia writes about live south of the US-Mexican border. However, they are not immune from the meanings that border proscribes. The effects of industrial and financial endeavors from companies and institutions to the North are the essence of his essays. His stories are of the multitudes in the migrant caravans escaping lives filled with violence and hunger. They are about families living in the aftermath of US-engineered coups and wars. Garcia reports from neighborhoods made of cardboard and tin next to refuse dumps, from refugee detention centers in Mexico and from the streets of cities throughout Central America. The people he talks to are nuns caring for abandoned children and fighting mines poisoning rivers and farmlands; children living on the fringes of gang-infested cities trying to go to school while taking care of siblings and other relatives. The pure horror of their lives goes unnoticed by most of the world, in part because the authorities hide it away but mostly because people do not want to look. Garcia's text, titled *A Different Kind of War: Uneasy Encounters in Mexico and Central America* is but a small part of a momentum to force people to look; to look and do something about it.

His lyrical prose transcends its journalistic task. The lives he enters and modestly profiles are humble lives. The book features the aforementioned nuns devoting their selves to the wretched of the earth. It also describes what might be seen as an unwarranted hope in the hearts of children who, despite the objective despair of their situation, tell Garcia of their desire to be a doctor or a nurse. Beyond the desperate nature of the lives Garcia writes about lurks a spirituality that his writing fashions into a beautifully wrought verse.

Many of the pieces in A Different Kind of War were originally written for newspapers connected to a religious faith, as are most of Garcia's subjects. It is within these people's lives that Karl Marx's description of religion as the" sigh of the oppressed " is made real. Spiritual belief is often the one of the few phenomena that gives them a reason to live; a hope that defies the despair of their lives. It is not something to be laughed at, but to be reckoned with. There's a reason people turn to ministers for guidance. Quite often that guidance suggests acquiescence. In Garcia's reports, the opposite is often true. Nuns and priests are engaged in the struggle for a more equitable existence; against the bloodshed and economic injustice they know so intimately—from their work and from their own lives.

The common thread in these two texts involves borders and capitalism. Both include profiles of individuals and communities struggling to make their lives better in the face of the obstacles placed in their way by borders and capitalism. Todd Miller provides an overview that discusses the political and economic system that profits from and enforce the regime of borders. J. Malcolm Garcia lets his wonderfully narrated stories speak for themselves. In both works, we find a beauty scuffling not necessarily to thrive, but to exist.

It's A Man's World

King Kong Theory—Virginie Despentes

There are at least two topics in the modern world I write in which tend to bring the knives out. One is the Israel-Palestine situation and the other is sexual/gender politics. The knives don't bother me, because it reminds me that people are reading my work. Indeed, their points are rarely sharp enough to do much but scratch the first layers of my skin.

That said, the book I am writing about here—titled *King Kong Theory*—seems to be written with the same attitude. In other words, it is pushing people to bring out the knives. Wield them from behind your toxic masculinity and your ambition-informed liberal feminism. Wield them from your need to demean your lover and the sex worker you pay online. Wield them from your university posts and your political campaign offices. Wield them from the backseat of your car parked in the "dangerous" part of town after that sex act you paid for is over. Wield them from the safety of your suburban home after your errant children have gone off to school. Wield them from Hollywood and a studio of porn.

King Kong Theory is a text that is decidedly anti-capitalist and a little bit punk. Like much of the left and anarchist writing from the west since the 1960s, individualism clashes with class understanding and political economics with cultural revolution. The author, Virginie Despentes, is a French novelist, who left her home for Paris when she was a teen; her punk lifestyle had outgrown her hometown, so to speak. Like so many people that age, she had a variety of jobs, including as a sex worker. It was the experiences she accrued during that time that informed her fiction, including one on rape which became a movie called F*ck Me and was ultimately banned in France. This particular title is a collection of essays on all of those topics and more.

The world Despentes describes in no uncertain terms is that of a woman under capitalism. In 2021, that is the only world there is for women to love and live in. It is a world that, despite all the feminist agitation women are still working for free. They are caring for children in their homes and cleaning those homes for free. This isn't liberal feminism. Nor is it bourgeois feminism. It's leave me the fuck alone while I rip down your capitalist patriarchy feminism. There are no holds barred and no idols considered sacred. The housework, childbearing and child raising without pay that is expected from women would not exist if feminism had completed its task of liberating women. But it didn't. Instead, it became another capitalist consumer scheme. Not always and not completely, but fairly uniformly.

A key understanding I got from this book is that, if one struggles long and hard enough as an individual and a group, they will achieve sexual freedom, even a form of liberation, under capitalism. However, they will still be under capitalism. That fact will completely effect their liberation as a class. Another thing I got from my read was that the patriarchal mindset is so pervasive, it has a way of turning feminist women into playacting for men and their fantasies. The latter is how Despentes describes Slut Walks and sex work. The latter, she writes, is not liberating, although it should be legal so that those who engage in it can have some actual protection from their pimps and johns, porn film directors and actors, and the police. Instead, sex work is a blatant example of capitalism at work. Everything is merely another commodity and how it gets to the marketplace is none of our goddamn business. Brutality, slavery, trafficking, unsafe and unhealthy working conditions—none of that matters as long as the customer get his jollies. After all, isn't the customer always right? That and the profit motive?

King Kong Theory should open your eyes to the confusion and hypocrisy of modern feminism and the lives of women and girls in the capitalist economy. In fact, it should rip your eyelids off your face; that is the intention with which it is written. While your eyelids are bleeding, Despentes' words will likewise expose the grip of the profit motive on the bodies and minds of women, girls, men, boys and every other gender in this twenty-first century. The conspiracy of patriarchy and capital is a conspiracy as old as the gods of Abraham and as new as the last episode of virtually any television show that stars a female in almost any role. As Despentes makes crystal clear, it won't be going away without a major fight. History affirms that position.

Rewriting History in the Land Called California

We Are the Land: A History of Native California—Damon B.
Akins & William J. Bauer, Jr.

I lived in the San Francisco Bay Area of California for eight years during the 1970s and 1980s. One of the reasons I moved there in the first place was because of its radical history, much of it fairly recent and much of it still alive at the time. It was one of the few places I have lived in the United States where a fair amount of that history was somewhat common knowledge, even mainstream—the Black Panther Party, Free Speech Movement, People's Park, Haight-Ashbury and the counterculture come to mind. While I lived there, an awareness of the historical role of the Latino population in California was on the rise. One group whose history was less known and mostly barely acknowledged was that of the original inhabitants of the land. It was as if the indigenous people whose lives had been disrupted and their lands stolen had never existed. This was in spite of various efforts by the descendants of some First Peoples to reverse that erasure. I had never lived in a place where the histories of Native Americans (no matter how distorted) had been so completely erased.

It was through an Ojibwa fellow I knew for a short time that I learned the names of some of the California Native peoples tribes: the Ohlone, the Shoshone, the Nisenan were just the beginning of a long list of Native Peoples group identities. Unfortunately, even armed with these names, the actual histories were still difficult to discover. There didn't seem to be many books written about any of them. Most municipalities built on land taken from the indigenous ancestors gave little or no acknowledgment of who was there before the European and American occupiers. No museums existed dedicated to this history existed while the museums that did exist celebrating California's colonial history barely mentioned those the colonizers found when they arrived.

A new book, titled *We Are the Land: A History of Native California*, is an attempt to fill in this historical gap. Authored by historians Damon B. Akins and William J. Bauer, Jr., the text is a comprehensive, decades-spanning discussion of Native People's history in the territory now known as California. Each chapter is deeply researched via both primary and secondary sources. The narrative is academic in approach, but mostly conversational in tone, making it accessible to the general public. Like many texts concerning complex and even complicated histories, the challenge to the authors is to create a readable and complete story that provides both detail and context. Given the difficulty of the task—from plowing through research to composing an interesting and concise chronicle—Akins and Bauer have written a classic.

This is a history seen through the lenses of indigenous communities and individual storytellers, not the eyes of great capitalists and invaders. The indigenous history prior to the European and American invasion is told via legends and remembrance. The history of these same peoples becomes one of resistance to and accommodation with those intruders once the first contact is made. This is similar to other such texts like Roxanne Dunbar Ortiz's An Indigenous People's History of the United States. Of course, it seems ridiculous to think any other approach could be accurate, especially in the twenty-first century. However, the reader knows that a small but powerful element of the ruling elite vehemently oppose histories that tell the truth about the brutal European and the US conquest of the new world. After all, such truths give lie to their holy legends about American exceptionalism.

The book is mostly arranged chronologically. However, interspersed between the chronology are chapters focused on the history of individual California cities: Ukiah, Los Angeles, Berkeley and Oakland, Sacramento, etc. Each of these chapters summarizes the particular history of the Native Peoples who lived there and the results of their interaction with the Spanish, the Americans and even the Russians, who traded with various coastal peoples. Attention is paid to the ecology of the area and its effect on the relations between indigenous people and the foreign invader. One thing becomes quite clear as the reader delves further into the text—settlers, prospectors, politicians and the US Army supported each other intentionally and otherwise in the genocide of California's indigenous people. The massacres by settlers were joined with rewards offered by the government for trophies of body parts from dead Indians. Laws intentionally misnamed to create an illusion that they were designed to protect Native People's actually exacerbated their removal from their lands, the kidnapping of their children and the disruption of their culture and economy. Although the Spanish missions were devastating to Native Peoples during and after their existence, it was the infamous gold rush that legend says began in Sutter's Mill that seems to have been the most destructive in all regards. The land rush that followed only hastened the ultimate goal of erasing the Native People from the land and from history.

Even though We are the Land may not necessarily have been conceived and written as a consciously radical history, it is one. The very fact of its existence and its approach to the history of a people whose history has been intentionally erased and replaced by that of the conqueror ultimately makes this text a radical one. Not only is it a much needed and important retelling of the invader's history from the perspective of the invaded, it is also a relocation of the region's indigenous peoples from a history based on their erasure to a history based on their preeminence.

The Myth of the Atomic Genie

The Wretched Atom: America's Global Gamble with Peaceful Nuclear Technology—Jacob Darwin Hamblin

It was forty years ago this coming September that I was busted along with a couple thousand others protesting the Diablo Canyon Nuclear Power Plant near San Luis Obispo, California. The protests were one of the larger civil disobedience/direct action undertakings of the anti-nuclear movement in the United States. The politics of the protesters were eclectic, while the approach of the organizers tended towards the timid, at least in my opinion. Nonetheless, the action itself was a week's worth of constant harassment of those powers intent on opening a plant built way too close to an active earthquake fault. Although the protests did not force PG&E to shut down the plant, they did end up creating enough of a stir that scientists and engineers opposed to the plant's existence were able to find a major design flaw. That flaw kept the plant closed for a few more years. Although it finally did go online, the Diablo Canyon plant is scheduled for shutdown beginning in 2024.

For those of us growing up in the 1950s and 1960s, nuclear power was presented as a solution to all of our ills. Hunger, poverty, cheap electricity—all of these would be resolved if only nuclear energy was established in the manner the industry and its sycophants described. Propaganda extolling the benefits of the so-called peaceful atom included comic books given to schoolchildren and field trips to nuclear power plants. The dangers of radioactive waste and the possibility of meltdowns were dismissed or went unmentioned. It took a number of years of organizing and education by anti-nuclear activists to make those things part of the conversation. Also not mentioned was the war industry's role in promoting nuclear energy—a role ignored today by so-called green campaigners who along with industry spokespeople are once again trying to convince the world's public that nuclear power is safe and the best way to combat global climate change.

In recent years, the warming of the planet has caused tremendous changes to weather patterns, many of them harmful to human, animal and plant life. While some search for ways to diminish their impact on this climate change, the truth of the matter is that the very nature of the worldwide capitalist economy makes their attempts virtually meaningless. Scientists from various disciplines search for means to slow down the warming while charlatans deny it exists and capitalists continue to put their profits ahead of everything. This places some of them in the denial camp while others finagle ways to make some coin while ostensibly helping the planet survive. Solar, geothermal and wind energy are increasing in output while the champions of nuclear energy make the same arguments in support of that form of power they have always made. It has once again become necessary to point out its shortcomings to the general public.

Essential to the arguments against nuclear power is its history. This is where a new book titled *The Wretched Atom: America's Global Gamble with Peaceful Nuclear Technology* comes in. Written by Oregon State University history professor Jacob Darwin Hamblin, this text describes how the concept of peaceful nuclear energy was conceived, developed and sold. The tale he narrates includes government and industry manipulation of the truth, scientists and bureaucrats religious-like proselytizing to sell nuclear energy, and the neocolonialist nature of the decision-making by the powers involved in exporting this energy to other nations. It is a story fraught with racism, hubris and imperial arrogance. Conversely, it is also a narrative in which nuclear weapons became symbols of sovereignty and strength to governments of formerly colonized states. There is economic blackmail under the aegis of none other than Henry Kissinger and there is blatant manipulation of governments in the Global North by Israelis intent on building the bomb.

Hamblin frames his text around the program innocently (and deceptively) called Atoms for Peace. This program began almost immediately after the end of the Second World War—a war which ended in Japan with the incineration of two cities and over 300, 000 people in two nuclear attacks by the US military. Despite the misguided hopes of some who thought the war and its ending would bring about a new world which made disarmament a primary goal for the future, the opposite occurred. Instead of disarmament, the race to develop nuclear weapons became the goal of several nations. Coinciding with this race was a desire by nuclear scientists and their supporters in government to figure out other uses for this dangerous form of power. According to these advocates, nuclear energy could solve virtually all of the world's problems; hunger, homelessness and epidemic might all be erased should this power be harnessed. Of course, very little was said about the downside—nuclear waste, meltdowns, security, and so on. Nor was much said about the relationship between nuclear energy and the nuclear arms race. This was intentional, as surely as this connection is still barely mentioned by those who support a rebirth of nuclear power today.

During the peak of the antinuclear movement in the late 1970s and 1980s, many of the objections to nuclear energy focused on the uncertainties and real dangers associated with nuclear fission. However, some protesters also objected to it because of the unwarranted centralized power it gave to the governments and industry involved in its development and proliferation. As Hamblin makes quite clear, this centralization of control is a large part of nuclear power's appeal to government and military officials that support it. In Hamblin's history he describes the manipulation of countries in the Global South by the governments of the North in the former's quest for nuclear capabilities. It is a tale which serves as both metaphor and a microcosm of the unequal nature of those relationships.

The Wretched Atom takes its name from the title of revolutionary anti-colonialist Frantz Fanon's book The Wretched of the Earth. In his conclusion, author Hamblin writes this: "Frantz Fanon warned in the 1960s that the 'wretched' or 'damned' of the earth would be offered dreams of rapid advance and of economic miracles. That surely has been true of the atom." (238) Hamblin makes it equally clear that the atom has also been one more tool of the world's most powerful nations to keep the rest of the world under their control. Hamblin speculates at the book's beginning as to whether or not his history id pro or anti-nuke. He then writes that his approach is to be objective. It is this reviewer's contention that in its objectivity, The Wretched Atom and the history it relates is as anti-nuclear as those of us arrested at Diablo Canyon in 1981 were.

Intrepid Trips, Indeed

Cronies, A Burlesque: Adventures with Ken Kesey, Neal Cassady, the Merry Pranksters and the Grateful Dead—Ken Babbs

It's a crooked road, a long strange trip with no left (or right) turn unstoned. A trip of a celestial and even extraterrestrial nature where you never leave the ground. An intrepid trip without any guides, just some clown in the driver's seat. And that clown could be you. I first heard about Ken Kesey and the Merry Band of Pranksters when I was in high school. 1969. Freshman year. A book called The Electric Kool Aid Acid Test showed up at the newsstand in the local drug store. I'm gonna' say it cost me ninety five cents to bring it home and climb inside a bus filled with characters on a journey my fourteen year-old mind found fascinating. I had yet to smoke anything other than a Winston, but my curiosity was piqued.

The next few years, as I dove deeper into the world of the counterculture I learned that that book's author Tom Wolfe was a damn good observer, a pretty decent journalist if you liked this stuff they called the New Journalism, and anything but a hippie freak. I read that book every summer in high school, the style and the story imprinted in my brain. As the 1970s wore on, I watched as the world of the grey flannel suits fought against the world of blue jeans, long hair and marijuana. I knew which side I was on. It wasn't the ones wearing suits (figuratively speaking). Unlike the political world of the time—which ultimately put "if there's going to be a bloodbath, let's get it over with" Ronald Reagan into the White House in 1980—there were no clear cut victors in the cultural struggle. Capitalists in both realms figured out ways to sell the pieces of the counterculture that were salable. And the people bought it.

As for me, I moved to the Bay Area, where the counterculture was still hanging on. I began meeting some of the people I had only read about. I played it cool, listening to their stories while hanging out drinking beer in People's Park, crashing at the Hog Farm house, at concerts big and small, the White Panther squats and the parties I ended up at. The storytellers included acid manufacturers recently out of prison, Black Panthers tending bar, hippie women turned Christian, street hustlers who fought the cops in the Haight uprisings and then People's Park, college professors, working musicians and burnt out rock musicians whose bands had left them behind. Every collection of freaks had their memories and every freak had their own version of what went down. Still, certain stories and storytellers were paramount. Like the book of Genesis or the creation stories of the Tlingit, those stories were origin stories. Those were the ones I wanted to hear, to collect and remember. This interest remained even as those who knew them left their earthly existence, taking their tales with.

Now, in the year 2021, a book by one of the earliest Merry Pranksters sits ready to hit the shelves. Titled *Cronies, A Burlesque: Adventures with Ken Kesey, Neal Cassady, the Merry Pranksters and the Grateful Dead,* it is the story of the Pranksters as recalled by Ken Babbs, Kesey's cohort in multiple escapades both foolish and fun, bizarre and benign; all of them intended to unbind the mind of modern misery. It's the story of a trip and a story of the trip. From a bus named Further and its pilot Neal Casady who was also known as Dean Moriarty. There's Babbs' recollection of the bus trip across the USA that inspired not just a book or two but thousands of other trips across the star spangled nation whose legacy is schizophrenic at best and psychotic too. Cronies describes a journey of two friends placed together by the spirits inside psychedelic medicines and the Wallace Stegner Creative Writing seminar. Babbs takes the reader from Stanford University to the ever mounting flame of consciousness inside all of us. Yippie yi yo ti yay.

The author calls his book a burlesque, explaining the word's use with a brief definition: "an historical accounting with additions, exaggerations, embellishments and inventions." In other words, memories as he remembers them…or not. In a manner of speaking, it's like the old guys at the coffee shop telling stories about the war, their jobs, their cars or women they have known. It's mostly true, but memory is a funny thing.

My dad used to say before he started up a tale: "I may have told you this before, so I hope I make it as interesting as the last time you heard it." It's one of things I borrowed from him a few years back and use more and more as the years pile up. Like him, I hope I make my stories interesting.

Needless to say, Ken Babbs has certainly made his story interesting. The moments he relates include tales from the aforementioned bus trip, the Woodstock festival, the Acid Tests, working with and for the Grateful Dead, and a multitude of other moments the reader may or may not have heard about. It's a rip-snorting tale tempered by the wisdom of time and informed by the psychedelic enthusiasm of a culture founded in youth but defined by eternity. There are moments when the story being told reflects the sexism of the time and there are other moments that reveal today's differences from the decades that have passed. Cronies is part tall tale, a memoir, and a song of brotherly love and camaraderie. It's about a time when art and music meshed with acid in search of an ecstatic revival of the human spirit lost in the cloud of atomic war.

It's too early in human time to tell what this tale means, but this telling of the tale is well worth the time.

Peter Weiss and His Pièce de Résistance

The Aesthetics of Resistance(v.2)—Peter Weiss

Every once in a while a book is published that not only tells a different story about the world we live in, but does so in a manner that is inimitable and unique to the point of being without peer. Peter Weiss's fiction trilogy *The Aesthetics of Resistance* may very well be just such a book. Originally published in German during the years 1975 to 1981, the second volume was recently published in an English translation in 2020 by Duke University Press (Volume One was published in English in 2005). It has been worth the wait.

Weiss, who is perhaps best known in the English-speaking world for his dramatic masterpiece The Assassination and Persecution of Jean Paul Marat as Performed by the Inmates of the Asylum of Charenton Under the Direction of the Marquis de Sade (Marat/Sade), places his story in The Aesthetics of Resistance in Europe during the years 1937-1945, give or take. The narrator, the sole fictional character, shares some life history with Weiss himself. He is a young man whose leftist politics inform his resistance to fascism in Germany, Spain and elsewhere. Those politics are also what compel his travels from Berlin to Spain where he fights for the Republicans against the fascist Falange until he is exiled to France after the Republican defeat by the fascist forces.

This is where the second volume begins. We find the narrator at the Louvre in front of the Gericault painting Raft of the Medusa; a painting depicting survivors of a shipwreck on a raft. Through his narrator, Weiss takes a deep look at the artwork, describing the obvious pain and despair of those on the raft. The wrenched faces, the fate of the partially disrobed woman clinging to the mast, the circumstances on the ship from which they were cast. All of this becomes a means through which the narrator introduces the reader to his situation, the situation of other political and economic refugees and the debates on the European Left in a world where fascists and their allies are sharpening their swords, enflaming the masses with their rhetoric of racial purity and hate, and intensifying their grip on the continent's political reality. Those debates reflect a Left that, while stronger than the Left of today, is split between those who rationalize and support the conclusions of the newly established Soviet Union, those who oppose Moscow's approach preferring instead a compromise with the capitalists, and those who align themselves with neither.

This debate is played out in these pages while the European powers maneuver into positions for the war their actions are leading to. Understood by the capitalist governments of Europe is that their greatest shared enemy is the revolution the Soviet Union represents—its socialist government being a threat to capitalism in all of its political forms. Communist Party members wrestle with Moscow's decision to sign a non-aggression pact with Berlin and are forced to develop convoluted defenses of the pact with the Nazi regime in their media. As far as those to the left of the Communist Party are concerned, the fascists are their first and worst enemy. Meanwhile, the Social Democrats and capitalists remain a permanent focus of their ire. The Social Democrats because they are only too willing to accommodate the financial interests that assume their domination and the capitalists because, well, they are capitalists.

The narrator, who is never named, exists in this uncertain political world. His personal world is even less certain. The first book of the trilogy closed with him leaving Spain after Generalissimo Franco and his Falangists have reclaimed the capital Madrid. The second book opens with the narrator figuring out how to exist as a homeless exile in Paris. Never a member of the Communist Party, his politics agree more with it than the Social Democrats, whose turn towards the right has become even sharper in the face of the Nazi upsurge and assumption of state power in Germany. However, it is his connection to the Social Democrats via his father's status in that party which makes his escape from France possible. Ultimately, he ends up as a worker in a small metallurgical factory in Stockholm. One of his tasks when he is not working is to carry messages for the Party, which is illegal and therefore underground. It is this latter role that finds him delivering copy to a Party member named Rosner, who edits the Party paper distributed to Swedish workers. It is also in Stockholm where he begins attending meetings of intellectuals and workers at the home of the exiled writer Bertolt Brecht. Brecht, whose play Mutter Courage und Ihrer Kinder was recently produced, is working on another play based on the life of a Swedish mine owner/worker named Engelbrekt. Despite his class identity, Engelbrekt became a hero of the miners, peasants and other downtrodden Swedes in the Middle Ages for leading a rebellion against the nobility, German pretenders and the newly forming bourgeoisie. Weiss expertly weaves the story of Engelbrekt and his rebellion into a metaphor for the situation at the time his fiction is taking place.

Informing the narrative—and crucial to its telling—is the author's contention that not only is resistance to the powers that rule human lives essential to remain human, it is art that both maintains and provides beauty to such resistance. Furthermore, it is art that can provoke that resistance even in humanity's darkest times. Those who would turn art into a function of political repression deny its potential as a weapon of liberation. This is true whether one is considering the Stalinist and Nazi style of heroic realism or the seduction and fetishizing of objects synonymous with capitalist advertisements.

While reading The Aesthetics of Resistance I couldn't help but be reminded of Jean Paul Sartre's Roads to Freedom trilogy; a semi-autobiographical fiction of a Frenchman living during almost exactly the same time period. Both works reflect the uncertainty and confusion of the twentieth century's years of fascism, if not of modernity itself. Sartre's protagonists linger in a doubt defined by despair, while Weiss's act from a place defined by resistance to the same human horror that leaves Sartre's characters fumbling. By doing this, the reader is reminded that it is that resistance that keeps the human race alive as surely as the lack thereof would mean a quick and almost certain end to us all. At once a compelling tale of that resistance and an informative leftist history of the period it is situated in, Weiss's Aesthetics of Resistance is not just his piéce de résistance, but a piéce de résistance of the twentieth century.

Fascism is a Movement, Not Just a Man

Rising Fascism in America: It Can Happen Here—Anthony DiMaggio

In the wake of the Trump White House years, is the United States a fascist country? No, but it is certainly much closer to being one than it was before 2016. As Anthony DiMaggio carefully explains in his newest book *Rising Fascism in America: It Can Happen Here*, Trump's campaign and presidency prove the existence of an uncomfortably large number of US residents who not only would have few problems with a fascist government, but are either already fascist or leaning in that direction. Similarly, the Republican party is the mainstream vehicle for this political transition. The fealty to Trump in the GOP despite his loss in November and the right-wing uprising on January 6, 2022 in the Capitol qualifies as the main indication of this US political trend.

The reasons for the ascent of this element in US politics are arguably many in number, but the essential element in virtually every explanation provided in DiMaggio's study is white supremacy and the supremacists' fear of losing it. Demographics make it clear that the United States will be a nation composed of people who do not consider themselves white in a few decades. To put it succinctly: this scares the hell out of many US citizens who do consider themselves white. This element of the population has always had a certain power in US politics. Indeed, it can be safely stated that it is that element that wrote some of the most recalcitrant parts of the US Constitution; recalcitrant because courts have upheld certain racist interpretations of US law more often than otherwise. The consequence of this is that in 2022 civil rights activists find themselves fighting to protect the right of every adult US citizen to vote.

Yes, a battle that most citizens believed resolved fifty years ago is being fought once again, in large part because the Voting Rights Act that ended restrictions based on skin color and income in the 1960s was struck down by the Supreme Court in 2013. According to the court, it was no longer needed because people were no longer being prevented from voting based on those reasons. Of course, once the law was invalid, the successors of the white supremacists who passed the legislation struck down by the Voting Rights Act got back to work creating ways to prevent Black voters from voting. They know that curtailing voting rights is the only way they can stay in power and enforce their racist agenda.

As DiMaggio and many others have pointed out, the Trump campaign not only represents this element of the US polity, it is the foundation of their politics and organizing. His ending up in the White House was more than just a victory for those forces; it was a call to battle that brought together the KKK, alt-right groups and individuals, right-wing Christians of all denominations, pro-Zionist Jewish citizens, even Nazis and other such fascist groupings. Bringing up the rear was most of the remainder of the Republican party. Sensing a means to get back into the White House and push through more of their reactionary, pro-corporate/anti-labor agenda, these donors, Senators, congresspeople and their supporters denied the obvious racism of Trump and his most avid supporters and jumped on the campaign bandwagon. We are living with the results of that unholy union.

As DiMaggio makes clear throughout his text, we will be living with it for a while. Fascism requires a popular movement behind it, which is what Trumpism is, after all. This understanding is crucial to DiMaggio's certainty that Donald Trump and his supporters are fascist. Unlike most mainstream analysts and commentators who deny that the US can be fascist because it does not have a completely fascist government, DiMaggio looks at the entire phenomenon of Trump and Trumpism. In doing so, he examines Qanon, groups like the Proud Boys, traditional US white supremacist groups like the KKK, right wing Christians and right wing Republicans. The coalescence of these folks around the figure of Donald Trump created the movement now called Trumpism. In an examination of Trumpism that draws from history, political science and sociology, DiMaggio eloquently argues that yes, Trumpism is a fascist movement.

As it shouldn't, Rising Fascism in America does not leave the

294

Democratic party and its sycophants off the hook. In a chapter appropriately titled "The Enablers," the author takes the Democrats, the so-called liberal media, and much of the liberal establishment in the US to task for their refusal to call Trumpism a fascist moment and deal with it as such. Instead, they help maintain the pretense that his politics were and are politics as normal. Particularly nasty politics, but still politics within the norm. Even after the violent, ultimately fascist riot in and around the Capitol on January 6, 2022, the number of non-Trumpists willing to go ahead without insisting Trump be put on trial proves DiMaggio's contention that too much of the US polity is enabling the fascist presence in the US not only to exist, but to grow. In addition, argues DiMaggio, the neoliberal capitalist economy provides a fertile ground for the politics of fascism.

Most readers are probably familiar with the Sinclair Lewis novel titled It Can't Happen Here, which describes a fictional fascist movement taking power in the 1930s in the United States. DiMaggio begins each chapter in Rising Fascism in America with a discussion of a part of the novel. The similarities with his discussions of Trump and Trumpism are impossible to miss. Except, of course, neither Trump or Trumpism are fiction. Indeed, both are only too real. Furthermore, as DiMaggio makes clear, they will not be thrown into the dustbin of history without a mass popular movement that expands beyond antifa in the streets, expressions of shock and shame by politicians and mainstream media, and pretending it will go away on its own.

Gwangju, May 1980: A Genuine Movement for Democracy

Gwangju Uprising: The Rebellion for Democracy in South Korea—Hwang Sok-Yong, Lee Jae-Eui, Jwon Yong-Ho

The spring of 1980 saw president Jimmy Carter foundering as he attempted to convince the citizens of the world that his human rights rhetoric did not conflict with his ever more aggressive foreign policy With the possible exception of Nicaragua, where the revolutionary forces had finally overthrown the decades-long Somoza dictatorship, Washington's history of invasion and murder was keeping the White House and it's imperial agencies barreling to an ever aggressive and repressive policy designed to keep the US in control. The infiltration and creation of democracy movements by Washington was a developing policy but most such movements were actual movements for democracy, not just a means for US interests to get their dirty paws into a country. The most dramatic of these movements was actually against a dictatorship supported by Washington. It took place in May 1980 in Gwangju, South Korea.

It is easy to recall how little was reported about this uprising while it was occurring. The South Korean military dictatorship of Chun Doo-hwan clamped down on domestic media immediately. At first, the international media accepted the reports provided by the military. Eventually, certain reporters broke through the censors and were able to get into Gwangju and report the scenes they witnessed to the greater world. I was living in Berkeley, CA at the time; it was through some friends of mine who were members of a Korean leftist organization that I received my information. In the years that followed, the narrative regarding the Gwangju uprising was controlled by the right wing Seoul government. In spite of the repressive atmosphere and laws, a group of participants (Hwang Sok-Yong, Lee Jae-Eui, Jwon Yong-Ho) published a detailed description of the uprising, its repression and its meaning in 1985. This effort was titled Beyond Death, Beyond the Darkness of the Age and followed at least one other effort titled Gwangju White Papers which was published and circulated underground beginning in 1981.

As far as the English-speaking world is concerned, perhaps the best account of the uprising appeared in scholar/activist George Katsiaficas' 2012 release titled Asia's Unknown Uprisings Volume 1: South Korean Social Movements in the 20th Century. Katsiaficas, who lived in Korea for a few years while writing his text, is known for his extrapolation and expansion of Herbert Marcuse's works into what he called the eros effect to explain why worldwide revolutionary moments like those in the year 1968 occur. One can now add a new English translation of Beyond Death, Beyond the Darkness of the Age to Katsiaficas' work. Titled *Gwangju Uprising: The Rebellion for Democracy in South Korea*, this publication not only provides the reader with an incredible history of the ten days in May 1980 when the uprising occurred, it does so by keeping the spirit of the uprising intact.

The text provides a day-by-day, even hour-by-hour descriptions of the provocations of the military and the responses of the crowds. From its opening moments at a local university up to the final attack and surrender of the protesters, the narrative is fast-paced yet precise in its description. The book opens with a discussion of the South Korean history of autocratic rule propped up by Washington and its military ever since the nation's creation. The end of the Park Chung Ree dictatorship is briefly discussed with the note that the democratic promise of the next president was quickly quashed when part of the Republic of Korea's (ROK) military staged a coup and returned the population to its previous oppressed situation. Despite protests by students and workers across the country, it was the one in Gwangju which would spread to the entirety of the city's population while producing murderous repression from the ROK military.

I couldn't help but be reminded of John Reed's classic journalism on Russia's October Revolution, Ten Days That Shook the World or even the slender text by Alexander Cockburn and Jeffrey St. Clair reporting the

1999 uprising in Seattle against the World Trade Organization, 5 Days That Shook the World: Seattle and Beyond. Still, this book goes beyond these titles in its depth and breath discussing what was perhaps one of the greatest post-Sixties movements until the series of anti-capitalist globalization protests that shook up the world from 1999-2001. Besides its role as a journal, it also serves as a handbook—a manual, if you will—of how such events unfold and how they are run. The questions of arms versus non-violent means are discussed and presented as the discussions unfold in reaction to the repression and brutality of the police and soldiers. In addition, the authors utilize the testimonies of troops who were put on trial for their actions in Gwangju many years later, when a democratic and progressive government was in power in Seoul. Furthermore, the attempts by South Korea's right wing and its supporters in the US to label the uprising a communist rebellion engineered by the government in Pyongyang are answered. Indeed, the return of a right wing regime to Seoul in the 2010s was a primary motivation in publishing the revised edition of Beyond Death, Beyond the Darkness of the Age, from which the text being reviewed was translated. Just as it was then, these governments were fully supported by Washington. The last election saw a more democratic government get elected. One wonders if the will of the people will finally prevail over the ultra-right in South Korea and the US government in DC. If the spirit of those described in this text has its way, it will.

Rousing the Power of the Rank and File

Fighting Times: Organizing on the Front Lines of the Class War—
Jonathan Melrod

In the 1970s thousands of leftists—many of them members of various communist groups that came out of the dissolution of Students for a Democratic Society(SDS) –went to work in the industrial sector of the US. The intention was to organize the working class into a revolutionary element of a potential revolution. Many believed that revolution would take place in their lifetimes. Our current reality reminds us every day that it did not. Despite this failure, the fact is that these young leftists did influence the US labor movement in a positive way, moving a substantial portion of the unionized rank and file out of complacency. Their successes in creating a workplace where the workers had the power to determine their working lives were many. Unfortunately, the capitalist powers still had the upper hand and by the mid-1980s were back in control, demanding and receiving concessions from unions by threatening to move jobs. As we all know, many went ahead and moved the jobs anyhow.

I have a few friends who took this route. Most of them were in the Revolutionary Union (RU). As for myself, I was already working a shit job as a short order cook at an IHOP. After I quit that job and worked at Howard Johnson's—where we walked out because of a racist manager—I eventually did go to work at an industrial site. My first such job was at a brick factory where I watched bricks go by on a conveyor belt. My task was to pull the malformed bricks off the belt. As the orders piled in, the belt moved faster and more malformed bricks got past me. I left after two weeks. Next, I worked at a place that made preformed concrete balconies for apartment buildings. The job was less boring but physically more taxing. However, I had a goal in mind. I was going to California with a friend in three months. That was my light at the end of the tunnel. I made my three months worth of pay and left. I would occasionally work other industrial jobs through the day labor office the eight years I lived in California. When I moved north to Washington State in 1985, I ended up assembling circuit boards for a subcontractor whose primary client was a new company called Microsoft.

Some of these jobs sucked more than others, but they all sucked. Being a temporary worker most of the time, I used that as an excuse and told myself I did not have time to attempt any organizing. Before I took the job in Washington state, I signed what was essentially an illegal yellow dog contract in which I promised not to talk union at all. I broke the promise, but it didn't matter. The people who worked there were the castoffs from a major union busting campaign undertaken at the local Simpson lumber mill right before I moved there. The International Woodworkers of America (IWA) had conceded hundreds of jobs and most of its future operations in the town. Consequently, my co-workers at the circuit board assembly plant were afraid of unionizing and skeptical that a union could really do much about anything, anyhow.

Jonathan Melrod was someone who did go to work on an industrial shop floor and stuck it out for over a decade, organizing a militant and democratic rank and file force within his union local. His new book, titled *Fighting Times: Organizing on the Front Lines of the Class War*, tells the story of those times. After graduating from the University of Wisconsin in Madison, where he was actively engaged in the antiwar movement and various counterculture battles against the police and the structures they protect, Melrod joined the RU and began looking for work. His intention was to organize working people into a movement that fought for their rights on the shop floor, with a future goal of that movement creating a communist revolution in the United States. Of course, fulfillment of the second goal never came close. However, the creation of a fighting rank and file movement was achieved.

Melrod begins his tale in Washington, DC, where he grew up. He briefly discusses going to desegregation protests in the area, including one at Glen Echo Amusement Park in nearby Maryland. After entering college in 1966, he quickly became involved in a growing antiwar movement in Madison, Wisconsin. By the time he graduated in 1970, he was being watched by the FBI and other law enforcement agencies. He was also part of the Revolutionary Unions movement that would soon evolve into the national organization abbreviated as RU. This would be the motivation for his entry into the industrial workforce. After getting a job at the now defunct American Motors Company (AMC) in Milwaukee, he began organizing a radical caucus within his local. His efforts were not appreciated by the local union officials who seemed fine with things as they were. Nor were his efforts appreciated by AMC. In fact, he got fired after organizing a campaign against a speedup of the assembly line. Part of the reason for his firing was the FBI telling management and union leadership that Melrod was a communist. One of his co-workers was also fired, mostly because he was working closely with Melrod. Although the two were eventually rehired (after a long public and legal campaign) with back pay, Melrod needed work. So, he ended up working at a tannery. His description of the work and the site reminded me of the panel depicting Hell from Hieronymus Bosch's triptych known today as The Garden of Earthly Delights. Maggot-infested hides, poisonous liquids and fumes, pits filled with these liquids. It was with relief that he went back to work on the AMC line when he was reinstated.

Of course, like any organizer worth their salt, Melrod not only learned from his previous experience at AMC and his fruitless effort to talk union at the tannery, he applied the lessons to the rest of his time at AMC. The story he relates is one that includes confrontation with particularly obnoxious and dictatorial bosses, racist and sexist foremen and union members, an international office all too comfy with the very industry captains its members oppose, and a rank and file slowly but surely convinced they have genuine power that can only grow with its utilization. Excerpts from the caucus's newsletter are included as is a discussion are the attacks on the newsletter's right to publish. The reader is brought into the thick of these battles via Melrod's vivid prose and colorful descriptions. He describes the struggle to keep every member united against the company's attempts to divide them along racial, gender and political lines. As someone who has been involved in organizing drives and is currently the head of his union local, the episodes he discusses were both familiar and instructive.

Indeed, if one were to explain to a working person interested in organizing a union why they should read this book, the key word would be instructive. The tactics so vividly written down in this text remain useful and appropriate. They will remain that way as long as there are managers and supervisors who make it their duty to harass and belittle workers, CEOs and boards of directors whose pursuit of profit encourages those activities, and national union leadership that identifies more with the company board of directors than with the rank and file whose dues pay their often exorbitant salaries. Not only has Jonathan Melrod told a good story in his book Fighting Times, he has also provided today's workers with a guide to workplace organizing that is inspiring, practical and entertaining to read.

Unnatural Consequences

Natural Consequences: Intimate Essays for a Planet in Peril—
Char Miller

An unfortunate part of modern life is living with the knowledge that the planet we live on is quite obviously suffering from the ventures of humankind. The destruction wrought in the pursuit of profit and the name of progress continues every moment of every day. The benefits are now mostly outweighed by the damage of these endeavors. Some of us watch and fret, some just watch, and some just don't seem to care, even though the vehemence of their denials seems to indicate their belief in the truth of the claims. Those who do care wonder what they can do and if anything they do at this point in time would even matter.

We read newspapers, journals and watch video reports discussing and detailing the damage. We hear scientists raising alarms and politicians demanding our dollars. The content is often overly technical and the context is one of fear. The protests are naturally strident and the official promises are bureaucratically bland. Very rarely a voice comes forth, expressing the fears and the facts in a lyrically sensitive manner,

Char Miller is one such voice. His years of prose detailing the dangers of fracking, the commercial reasons those dangers are denied and the struggles against this industrial destruction comprise a fair amount of his recently published text titled *Natural Consequences: Intimate Essays for a Planet in Peril*. As a resident Southern California, he is also witness to the devastation caused by the excesses of US capitalist culture that most of his fellow residents seem to take for granted. Among those excesses are too many motor vehicles on too many giant highways, not enough water but a refusal to conserve what water there is, and a human hubris that is only exacerbated by an economic system that rewards environmental destruction in the short term while rejecting and silencing those who search for more long term and sustainable approaches to humanity's presence on the planet.

Having lived in southern California for six or seven months back in the 1970s, I can visualize some of the places Miller writes about. I recall the sense back then that that part of the earth was being sucked dry and the air above it was not exactly how air should be. My connection to the highways was one where as a hitchhiker I appreciated their utility but cursed their domination of the region's surface, After all, it was the smaller roads that were easier to hitchhike on, not the multi-lane freeways with entrance ramps as confusing as the working-class neighborhoods that looked remarkably similar to each other, with only street markers differentiating them from each other.

Miller's day job, if you will, is as a professor of environmental analysis and history at Pomona College. The college is in a city that sits east of Los Angeles right off Interstate 10 between Los Angeles and San Bernardino.. My memories of the region include a lot of concrete, some mountains in the near distance and San Bernardino up the road. Miller's essays in Natural Consequences fill in the huge blocks of description my memory never held. His love for the region, its landscapes, and wildlife is eloquently written down in the text. So, too is a sense of foreboding and even hopelessness despite his natural optimism because of what humanity and its economics have done to erode and even destroy.

There are reflections on various political endeavors whose goal is the protection of the region's dwindling habitat and resources. The words written about these campaigns describe a scenario only too familiar: human arrogance fueled by profits and greed; all of which are accompanied by a refusal to consider long term solutions because such solutions do not turn in the same profits. Instead of keeping public lands and the water flowing through those lands owned by the public, the privateers in development and banking demand more privatization or, at least, the siphoning of the water from those lands, consequently changing them from important resources designed by nature to sustain life on and under the surface into dust. One essay describes a water reclamation project rejected for a project that will ultimately suck an underground stream dry. When one considers the constant state of drought in California, the irresponsibility of such decisions begs the question of not just how little the profiteers care about future generations, but of how much do they even care about their own lives. One is reminded of how dangerous human hubris actually is while also wondering how blind and foolish can the pursuit of money and power actually make humanity be.

The beauty of this book can be found in Miller's descriptions of flora and fauna he discovers in his wanderings. The unique ecology of the Los Angeles Mountains comes alive in his telling. Likewise, the urgent need to save this world he describes is also situated in the lucid and simple elegance of his prose. Miller reminds us that not only should this beauty be saved for its own sake, but for the sake of the planet and its inhabitants, too.

New Look at the Strategy of the Civil Rights Movement

Waging a Good War: A Military History of the Civil Rights Movement, 1954-1968—Thomas Ricks

Thomas Ricks is a military historian. His writing usually explores the dynamics of military strategies in war. His book on the first couple years of the US invasion and occupation of Iraq titled Fiasco: The American Military Adventure in Iraq, 2003 to 2005, was both bold in its challenge to the conventional Pentagon narrative and revealing in its detail of the warmakers approaches. Ricks emphasized the importance of strategy and the pitfalls of military operations that either lack a coherent strategy or apply one that isn't relevant to the actual political or military situation.

Given this previous focus in his work on war, the military and those who execute those endeavors, it might surprise the reader that Ricks' newest work is what he calls "a military history of the civil rights movement." After all, if there is a movement in the United States other than the antiwar movement that one is unlikely to associate with the military, it would probably not be the movement against racial apartheid and for equal rights for Black citizens. Indeed, until this text made me consider that history in a new light, the only connection I could think of between the civil rights movement and the military was the latter's use in keeping the southern police forces and civilian racists at bay during the protests that define that movement.

In writing this book, titled *Waging a Good War: A Military History of the Civil Rights Movement, 1954-1968,* Ricks has composed a masterful history of the civil rights movement. It is a history that details several of the campaigns–famous, infamous and otherwise–associated with that history. From the Montgomery Bus Boycott that first pushed

Martin Luther King, Jr. into the national spotlight and the crosshairs of the Klan and the FBI to the Memphis sanitation workers' strike in 1968 where Dr. King was assassinated, the author provides a narrative that is both rich in detail and emotionally wrought. Equally so, he provides a strategic analysis of the numerous campaigns that make up the text, discussing the strengths and weaknesses of each campaign while simultaneously keeping his perspective on the long term goals of the movement over the years.

In his introduction, Ricks tells the reader that by framing the movement in terms of strategy and tactics, his research uncovered and highlighted personalities not nearly as well known as men like King or women like Mississippi freedom fighter Fannie Lou Hamer. Those individuals–James Lawson, Diane Nash, Bayard Rustin, James Bevel and Bob Moses, to name a few–debated and formed strategies, learning from their mistakes and their victories. It was their advice, say as to whether to go ahead with a series of protests in a particular place or to postpone them, that guided the leaders like King. Likewise, it was these women and men who found and encouraged local activists, seeking their knowledge and input before going ahead with a campaign. It was these local folks who most often faced the most danger from racist vigilantes, politicians and law enforcement. The number of local activists who were killed by the forces of reaction in this struggle will probably never be known.

One might think that by taking the approach it does, Waging a Good War would be a boring read; too much analysis and not enough action. Nothing could be further from the truth. This book is what they call a page-turner. The fear of the marchers when walking into a gauntlet of Alabama sheriffs and troopers, the bravado of the children and adolescents facing down Bull Connor's police dogs and firehoses, the despair of the freedom fighters in Mississippi and the silent strength of the freedom riders as they pull into bus stations across the South–Ricks' narrative makes these and other scenes as real as the images that flashed on television screens across the nation during those years. Images that served both as a testament to the ugliness of US white supremacy and as an organizing tool for the movement.

Still, this book is much more than a history. It is also a savage reminder of how entrenched white supremacy is in the social, political and economic life of the United States. While reading Waging the Good War, one cannot help but be reminded of the ongoing symptoms of this fact: racist language in political campaigns, too many police killings of unarmed Black men and women to count, public rallies and marches by groups of ultra-right formations informed by white supremacist theory and excused by too much of the mainstream media, even cheered by that media's more extreme elements. In other words, this text is not just a step into history that not only informs the present, but also a reminder of what remains to be done. Furthermore, by framing his work in terms of how military strategists tend to think, Ricks has also provided today's anti-racist activists with a manual on organizing. While obviously not a template we can just put today's situation neatly inside, the essential approaches illuminated here should definitely be considered as the struggle continues.

Women, Communism and the USA

Organize, Fight, Win: Black Communist Women's Political Writing—eds. Charisse Burden-Stelly & Jodi Dean

Black working class women in the United States face a triple oppression – as workers, as Black people and as women. These particulars are not necessarily ranked in any hierarchy, but it is the combination of all three that create the special oppression faced by this group of US residents. One of the first political formations in the country to recognize and attempt to address this reality was the Communist Party of the USA (CPUSA). Indeed, it was the CPUSA's work on this aspect of the economic and political reality in the US that informed a fair amount of the work by the US Left in the 1960s and 1970s regarding racial oppression. It has been an ongoing trend for many on the US Left to disparage the history of the CPUSA for its failures in theory and in practice. By doing this, these detractors fail to acknowledge its genuinely radical and quite important role in the working class and Black liberation movements beginning between the two world wars of the twentieth century.

A newly published work titled *Organize, Fight, Win: Black Communist Women's Political Writing* and edited by Charisse Burden-Stelly and Jodi Dean is a valiant effort to remedy this situation. By highlighting a number of primary sources, today's reader is able to consider the actual words and thoughts of the CPUSA with minimal filters that might reinterpret the meaning of the concepts being discussed. Burden-Stelly is the co-author (with Gerald Horne) of WEB DuBois: A Life in American History. Jodi Dean is the author of several books addressing communism in the modern era, including The Communist Horizon and Comrade. Their selections in this text include excerpts from various newsletters and newspapers, along with excerpts from CPUSA theoretical papers and meetings and a couple different books.

Given that until recently, the majority of Black women in the United States were employed as domestic workers, a fair number of the pieces in Organize, Fight, Win discuss the nature of these workers' exploitation and attempts to organize them. A phenomenon known as the Bronx Slave Market is mentioned more than one and there is even one article that details the mechanics of this endeavor. In essence, this so-called market reminded this reviewer of those street corners and Home Depot parking lots where undocumented and other workers congregate today in the hopes a homeowner will hire them. The selections tell of the job seekers underbidding each other in an attempt to earn at least some money so they can feed their families and males offering them better pay if the women engage in sexual activity. In response to this exploitation, various attempts to organize the domestic workers are discussed, revealing varying limits of success.

One of the writers that appears frequently in this book is Claudia Jones. Jones was born Claudia Vera Cumberbatch in Trinidad, but changed her surname to Jones when she became a political activist. Her entry into the CPUSA began with her work in the campaign to free the Scottsboro Boys, nine young Black men falsely accused of rape in Alabama in 1931. Jones ultimately became the executive secretary of the Women's National Commission, secretary for the Women's Commission of the CPUSA and the National Peace Council. In 1953, she took over the editorship of the party journal Negro Affairs. After being charged and found guilty of sedition under the anti-communist McCarran Act in 1950, she served several months in prison. After her release, she was charged under another anti-communist law called the Smith Act. After serving more time, Jones exiled herself to the United Kingdom. Her writing in this collection includes an article on the right to self-determination for Black people in the United States, a discussion about CPUSA's organization of women workers, and a long discussion about imperialism, militarism and the movement against war written in 1950 as Washington's intimidation of the popular forces in Korea headed towards all-out war.

Besides showcasing the importance of organizing Black women, Organize, Fight, Win provides numerous examples of not only how seriously the CPUSA took this work, but also how they supported women's input on this and other questions. It's not to say the Party was free of sexism, but it does seem to illustrate that the struggle against sexism in the ranks was understood to exist and that the participation of women in that struggle was an important piece if it was to be defeated. The fact this work was emphasized during a period when the Left in the US was under attack in the courts, Congress and the media is testament to that importance. Speaking of the persecution, there is an excerpt from Esther Cooper Jackson's reflection on her husband James E. Jackson after his arrest for his political beliefs and activism. In that piece, she reflects on the murder of Harry Moore and his wife after racists bombed there home in Florida. Noting that the FBI had yet to find the perpetrators of that crime, she contrasts it to their pursuit of her husband and other Leftists fighting from civil rights and an end to racial apartheid in the United States. Other writers mention the harassment of singer and communist activist Paul Robeson and his prosecution by the US government. The authoritarian police state represented best by the FBI unleashed much of its force against the Black liberation movement while ignoring if not openly supporting white supremacist groups like the Ku Klux Klan.

This text is an important addition to the history of the United States, especially as regards the struggle for Black residents' freedom and equality. The fact that all of the work included in this book is written by communists is also important in that it proves the important role they played in the struggle during the period represented. However, more than just a look at that legacy, Organize, Fight, Win is also a working textbook for the current and future state of the fight for liberation and against the economic system of capitalism; a system that is the basis of most every other oppression, especially those targeting Black and Brown people.

Work of National Importance

War by Other Means: The Pacifists of the Greatest Generation
who Revolutionized Resistance—Daniel Akst

If those of us who are against war in the second decade of the twenty-first century feel outnumbered by a factor of a few million, imagine what those who were against World War Two felt. A popular antiwar sentiment in the United States and other nations that arose after the insane bloodshed of the so-called Great War was replaced with an even more popular desire to wage war against fascist Europe. Even though the antiwar movement was correct in its appraisal of the war being the result of the world's capitalist governments' desire for dominance over other nations, the brutal fact of nazism made their call for no war equivalent to a child's whisper in the wilderness. Still, the most militant and committed antiwarriors of them all waged what Daniel Akst aptly calls a war by other means. These individuals would be jailed and otherwise prosecuted for their stance, all the while setting the stage for a future where they would play prominent roles in the struggle for civil rights and against the US war in Vietnam.

Akst's new book, titled *War by Other Means: The Pacifists of the Greatest Generation who Revolutionized Resistance*, is a fascinating and detailed history of this movement. By focusing on the best known organizers, Akst tells the story of pacifism in the United States from the 1930s up through the 1960s. Those names–Dorothy Day, David Dellinger, Dwight McDonald and Bayard Rustin among others–are as important to twentieth century US history as any politician or general that ever convinced others to go to war. His narrative highlights the role of peace churches like the Quakers and Mennonites in the expansion of conscientious objector status and the shortcomings of that expansion. More importantly, he details several acts of resistance in the camps, farms, hospitals and prisons by those who refused to fight. Likewise, he discusses the good works that the resisters performed in hospitals and mental health facilities and their development of an idealized community that transcended their confines. That community ultimately set the stage for the antiwar and anti-racist movements of the 1960s and 1970s. It was their moral outrage, philosophical justifications and organizing approaches that would form the basis for one of the most popular movements against a nation's war in human history.

The resisters portrayed here–and the thousands of others whose names are known mostly to their family and friends–were heroes in a manner beyond the comprehension of most human beings. I would argue, based on my experience, that incomprehension is especially true when considering citizens of the United States. After all, in the minds of most US residents, their military has never lost a war. Furthermore, it is a nation founded and sustained by continuous expansion fueled by war. Consequently, war seems to work to their benefit. The current time is certainly no exception. Indeed, the past fifty years has seen Washington engaged in some kind of military conflict with nary a pause.

The biographies in the text are biographies of radical pacifists who believed in using militant nonviolent resistance to oppose the war machine. Some of these women and men were religiously inspired while others inspiration came from more secular philosophies. All considered war an abomination; modern warfare being even more so. Indeed, Catholic pacifists argued that modern weaponry, especially nuclear ones, rendered the Catholic requirements for a so-called just war moot. Their reasoning was based on the fifth element of the "just war" doctrine, which states that the end desired by a nation waging a war must be proportional to the means used. If one recalls, the Vatican made this argument at the outset of the second US war on Iraq in 2003.

War By Other Means is an excellent and detailed history of the US pacifist movement since the 1930s. Yet, the author's tale is somewhat colored by the politics that seep through in his narrative. These are politics that do not stray far from the accepted, official telling. Indeed, it is that they essentially reflect a liberal understanding of the State that limits a deeper discussion of the politics and economics. Akst often repeats the mainstream understanding of political events without question even though evidence exists that challenges that understanding and renders it at best questionable. One example that sticks in my mind is when he states the Korean conflict began when Pyongyang's forces "invaded" what is called South Korea on June 25, 1950. This declaration ignores the mountain of evidence suggesting US-backed forces had engaged in similar actions going north for months if not years. In other words, the date of June 25, 1950 is mostly a fiction when discussing that conflict. (Interestingly, the beginning of the current conflict in Ukraine is portrayed similarly, despite evidence showing the conflict's beginning is much less clear than Washington and its media voices would like us to think.) Besides accepting the mainstream narrative on various world events without challenging that description, Mr. Akst's understanding of communism and Marxism seems superficial; he seems to equate the US Communist Party in its Stalinist phase with Marxism. To be fair, perhaps his understanding of Marxism is not the same as mine. In fact, it seems to be an understanding that is not based on personal experience, but on the impressions of others. While this anti-communism and mainstream liberal portrayal of US history do not detract from the overall excellence of the narrative, this reviewer found them a distraction.

Still, this text is an important, detailed and captivatingly told history of an under examined piece of US history. It raises questions about war and peace, allegiance and conscience, nation and humanity. It is certainly worth your time.

Wealth, Power and Climate Change

Future on Fire: Capitalism and the Politics of Climate Change—
David Camfield

I like clarity. On the question of the politics of climate change under capitalism, David Camfield's new book *Future on Fire: Capitalism and the Politics of Climate Change* provides exactly that. In addition, the book is brief and very much to the point. The topic is climate change, the target is the system of capitalism and the point is that the issue is a political issue and that political power is what will halt humanity's quickening race to self-destruction. Not the political power of politicians and bureaucrats who suckle on capitalism's teat, but the political power of social movements; social movements that are slowly but surely being built. Social movements that require tenacity, a political and economic understanding of how the powerful see the planet and its residents, and reject corporate and other non-solutions to the crisis.

Camfield begins this text with a reminder of where the planet is at the current moment. He discusses heat rise and the need to curtail CO_2 emissions. Reasons why the planet is experiencing rapid increases in both are looked at and placed in perspective: population growth, economic growth, fossil fuels. Naturally, each of the reasons he presents are elements that contribute to the crisis. Addressing one or the other of them might help but, as Camfield makes abundantly clear, the primary culprit in the demise of the planet as we know it is the economic system of capitalism; its exploitation of the environment, of human labor and, most importantly, its need to constantly expand in order to survive. The metaphor of cancer is an appropriate and oft-used one when it comes to acknowledging capitalism's destruction. What cancer cells do to the human body is what capitalism is doing to the planet and the multiple environmental systems it requires to exist as a healthy entity.

Given this, it becomes quite obvious that capitalism must go. Like others sounding the alarm on climate change and its effect on humans and the planet we live on, Camfield makes explicit that those who will suffer first (and probably the most) are those most at the mercy of capitalism. He explains it like this: "As rising waters, drought, and other effects of climate change drive more people to move, the impact on people will depend on their wealth and power."(5) Expanding outward, his dynamic is applied to communities and even entire populations living in certain regions on earth. Therefore, he argues, the most effective way to address climate change must include a re-ordering of the social order. Already, we know the wealthiest among us are making plans to leave the rest of their fellow humans behind when the shit of climate disaster hits the fan. Some are thinking about moving to other planets while others just figure on heading to luxury fortresses in the hills.

Obviously, Camfield's prescription is a tall order, especially when one considers the state of the movement addressing climate change today. At best, it is confused. There are those looking at a green new deal which in its most radical forms does demand a re-ordering of society. There are others hoping for something more moderate. Among the latter element and in many other manifestations of this movement, very few are seriously addressing the essence of the problem, pretending instead that capitalism is compatible with a livable future on earth. Even among those acknowledging the need for capitalism to go if climate change is to be seriously addressed, there are those that support capitalism's wars. War and the preparation for war are some of the worst contributors to earth's failing ecosystem, both in terms of the damage wars cause and the amount of money spent on them—money that could be used to address the negative effects of climate change.

One note of hope that Camfield sounds that others writing on the subject rarely address is that even if we don't reach certain goals considered important to slowing down and ultimately halting climate change, the planet is still worth saving. In a chapter he titles "Even a Ravaged Planet is Worth Fighting For," the author points out that the world will not end if those goals aren't reached. This fact would make it even clearer that the need to restructure human society along lines that remove profit as its motivation even greater. There will still be billions of people living on the planet and their future would still need to be assured. The date of 2030 suggested by scientists and others as crucial to reducing greenhouse and other emissions is not an "end of the world" date, but a marker. While we should of course be organizing and fighting to come close to the goals symbolized by that date, we should also be thinking of our work beyond that date, especially since the possibility of warming over two percent seems more likely with each passing day. The defeat of capitalism and its replacement with a system based on humanity's needs will be even more urgent, not less.

J. Edgar Did Not Dig No Rock and Roll

The Whole World in an Uproar—Aaron J. Leonard

There was a cultural revolution in the United States in the 1960s and 1970s. It began in the 1950s, not with Elvis as much as with Little Richard and Chuck Berry. Not only were these two artists Black, they were singing about sexuality and flaunting theirs on the stage. Elvis picked up on it–and probably felt it as genuinely as the other two. A little more than ten years later in 1968, Elvis was just a Las Vegas attraction and Little Richard was doing a gospel thing. Chuck Berry, on the other hand, was still playing his guitar like he was a-ringin' a bell, despite some time in prison earlier in the decade. His licks were borrowed and expanded on by guitarists like Keith Richards and John Lennon, who recognized him in their playing as the true king of rock. In fact, Bob Dylan remarked on his radio show once that if rock and roll was called something different, it should be called Chuck Berry. (Bob Dylan Theme Time Radio Hour–Eyes. It's on YouTube)

Mostly white and mostly male, rock music was turning the culture of the US (and by default much of what we call the West) upside down and inside out. Mop-tops from Britain were tripping on LSD and growing out their hair, poets in the USA were singing songs beyond the understanding of the old and straight (and the young and straight, for that matter). Revolution was being debated in some pop songs and urged on in others. A counterculture with politics as confused as the understanding of its adherents' parents was tossing out the old and blasting in the new. One thing was certain. The counterculture had no use for the US war in Vietnam and it liked smoking marijuana. In addition, most of its partisans dug Black America and thought it should be free. Many of its artists made these positions clear, either through their work, their statements or the way they lived..

If nothing else, the support for Black freedom was enough to garner the attention of the Federal Bureau of Investigation's director J. Edgar Hoover. His racism was quite well-known well before the decades in question. His ultimate obsession with it and the consequent focus on it by the Bureau would continue after Hoover's death in 1972. It would also be the cause of numerous murders of Black radicals, the snitch-jacketing of others, illegal surveillance of civil rights leaders like Martin Luther King, Jr. the framing of activists and a multitude of other excesses by the FBI and other law enforcement agencies.

As author Aaron Leonard describes in his newest book *The Whole World in an Uproar*, the FBI also spent a fair amount of its time watching and investigating certain musicians whose politics and countercultural activities drew its prurient and political interest. Like Leonard's previous texts Heavy Radicals, The Folk Singers and the Bureau, and A Threat of the First Magnitude: FBI Counterintelligence & Infiltration From the Communist Party to the Revolutionary Union – 1962-1974, he utilizes the Bureau's own notes and reports as the backbone of his research. Unlike those previous works, most of the persons and groups discussed in The Whole World in an Uproar did not belong to leftist political groups or exist in relatively "normal" lifestyles. This made them more difficult to infiltrate and harder to classify according to traditional criteria. That in itself created circumstances that were occasionally comical or completely off the mark.

In his preface, the author discusses how these differences caused him to modify his approach, too. He tells the reader: "this book turned out to be a different one from that originally conceived. It also marks a departure, to a degree, from my work so far...." Consequently, his references included many other sources, ranging from memoirs to music and regular media sources. In the end, Leonard tells a much grander tale than one that would have stuck more closely to FBI sources, precisely because so many of its subjects existed outside of traditional FBI understanding. After all, that was the essential nature of the cultural revolution, the counterculture of the long Sixties–creating and existing outside of the traditional understanding in US and western culture.

In writing Whole World in an Uproar, Leonard presents a greater structure of repression beyond that undertaken by law enforcement agencies like the FBI. His narrative illustrates the overall culture of cultural repression existing in modern societies. By presenting stories of events, movements, bands and musicians from Buffy St. Marie to Bob Dylan, Jim Morrison and the Doors to the Fugs, the Beatles and the Rolling Stones, the 1967 March on the Pentagon to Woodstock, the Black Panther Party to the Yippies and the Students for a Democratic Society Leonard provides the reader with an extensive yet concise survey of the popular music of the period and its meaning. It was a meaning that meant one thing to those in power and their enforcers and something quite different to those playing the music, dancing to the music and spreading the culture within which the music thrived.

Repression in this period meant anything from busting people for marijuana (yes it used to be very illegal in the US) to setting them up on drug charges. This was experienced by members of the Rolling Stones, the Beatles, Abbie Hoffman, the Grateful Dead, myself and millions of others. It also took the form of conspiracy to riot charges or framing Black Panthers for murder. The person that busted you could be a long-haired acquaintance or a jackbooted highway patrolman, an undercover girlfriend or a high-school principal. If you were not white-skinned your chances of going to prison were–just as they are today–considerably greater than if you were white-skinned. The uniformed cop who knocked you down at a protest or the undercover who busted you at a rock concert for smoking weed didn't seem to care as much. Indeed, they often seemed to delight in hurting those they cuffed and tossed into the back of their vehicles.

Aaron J. Leonard has written a very readable history of the period we call the Sixties. What it occasionally lacks in detail, it makes up for in temperament. He skillfully captures the spirit of the time while filling in many details regarding the reaction of the reactionaries to the attack on puritanical and political restraints instigated and carried out by the counterculture and New Left. Like Grace Slick of the Jefferson Airplane sang in their song "Volunteers of America," the forces of the Sixties cultural revolution really were "outlaws in the eyes of Amerika." Whole World in an Uproar is a great trip back for those who were there and, more importantly, an excellent and very readable history for those who weren't.

Many Millions Gone

Endless Holocausts: Mass Death in the History of the United States Empire—David Michael Smith

It's a relatively familiar recitation to those who study an honest history of the United States.

It begins with the first encampment of British colonists in what became Plymouth, MA and Jamestown, VA.; the failure of the latter colony and the success of the former thanks to the Pequot peoples in the region in a tale remade as the Thanksgiving legend. The expansion westward and the bloody heroism of men like Davy Crockett, the blessings of men like John Winthrop and the false military prowess of killers like Custer. Then there's the politicians with their fancy words writing and talking about freedom, justice and governance; all while they profit from the trade in human beings and the theft and sale of lands that were never theirs to take or sell.

Yes, it's a familiar litany to those who acknowledge the genocidal history of this nation under its murdering god. Even those who try to eliminate this history from that taught in schools and shared by the real and figurative descendants of those who conquered know the nature of it. That is why they fight so hard to keep it from their children and those who immigrate here now. After all, knowledge of such truth could mean the end of their assumed domination of the nation and its riches. So, instead, the brutal truth is either eliminated or diluted, as if there can be some justification for the legacy of death and destruction celebrated every Fourth of July in these United States.

This is why a new book from author David Michael Smith is so important. Titled *Endless Holocausts: Mass Death in the History of the United States Empire,* this book is a history book like no other. It is harsh.

It is relentless. It cannot be any other way. The endless death described in its pages does not allow another interpretation. The only other text that comes close to this effort in its scope of crimes against humanity undertaken in the name of the American Way is Richard Drinnon's icon-oclastic 1980 classic Facing West: The Metaphysics of Indian-Hating and Empire-Building, wherein the author draws the ever-so-straight line from the slaughter of northern America's indigenous people to the slaughter of Koreans and Vietnamese in Washington's wars in Asia.

Smith's book, while not as evocatively narrated as Drinnon's, is more expansive in terms of what he labels holocausts (and it's a fair termi-nology) while also quite clear in the numbers of deaths involved. In addition, given the January 2023 publication date of Smith's Endless Holocausts, the line drawn by both authors that begins in the seven-teenth century is updated by forty years to the current bloodletting in the name of expanding Washington's empire. After all, Facing West was last reprinted in 1997. For those paying attention, that year was a few years before the second US invasion of Iraq, the invasion of Afghanistan, the numerous other military operations in the name of the war on terror, and the imperial expansion of NATO up to the current conflict in Ukraine. In addition, Smith includes a section that enumerates and discusses the ongoing war on the Black people in the US, immigrants, working people and political dissidents, especially those on the left.

After reading this book, there is no way to pretend that those who call the United States the world's most violent, most genocidal nation are telling anything but the truth. The numbers of deaths in the name of whatever it is Washington claims to kill for–freedom, democracy, the rules-based order, free enterprise, ad infinitum–is more than mind boggling; it's unfathomable. That in itself is the danger of these types of enumerations. Like a multi-trillion dollar national debt, the millions killed in the name of truth, freedom and the American way is a chal-lenge to get a hold of. When one considers that much of that debt is directly related to the warrior mission the United States wears proudly while denying its murderous past, it remains essential that each individ-ual number in these morbid statistics is a life taken, a family broken and a home destroyed. And, somewhere, a dollar made by a war profiteer masquerading as a defender of freedom.

David Michael Smith and Monthly Review Press have done us a favor by publishing this book. Not only is it honestly refreshing, it is perhaps the most important history of the United States published in recent years. There are no excuses here, no rationales; just an accounting of the essential truth in the making and maintenance of the US empire. Millions dead with little to no mercy. Patriotism and its false glories are removed from the telling, leaving the reader with nothing but facts shorn of myth and history minus embellishment too often disguised as truth. It should be near the top of the list for anyone who claims US history as the reason they fly their stars and stripes and cheer the wars fought in its name.

Maggie Thatcher Sucked, But the Music She Inspired Didn't

The Fascist Groove Thing: A History of Thatcher's Britain in 21 Mixtapes—High Hodges

Maggie Thatcher's rule in Britain was, like the same years in Ronnie Reagan's United States, a vicious attempt to move their nations as far right as they could. The process they began continues today with a ruthlessness that is only matched by its idiotic insistence that it is beneficial for the very demographic that has probably lost the most–the white working class. On the other hand, the attacks on working people and their unions, the theft of their nation's wealth by the wealthiest people in the world, the blatant racism and the intensified love affair with nuclear weapons and power created some of the best political popular music since the Sixties, at least in Britain.

It is that music which inspires and informs Hugh Hodges recent book, titled *The Fascist Groove Thing: A History of Thatcher's Britain in 21 Mixtapes*. Likewise, it is the history of Margaret Thatcher and her brand of selfishness packaged as politics that inspired and informed the music on those mixtapes. From Heaven 17's recording of "(We Don't Need This) Fascist Groove Thing" to Linton Kwesi Johnson's radical reggae putting the police in their place and from the brash, even abrasive sounds of Penny Rimbaud and his band Crass to the Tom Robinson Band's straight out rock against racism and homophobia, author Hodge's story of the opening decade of neoliberal capitalism in Britain makes one thing clear: not everyone was buying the repackaged version of robber baron capitalism Maggie and her heartless henchmen were selling.

Unfortunately, it didn't seem to matter whether or not everyone bought it. That is quite obvious if one takes a look around the world we live in today. Neoliberal capitalism has not so much remade the world as it has destroyed it. This is as true in Oklahoma City as it is in Yorkshire; as true in Paris as it is in Mumbai. To paraphrase Bob Dylan, money doesn't just talk or swear, it has destroyed. It has destroyed the livelihoods of working people and it has destroyed their living space through a business approach that rejects regulation, thereby ensuring greater environmental destruction. It has devalued culture unless it's corporate and made a mockery of art in every sphere. In other words, the world today is more Thatcherite and more Reaganite than it was when either of them were in power.

As The Fascist Groove Thing tells the reader, this began in 1979, when Maggie and her band of crooks won the British election. There were already plenty of signs that the welfare capitalist state that Britain had built after the destruction of World War Two was shaky. The triumphant western capitalist system set up in favor of Wall Street and Washington had suffered some serious assaults on its reign. The period of relative affluence among working class white people was waning. While this affluence looked different in Britain than it did in the United States, the reality facing the rulers in both countries was that they were going to have to go after the workers if the rulers were going to keep their mansions (or whatever it is they have). Disgruntled and disenfranchised youth were the first to express their anger. After all, they were the first to be disenfranchised. The Sex Pistols 1977 single "Anarchy in the UK," while not much of a political treatise, was certainly a loud and angry howl. It was intended to offend and it did. However, it was another record from 1977 that was both more directed and more musical. The band and the record were called The Clash. The single "White Riot" was a response to a police riot at the predominantly West Indian Notting Hill Carnival in 1976. Arguably, it is The Clash whose leftist political lyrics and catchy hooks–from fifties rock and roll to Jamaican dub–that would do more to define the resistance to Thatcher's economic and race policies than any other band.

This book is about a lot more than that, though. The author's familiarity with British popular music is obvious before one is twenty pages into the text. Hardcore punk, ska, novelty tunes, Irish punk and noise; it's all covered. That coverage isn't just songs overlaid on historical events or the opposite of that. There is critical discussion of the various protest movements. The women of Greenham Common and their years-long protest against nuclear weapons are discussed along with the massive anti-nuclear protests across Britain and Europe after Washington began placing nuclear-tipped missiles on British and European soil (a decision that was ultimately reversed.) The closing of the mines and the attacks on the miners' union are as much a focus in this book as they were of numerous musicians during the conflict. This was Thatcher's first major salvo against the working class. In a way, the firing of the striking air traffic controllers by Ronald Reagan was but a poor imitation of what Iron Lady Thatcher did to the miners. The line had been drawn and the vitriol would only intensify. Fortunately, for the Brits who had no love for Thatcher's rule, their soundtrack would only get better and better.

The pointless war over the Falklands would provide Maggie with the support she needed for her next foray. Easy wars always seem to do that for dying empires. It would be the oppression of those subjects who came from the colonies that would provide some of the greatest moments of the history in these mixtapes. After racist attacks by police and British racists on immigrants along with the rise of the nazi National Front, a couple racist British politicians and some racist comments by Eric Clapton (not to mention David Bowie's comments about fascism), anti-racist rockers and reggae musicians began organizing Rock Against Racism(RAR). From my recollection, its efforts to make racism fringe again were fairly successful. Some on the left criticized what they considered RAR's white savior mentality. This was centered around the fact that RAR's organizing was mostly focused on white youth. Lost in this perception, though, is that the National Front was trying to organize white youth, not Blacks. Consequently, it made political and strategic sense to counter the racists' argument with one that emphasized white and non-white unity while keeping the focus on the true oppressor–the ruling class.

The Fascist Groove Thing is a political history, a music history and musical criticism all bound up in one fascinating book. The times it remembers and discusses are the roots of our current dystopian malaise. Like it was then, the music in these mixtapes is both tonic and topical, memory and manifesto. Author Hugh Hodges has done us a favor in writing it, both in terms of content and approach. If the story he tells does not satisfy the reader, there is a voluminous list for further reading and a massive discography.

(One more thing, even though I don't necessarily agree with everything that Spotify is, there is a soundtrack for this book on the platform that includes every song in every mixtape put together in the text.)

The US Conference of Catholic Bishops, Mammon and the Hippie Pope

A Theocracy of Intolerance and Hate

Playing God: American Catholic Bishops and the Far Right—Mary Jo McConahay

To use a word whose Catholic meaning I learned in second grade at St. Mary's Elementary while studying for my First Communion, let me make a small confession. It seems relevant to the response I have to Mary Jo McConahay's new book *Playing God: American Catholic Bishops and the Far Right*. That confession is this: I was raised as a traditional Catholic. Even though I only attended a total of three years of Catholic school, my father's devotion to the Church was translated to his children via weekly mass, CCD lessons(the equivalent of Sunday School) and lots of rosary recitation. Oh yeah, there were also strict observances during Lent and I also spent a few years as an altar boy. As I got older, my father and I debated Catholicism, the pope, Augustine, Thomas Aquinas, liberation theology and the meaning of the ten commandments all the way up until a night or two before he passed. Our primary differences in these discussions centered on the Church's homophobia, its refusal to consider women equal to men, its duplicity concerning war, and the expanding reactionary nature of the United States Conference of Catholic Bishops (USCCB).

On certain subjects, the stance of the USCCB was too much even for my father, who had come of age during the reign of Pope Pius XII at the Vatican. Besides that pope's seeming lack of concern for the fate of Jewish Europeans under the Nazis, Pius XII was a committed upholder of traditional Catholic values. In addition, he was bitterly opposed to communism in any form. The disparity between those years of my father's religious life and those that followed the liberalization of the Church under Pope John XXIII was quite stark. What followed John XXIII's death was a gradual return by the Vatican to something closer to the Catholicism my father had grown up with. That is, except on the questions of war, peace and poverty. Even the last pope before the current Francis, who was called Pope Benedict XVI, had issues with the nature of modern capitalism and the idolatry of mammon it demanded. He also questioned the US war on Iraq and doubted it would qualify as a just war according to Catholic theology.

Still, Benedict XVI mostly spoke on issues of what the Church calls personal morality. In other words, issues regarding sex, sexuality, gender, and procreation. He put these issues at the forefront of teaching in Catholic schools from kindergarten through graduate programs at universities. Personally, this just meant that my debates with my father about the Church and its teachings occasionally involved a few of my sisters, who were tired of going to Mass only to hear the priests in the conservative parish they attended use their pulpit to condemn women who preferred some control over their bodies. Of course, the Catholic church has never truly considered women equal to men, but priests saying Mass and using the pulpit to attack their person-hood was something new in our lifetimes. As McConahay suggests in Playing God, this incessant attack on the person-hood of women by these priests was (and is) much more the result of decisions by the USCCB to focus on abortion and contraception than it was the result of directions from the Vatican.

This brings us back to McConahay's text. The essential story in these pages is that not only does the USCCB not necessarily reflect the focus of the papacy, it doesn't even reflect the beliefs of its members or many of its priests. Instead, these bishops have allied themselves with the ultra-right Christian nationalist movement in the United States; a movement which saw its powers (if not its numbers) increase during the time Donald Trump was in the White House. Calling themselves traditionalists, these Catholics are anti-Muslim, anti-immigrant, anti-gay, and ultimately anti-women. This essentially fascist movement masquerading as a religious one sets the tone of way too many conversations in what the media terms the US culture wars. The fact that the Catholic hierarchy in the United States has signed on to this faction of the US polity is more than disturbing. The further fact that their domination of the US Catholic discourse means that young people seeking spiritual guidance could well end up accepting the bishop's political beliefs as doctrine is downright frightening.

The manner in which the transition from a spiritual body that challenged the economics of modern capitalism and imperial war along with what they considered moral corruption to one which now considers modern capitalism and its wars as morally neutral if not representations of God's work was not accidental. Nor was it something that occurred purely on the philosophical level via discussion, interpretation and writing. No, as Playing God makes clear, this transition was bankrolled by various wealthy Catholics in communion with the Koch brothers foundation, the extreme right-wing church organization Opus Dei, other Christian millionaires and organizations, and much of the Republican party. McConahay exposes the work of Domino's pizza magnate Tom Monaghan in this network of Christians, billionaire capitalists, Federalist Society leader Leonard Leo, and Clarence and Ginni Thomas. It is a seedy network that she describes. That seediness is not sanctified by the fact of its claim to religion or the rank of its most holy members, the United States Conference of Catholic Bishops. Indeed, the fact that it manipulates the desire of so many US residents for some kind of spiritual guidance in its quest for power and dominion makes it even more squalid. Jesus forgave Mary Magdalene and many another sinner. One has to wonder if these men who represent the Catholic Church in the United States would receive the same mercy.

Which brings me back to my father. After the coronation of Francis he was skeptical, especially because he had grown used to (and even accepted) the previous popes' continuation of the Church's essentially homophobic and misogynistic doctrine. In addition, his obsession with legal abortion only served to exacerbate his acceptance of that doctrine. Consequently, he began to go along with the anti-immigrant sentiment expressed in his circles. However, perhaps a year into Francis' reign, he revealed to me that he found Francis' emphasis on love to be much easier to live with than the focus on punishment Benedict tended to proclaim. I asked him what this meant to him in real life. He responded by saying that he had looked around the church at Mass and realized that many of his fellow worshipers were new immigrants to the United States. They spoke Spanish, French, different languages of Africa and even Arabic. It didn't matter what nation they were citizens of now or before; they were all children of his God. It's not so much that he had an epiphany, but that a new pope–a new spiritual leader–helped him remember what his gospel had taught him.

I listened then and thought to myself, I wonder when the US hierarchy of this church he is so devoted to will see what he had seen. I continue to wonder, even as they continue to circulate letters challenging and even defying the current Pope. Reading Playing God confirmed my concerns while also explaining the source of the money and the nature of the machinations of those who would make the Catholic church a part of their theocracy of intolerance and hate.

Poverty is Political

The Poverty Paradox: Understanding Economic Hardship Amid American Prosperity—Mark Robert Rank

Poverty is an ugly stain on the social fabric. It is also part of the economic equation that when added up is called capitalism. Even one of capitalism's first cheerleaders Adam Smith acknowledged that "no society can surely be flourishing and happy, of which the far greater part of the members are poor and miserable." The history of capitalism since that time has further proven that this economic system left unfettered cares little to none about how many people are poor and miserable. In its reasoning, this is a primary reason why most capitalist governments instituted some kind of social safety net for their citizens left by the wayside under capitalism's inequality. Despite any altruism that might have guided the legislation creating these safety nets, the bottom line is that these safety nets have kept the poor from overturning the capitalist regime in favor of one run by the workers. Despite this, there have always been exceeding self-righteous and greedy capitalists joined by similar thinking politicians working to end any kind of assistance to the poor. We have seen their ilk control governments of Britain and the US since the late 1970s.

Part of the methodology used by this element of society includes spreading their gospel of individualism. It is a gospel that rejects the rights of working people to organize, and classifies people according to how they wish to repress them. First and foremost, however, it blames the poor and the lowly paid for their own circumstances. In doing so, it rejects the very essence of capitalism—the idea that profit for the owner and the corporation comes from underpaying those who do the labor. Once this stance is taken, then anything the employer does to enhance their profit and further impoverish those who work for them is morally acceptable under these ethics. The role of government is to support this approach. This is especially true in the United States, a nation where the exploitation of labor by the wealthy is the accepted understanding by all of its residents. In part it is done via its social welfare programs; programs which are designed to embarrass and reproach those who are in need of them. In general, the essence of these programs is to place the blame on the individual for their poverty.

A recently published book, titled *The Poverty Paradox: Understanding Economic Hardship Amid American Prosperity*, challenges the common understanding described above. Instead, the author Mark Robert Rank begins with an understanding that poverty represents a failure on a structural level. This understanding naturally takes his text in a direction that means the solution for poverty is to be found by changing the structure. Before he begins to discuss potential solutions (short of a left-wing revolution), Mr. Rank presents a clear and potentially disheartening discussion of the odds against lower income working class families, specific to each generation and over time. These are the symptoms of an economic system designed by those with money to insure their money will remain in their families for generations. For working-class families, this means that once a family experiences something more than a short period of poverty and finds themselves returning to a dependence on ineffectual poverty programs and charity, the likelihood of them escaping this cycle decreases. As noted earlier, this is in large part because those programs are designed to maintain a certain percentage of poor people in society.

The author provides an analysis of statistics regarding poverty, wealth, and opportunity for different demographic groups. One common denominator in all of those concerning poverty and opportunity is that single women and Black Americans consistently face the most difficulty in taking advantage of opportunity and ending poverty. This increases when there are children involved. The reasons for this are many, but as Rank explains, can be boiled down to two essentials: racism and sexism. Black people are often rejected for jobs even if they are better qualified; women with children have no affordable and easy access to childcare. Of course, this means poor Black women with children find it even more difficult to improve their economic lot. In order to explain this reality, the author uses the metaphor of musical chairs—a game where people try to sit on fewer chairs than there are people while a song plays. When the song is over, whoever is not in a chair is left out of the game. Author Rank's description makes it clear the US economy begins with too few chairs for those who are already "disadvantaged because of their race, gender, family history and so on.

The Poverty Paradox describes a morally bankrupt nation. Not only is it failing its poorest and most disadvantaged, most of its politicians are unwilling to seriously address this. Instead, many of them are stepping up their attacks on the poor both in their words and their deeds. As I write this, millions of US residents are at risk of losing their Medicaid benefits and millions have already seen their SNAP/EBT payments decrease by over a third. Meanwhile, the price of food continues to rise with most of it going into the bank accounts of those who are gouging consumers in the name of profit. As far as Congress goes, a groundswell is strengthening among the right wing to continue the hundreds of billions worth of tax cuts benefiting the wealthiest while liberals and a fair number of rightwingers continue to hand billions and billions of dollars to the war machine and its conflicts around the world. This is an ultimately hopeful text. Mr. Rank provides relevant and important details of the inequality, how it works day to day. However, he does not challenge the fact of capitalism and the exploitation of labor and resources that define its essential nature. Like those of Bernie Sanders, Rank's prescriptions would be very helpful if they were implemented. Indeed, that possibility might be the only salvation left for this nation called the United States.

The Iranian Students Association and the End of the Shah

This Flame Within: Iranian Revolutionaries in the United States—Manijeh Moradian

The Iranian revolution in 1978-1980 was one of the watershed events of the last fifty years. It was also considerably more complex than the usually two-dimensional version presented in western conversation. In other words, it was much more than an overthrow of the Shah by religious fundamentalists who hated western influence and US interference. Despite the revisionist history told in most US takes on the events in Iran during the period, the Shah's modernization of Iran was not opposed by many of those involved in the movement to end his reign. However, virtually everyone involved was against the accumulation of wealth and power by the Shah and his class that modernization created. Furthermore, the brutality of his regime against dissenters intensified that opposition.

Volumes of literature have been published regarding the history of Iran, especially that history after World War Two. The primary event in that history is the election of Mossadegh as Prime Minister in 1951 on a left-leaning nationalist program that demanded nationalization of Iran's oil production and his subsequent CIA orchestrated overthrow in 1953. Once Mossadegh was removed and replaced by the Shah, the resistance to the Shah began. Likewise, so did Washington's military and economic domination of Iran. Indeed, Iran was one of the largest recipients of US military aid from 1954-1979. This aid was not provided just to project US imperial power in the oil-rich and politically precarious Middle East. It was also used by the Shah's government to crack down on dissent—dissent that came increasingly from the Left.

Perhaps the most represented social strata among the

radical opposition were high school and university students. As Manijeh Moradian details in her recently published text *This Flame Within: Iranian Revolutionaries in the United States*, student radicals were not only present in Iran's schools, but also across the global north. Indeed, she argues that it was Iranian student radicals that provided much of the radical anti-imperialist analysis in the early to mid-1960s student movements in countries like the United States and West Germany. The history she writes reveals the contradictions present in US imperialism's encouragement of the Shah's secular "modernization" project. In doing so, she discusses the role educational exchange programs between the United States and its client states were (and are) an integral part of Washington's soft imperial policy to win hearts and minds in its satellites. Of course, as this text makes clear, foreign students involved in such programs can turn them on their head and use their educational experience as a place for organizing opposition to the governments that hope to enlist them in their empire project.

The Iranian Student Association (ISA) was the number one organization for Iranian students in the US during the years of the Shah. It began in 1952 as a social organization created with the support of the Iranian embassy in the United States and the American Friends of the Middle East (AFME), which was later financially linked to the Central Intelligence Agency. By 1960, it was a politically radical organization dedicated to opposing the Shah and US imperialism. Author Moradian describes this transition via profiles of various members of the organization, discussions of the ISA's literature and its actions. The latter included protests against the Shah and his entourage during their US visits and disruptions of university graduation ceremonies in the US where the Shah was given honorary degrees for his role in supporting Washington's designs for empire—one of US higher education's fundamental roles then and now.

Like most leftist student groups, there would be fissures over theory and tactics inside the ISA. As would be expected, many of these differences reflected differences among the left in Iran. However, even these disruptions did not detract from the goal of ending the Shah's regime. It was this determination together with the paranoia of the Shah's regime and Washington's concern about the growing alliance between

US student radicals and the ISA radicals that provided a rationale that allowed Iran's secret police (SAVAK) to work in the United States. In addition to the instances of operations by SAVAK agents detailed in This Flame Within, I remember an instance at the University of Maryland in 1975 where an Iranian student was removed from a picket line protesting proposed budget cuts by two men in dark clothes. He was tossed into a black limousine. He returned to campus a couple days later. In a related incident, my father—who was an USAF officer working with the National Security Agency (NSA)–was visited by a couple men after I attended an ISA meeting as a representative of the anti-imperialist Revolutionary Student Brigade (RSB) . The topic of the meeting was how to protest a future visit to Washington by the Shah. To his credit, my father told them I was an adult and had my own politics; politics he disagreed with.

A considerably more violent example of the SAVAK's activities inside the US took place in 1977 during another visit from the ruler of Iran. I went to the first day of protests. I hitchhiked to DC from suburban Maryland with a friend who had been politically active since 1969 and very involved in the student strike at the University of Maryland after the US invasion of Cambodia in 1970. The fellow who gave us a ride was a member of the Sioux nation and had been involved in the November 1972 American Indian movement occupation of the Bureau of Indian Affairs. He spent a few months in prison and had given up on militant politics. Nonetheless, he drove us to the protest site, gave us some bandannas to help against tear gas and drove off. After a few speeches against the shah and US imperialism, cops on horseback started surrounding the park. Then hundreds of pro-shah protesters and SAVAK agents ran towards us waving sticks and piece of re-bar. The cops let them through. Fights broke out and tear gas filled e the air in one corner of the park. We did our best to defend ourselves as we sought an escape from the cops and the SAVAK.

Moradian's text is considerably more than stories about protests. Her profiles are discussions of the culture within the Iranian student community, the struggles of women to break out of traditional roles, and the relationship between the revolutionary movement in Iran and the US. There are also reflections on the interactions between US radical groups and the Iranian student radicals; interaction perhaps best expressed in the solidarity between the aforementioned RSB and the ISA in the mid-1970s through 1979, when the RSB's parent organization split into at least two different groups. Regarding the struggles of women to get beyond the roles society had assigned and too many male radicals had accepted: US women were struggling with the same issues. The nature of women's roles in the radical left during the 1960s and 1970s can perhaps best be explained in the words of an Iranian woman who described her experience as being empowering but not liberating.

Most readers know how the Iranian revolution went from a broad-based struggle that included leftists of all stripes, Shia Muslims, bourgeois liberals and social democrats to a theocracy that is both anti-imperialist and socially reactionary and essentially capitalist. Past interventions by foreign governments in this transition are still being uncovered while other interventions continue today. The Flame Within provides an excellent summary of the relationship between the Khomeini factions in the revolutionary movement and the Left. It also discusses the post-revolutionary diaspora and its role in reshaping the US understanding of the Iranian revolution.

Underlying the author's narrative is a tenet that is both unique and obvious, not just in the Iranian revolution, but in every left revolutionary movement in the world. That is that no ideology can (or should) ignore the relationship between women's freedom and the fundamental role it plays in human liberation from imperialism, racism, capitalism and other universal oppressions. It can't be stated forcefully enough—this is an important and instructive text. One doesn't have to agree with the entirety of the author's analysis or conclusion to understand that the discussions of mistakes of the revolutionary Iranian left regarding the liberation of women are important to today's and future radical left anti-imperialist movements.

338

Capitalism is Still the Problem

Capitalism: A Conversation in Critical Theory—Nancy Fraser &
Rahel Jaeggi

As far as the United States is concerned, today's Left is not only small, it's also quite confused. Sure, there are debates regarding the conflict being fought in Ukraine and the wisdom of organizing in the Democratic party, but I'm talking about more fundamental questions. Primary among them is the nature of class and how it should be addressed. The basic understanding in Marxism is that there are two classes under capitalism—the bourgeoisie and the working class. This dynamic places the workers in the position where the primary commodity they have to sell in a marketplace of commodities is their labor. This understanding also theoretically provides the worker with the freedom to sell their labor to the highest bidder. In other words, the employer who will pay the best wage and provide the most benefits. Of course, most workers don't actually have this luxury as individuals; it is only through organizing as a class that they can then (ideally) force the employer class to reach an arrangement most of the workers can agree on. Naturally, any such arrangement will only be agreed to by the employer if it divides the profit derived from the labor of the workers in the employer's favor. In other words, how much of the labor created by the worker will be stolen by the owners.

This relationship between employers and workers (the bourgeoisie and the working class when writ large) is one of the essential elements of capitalism. The other commonly understood element is the exploitation of the earth and its bounty. The wealth derived from this exploitation is understood as the process whereby enough wealth was accumulated by the unholy coalition of merchants, armies, traders and governments to shift the nature of Europe's economy away from feudalism towards capitalism. Marx called this process "primitive accumulation." As co-author Nancy Fraser states early on in the recently released book *Capitalism: A Conversation in Critical Theory*: "there is a whole back story about where capital comes from—a rather violent story of theft, dispossession and expropriation." (29) As the discussion on this particular topic continues, it not only becomes apparent that this process continues, it also includes historical activities beyond mining coal from the earth and other extractive operations. Indeed, it includes the creation of maintenance of the transatlantic slave trade and its development into a breeding and selling operation identical to the process used to raise beasts like cows and sheep. It also includes the colonization of much of the global south by northern governments, mostly Britain, and it is the economic rationale for the conquering of the western hemisphere and the genocide that involved. Both historically and in the present times, Fraser insists there cannot be wage exploitation in the traditional working class without expropriation elsewhere, be that through wage differences and precariarity among women, debt peonage, prison labor and non white workers, or ecological extraction and imperialist wars. Of course, all of those phenomena are part and parcel of modern capitalism.

The paragraphs above are the foundation of the text mentioned above. The book itself is framed as a discussion between two philosophers: Nancy Fraser from the New School for Social Research and Rahel Jaeggi of the Center for Humanities and Social Change at the Humboldt University of Berlin. The decision by the authors and editors to present this book of theory as a discussion was a wise one. It is that format which makes it accessible in a way that a more traditional exposition would not have. As I read this, I felt as if I was sitting in a room listening to a conversation unbound by any supposition other than that capitalism is a problem for the earth and those who exist on it. As the conversation progresses, it becomes clear that in order to resolve the problem of capitalism and its destructive nature, it is necessary to expand the current definitions of it. That is the task of this work. It is a task at which it succeeds, even as it leaves many questions left to answer. Those answers lie in this book and in the future of the struggle against capitalism.

In their search for a more expansive definition of capitalism, Fraser

340

and Jaeggi maneuver through different prisms: historically, morally, ethically and functionally. In doing this, they point out the weakness of each and the necessity of combining the views each of these prisms in order to come up with an expansive, inclusive and more honest understanding. In their examinations of these various ways of critiquing capitalism, various shortcomings of historical movements against capitalism are pointed out and considered. Likewise, the fascist movements of the last one hundred years are discussed in relation to the anti-capitalist aspects of their rhetoric. The nature of identity politics in modern politics is analyzed; both their possibilities for liberation and their reactionary possibilities. The exchanges between the two authors concerning the rise of right wing populist (fascist) movements echo dozens of conversations I have been part of or at least observed over the last few decades. Those conversations seem to have increased since the fact of trumpism and other right wing movements have surged in the global north. It is a discussion that is intertwined with the intensification of identity politics on the left. Fraser's analysis here is one that makes the most sense and one that she verbalizes better than anyone I have heard so far.

"In the decades since the 1970s," she states. "two different sets of struggles unfolded at about the same time in many countries of the capitalist core. The first set pitted labor against capital, which sought to break unions, drive down real wages, and relocate manufacturing to low-wage regions in the semi-periphery and precaritize work. This was an old-fashion class struggle, which has mainly been won by capital, at least for now. But unfolding to it in parallel to it was a second front, which pitted the forces of emancipation (in the form of new 'social movements' such as feminism, multiculturalism, LBGTQ rights, etc.) against defenders of "old-fashioned" family values and lifeworlds, many of whom were also on the losing end of the first struggle and the "cosmopolitanism" associated with the new globalizing economy. Caught up in the second struggle and largely oblivious to the first, hegemonic currents of the progressive movements dropped the ball on political economy, ignoring the structural transformation underway."(200)

Furthermore, the identity based movements moved away from the liberationist hopes from which they were born to a strategy demanding for a place at the ruling class table for individuals from these groups. It is a strategy that leaves the mechanics of exclusion and oppression in place for the majority of those in the groups affected.

This book isn't a book of answers; it is a book of questions and discussion resulting from those questions. The only certainty one might derive when they have finished reading it is that the only chance we have in defeating the ongoing march towards greater catastrophe wrought by human subjugation to capital is to be found in the struggle against capitalism and in organizing that struggle.

The 1970s and Popular Struggle

The Subversive Seventies—Michael Hardt

The 1970s was a decade of changes. Capitalism had its wings clipped by workers who understood their power and responded with a new mutation that became known as neoliberalism. The old colonial empires—already fading—suffered defeat. Foremost among the latter was Portugal, which not only lost its colonies, but saw the fascist regime it had been under overthrown by a leftist and popular coup. The US military saw its Vietnam adventure end in a television news special broadcast I will never forget. On the other hand, a popular revolution at the ballot box and in the streets of Chile was overthrown by the unholy conspiracy of the CIA, the White House and various US corporations. Thousands died during the coup and thousands more were imprisoned. The architects of neoliberal capitalism moved in and caused the lives of millions more to change for the worse—all in the name of profit and control. Lots of profit.

As someone who began the 1970s in ninth grade at a school whose students were mostly children of US military men stationed in Frankfurt am Main, BRD and ended the decade living with a half-dozen folks in a two-bedroom apartment next to the recycling center in Berkeley, CA., I feel I experienced the time through a variety of lenses. In his new book *The Subversive Seventies*, author Michael Hardt provides a similar experience to the reader. Also, like Hardt, my understanding of what was occurring around me and what I was often participating in was colored by a politically left and cultur-ally underground perspective. Although I had attended a teach-in and vigil against the US war in Vietnam during the 1969 October Moratorium Against the War, the first large and militant protest I

343

actually attended was a few days after the 1970 invasion of Cambodia by US forces. It began in downtown Frankfurt and made its way toward the headquarters of several US military commands that were housed in the IG Farben building—a building which was once the administrative headquarters of the war criminal chemical corporation IG Farben and was then where the US military ran its less than popular activities.

Hardt notes the shifting of the revolutionary focus from the industrial proletariat to students, lumpen, youth, women and third world movements that took place in the 1960s and 1970s. He points out that this was the case in every European nation except for Italy, where the workerist and Autonomen movements came out of the factories. In contrast to most other observers, Hardt argues that it was the intensified radicalization of workers that manifested itself in the late 1960s and early 1970s that convinced the capitalist class to shift their industrial activities overseas to places where there were few if any unions. As he reminds the reader, not only were the radical (even revolutionary) workers attempting to realign the factory floor via wildcat strikes and other "unauthorized" actions, these workers were also challenging the union bureaucracies. Those bureaucracies had given up their radical roots and political activities for decent salaries and complacent contracts. The radicals wanted more. They wanted to change society and the economic system that drove it. In other words, what had become a union conspiracy with capital needed to become an uprising against capitalism.

The Subversive Seventies is a global exploration. From the Fiat factory complex in Turin, Italy to the Lip watch factory in France; from the auto plants in Detroit to the auto plant in Lordstown, Ohio workers were on the rise. In the streets of Oakland, New York City, Chicago and many other US cities where the Black Panthers had organized to the streets of urban South Africa and Santiago, Chile, the revolutionary surge was both grassroots and widespread. Japanese radicals and farmers fought against an airport extension by camping on the land intended for the project. In Kwangju, Korea, the residents set up their own municipal government after being attacked and cut off by the regime in Seoul. It lasted less than a week, but it lives on in the spirit of the southern Korean left. The crackdowns by the states being challenged were quite

344

often brutal and even murderous. Some on the Left responded with their own armed attacks—the Weatherman/Weather Underground chose targets chosen for their connection to the US war on the Vietnamese, Black Americans and US imperialism in general. In Germany, the targets of the Rote Armee Fraktion were US military installations, law enforcement and capitalists with bloody hands. In Italy, the fascists took advantage of the fear produced by the Italian media and politicians; fascist bombings were calculated to cause mass casualties and blamed on the Left. Meanwhile the Left armed militants of the Rote Brigada captured and killed a politician when their demands were not met. It is Hardt's contention that these groups involved in armed struggle operated in ways which were appropriate to the situation, but it was the groups building popular organizations that held the key to a potentially new world. As we know, it was (and is) a world that the capitalists and their cohorts were intent on defeating.

Antinuclear struggles, feminist awakenings, gay liberation and liberation theologies are all incorporated into this clearly written and studiously researched discussion of the 1970s and the possibilities of popular power that decade represented. The fact that we are still fighting many of the battles introduced in this text does not detract from the successes of that decade or the lessons learned. It does remind us of the powers arrayed against; powers more entrenched and more desperate. This makes The Subversive Seventies both a history of the past and a portent of a potential future.

The Heartbreak of a Fatal Crash Compounded

A Day in the Life of Abed Salama: Anatomy of a Jerusalem Tragedy—Nathan Thrall

A school trip to an amusement park. The West Bank near Jerusalem. An extremely rainy day causing some parents to hesitate about sending their children on the trip. The children, however, are so excited about the day's potential fun they convince the hesitant parents to let them go. The bus hired to ferry the children to the park is old and in terrible condition; a condition made worse the weather which is flooding the roads and exposing its poor state. Because this is the West Bank, occupied by Israel since 1967, the route the driver must take is a circuitous one. After all, certain roads are for Israelis only in this land of separation and apartheid. What seems almost inevitable happens. The bus is hit by a runaway eighteen wheeler driven by an inexperienced driver with multiple violations on his record. It only gets worse. The school bus rolls over and bursts into flames. Israeli emergency services, including the police and the military, never come despite their close proximity to the accident. Palestinian services are further away and required to pass through checkpoints manned by the Israeli military and designed to slow down traffic from the Palestinian sectors to Israel and its illegal settlements. Bystanders join the driver and a school teacher in pulling children and faculty from the burning bus. What would be a tragedy in any place in the world becomes an indictment of the Israeli occupation—its racism and inhumanity.

This is the setting for the new book from Nathan Thrall. Titled *A Day in the Life of Abed Salama: Anatomy of a Jerusalem Tragedy*, this text describes the travails of Abed as he tries to find out the fate of his son Milad, a clever and lovable five year old involved in the bus crash.

346

This story line provides the author Thrall with an entry to the intricacies, inconveniences and outright maliciousness of the Israeli occupation of the West Bank. The aggressive intrusions and land thefts of the settlers, the obtuse, suspicious and often hateful behavior of the Israeli military, and the often servile nature of the Palestinian police under the Palestinian Authority (PA). But even more than this, it is a story of individuals and families interacting with each other to save their children despite their family feuds and differing political alignments. In Palestine, those alignments can often mean death given the nature of what is at stake.

The events in the book take place just after first Oslo accords between Israel and the Palestine Liberation Organization were signed. Abed Salama is a member of the Democratic Front for the Liberation of Palestine (DFLP), a secular leftist group. The other main organization in the PLO is the more popular Fatah, whose politics are not as leftist and, as it turns out, ultimately considerably more collaborationist. Indeed, it is Fatah's leader Yassir Arafat whose name became not only synonymous with the Accords, but also with those elements seen as giving into Tel Aviv's demands. Perhaps the greatest of these is the role of the Palestinian Authority, which is ultimately one that serves the Occupation, both in perception and fact. In the text, this dynamic is represented by Ibrahim Salama, who as a member of the Palestinian Authority refugee authority, works closely with the various Israeli military and civilian officials. In fact, he considers one of the Israelis as one of this closest friends. This works in his favor in the text because he is able to use that connection to get information from the otherwise uncooperative Israeli civilian and military authorities.

Then there are the women. Often involved in marriages to men not of their choosing and somewhat restricted by social expectations in their social circles, they carry on, finding joy in their roles as mothers and caregivers even while they hope for something better. Of course, this is not unlike the state of affairs for women around the world, although in a culture where arranged marriages are often still the preferred practice the women's sense of empowerment might suffer more. Yet, throughout the text, the women the reader is introduced to fulfill their maternal roles with love and efficiency. At the same time, the deadly accident exposes the fragile nature of the women's relationships with their husbands and families. Indeed, the mother of one of the children is ostracized from her in-laws because, in their search for a reason to the tragedy, they blame her for allowing the child to go on the school trip.

The story inside this book's covers is a tragedy; one that should never had to have been written. The heartlessness of the occupation, with its apartheid laws, separation walls, military incursions, deadly police raids and harsh imprisonments are part and parcel of the author Thrall's story. *A Day in the Life of Abed Salama* is a beautiful, heartbreaking and necessary tale made that much better by the his telling. This story reminds the reader of the humanity we all share. The tragic tale of the bus accident and the emotional and physical consequences for the children on the bus and their families could happen anywhere in the world. It is also true that only in the political reality of the Israeli Occupation could this tragedy occur in the manner it did. The description in prose both emotive and detailed of the parents' pain, fear and even anger makes that common humanity as real as if it were happening to the reader themselves. The harsh and cruel reality of the nature of Israel's occupation is omnipresent. So is its racism. So, too, are the individuals whose humanity ignores those cruel realities in their attempts to save the children.

Fascism in the 2020s

Late Fascism: Race, Capitalism and the Politics of Crisis—
Alberto Toscano

In 1976, the philosopher Herbert Marcuse wrote that "American fascism will probably be the first which comes to power by democratic means and with democratic support." A few years earlier, in a series of letters between Black Panther George Jackson, Angela Davis and Jackson's attorney John Thorne, Jackson wrote: "Fascism was the product of class struggle. It is an obvious extension of capitalism, a higher form of the old struggle — capitalism versus socialism. I think our failure to clearly isolate and define it may have something to do with our insistence on a full definition — in other words, looking for exactly identical symptoms from nation to nation. We have been consistently misled by fascism's nationalistic trappings." (*Blood in My Eye*)

Both of these statements are fundamental to the discussion of contemporary fascism that is the essence of Alberto Toscano's recent book titled *Late Fascism*. As the world watches the potential re-election of Donald Trump to the White House, the genocidal war against the Palestinians being waged by Israel with full support from the United States and the Biden administration, and the ongoing popularity of numerous far right movements around the globe, the question of fascism is both relevant and frighteningly current. Despite this, there seems to be no generalized understanding of fascism's modern manifestations or how to fight and prevent its potential rule, especially in the so-called West.

A very important, but often ignored or dismissed element of fascism is that it is a culmination of a certain direction capitalism can take. It is a direction that is directly related to certain crises that are built into the chaos that defines capitalism; a chaos that upends the working classes and those Marx called the petit bourgeoisie—small business people, technocrats and professionals—while enhancing the economic and political power of the capitalist class. The turmoil experienced by the former two strata mentioned above is such that it forces them towards political responses outside the comfortable choice presented by the bourgeois electoral system. In the Europe between the two great wars of the twentieth century, those choices were communism and fascism. Given communism's fundamental opposition to the economy and politics of the bourgeoisie, fascism became the politics of the formerly democratic bourgeois class. As Toscano points out, nothing makes this clearer than that fascism was invited in by the king and by Hindenburg in Germany. Indeed, it was the hatred of the communists that convinced Hindenberg to hand the chancellorship to Hitler and the Nazis. It was also that fear that convinced the ruling classes, their banks and corporations to support that handover. This fact left me with the thought that even if Trump loses in 2024, his followers will force the issue well beyond the stolen vote campaign of 2020, perhaps creating a compromise whereby he moves back into the White House to forestall major civil unrest.

Beyond the economics that leads capitalist countries to fascism are race and racial politics. Toscano discusses this in detail, reminding the reader of WEB DuBois' observation that European fascism in the twentieth century was born in colonialism. The treatment of the Roma, the Jews and others deemed undesirable by the Nazis and (in different degrees and with different foci) the Italian fascists had been honed over decades of European colonialism in the Americas, Africa and Asia. It is an oft-repeated trope that Hitler acknowledged the US genocidal wars against the indigenous peoples of North America that provided him with the template for what became known as the Holocaust. Richard Rubenstein's classic work The Cunning of History expands on this idea by linking the Nazi work camps to US and Brazilian slavery and its mechanization of humanity.

A couple of the more interesting and important additions to the ongoing discussion of fascism one finds in Late Fascism is Toscano's assertion that fascism does not completely obliterate freedom. Indeed, Toscano argues that fascism actually increases freedom, not only of those at the top and in the Party, but also those whose interests it represents—white supremacists (Hindus in India), the petit bourgeoisie and others who benefit from its relaxation of environmental and labor regulations put in place by the liberal state. Of course, like all manifestations of capitalism, the only unquestioned rights belong to property and those who own it. Capital's response to challenges to this fundamental right have been temporary at best. One need only look at the history of the global north since the end of World War Two to understand this. Social democracy and its manifestation as the welfare state began to be seriously dismantled with the advent of neoliberalism in the late 1970s. The ongoing social upheaval caused by the privatization and ultimate destruction of most government support systems has not only caused massive inequality, it has as its ultimate goal the reduction of the government to its essential roles: war and repression. Given this, a fascist government is the ideal means to produce such a system.

Late Fascism takes a deep look at fascism. It considers its inherent contradictions and its various manifestations in the modern world. Instead of insisting definition that relies on a detailed set of conditions taken from history, the author incorporates those historical manifestations into various contemporary movements and conditions in a valiant and important attempt to define current future fascisms. The Italian fascist Benito Mussolini once noted that fascism is anti-socialist, that is to say liberal. (57) That, I believe, is an essential truth not only fundamental to Toscano's text, but to any genuine understanding of fascism and how to fight it.

This final piece is a consideration of some of Marc Estrin's fiction. It scynchronistically appeared in *Counterpunch* magazine online the morning after Marc passed on August 10, 2025. Marc was a co-founder (with Donna Bister) of Fomite Press, a wonderful editor and a longtime friend.

Marc Estrin's Fictions of Alienation

Insect Dreams

The Education of Arnold Hitler

The Annotated Nose

The Good Dr. Guillotin

"People are up to their ears in facts. What they want is story; what they need is story." So explains the fictional author to his audience near the beginning of Marc Estrin's 2008 novel *The Annotated Nose*. It might seem cliche to suggest here that it is in the story that the truth often lies. Yet the truth (there's that word again) is that this is a fact more than many of us will, upon reflection, acknowledge. While he might publicly reject the notion, Estrin has revealed many truths in his novels and tales. He does this through the magic of fiction and his often magical use of words and the concepts words describe. Informing it all is an underlying theme that contemplates the so-called Other while exploring the Other's role in revealing certain truths, both through the Other's existence and its interaction with the majority.

The task Estrin has given himself is one that requires a keen sense of life's contradictions; of history's role in creating the future, often in ways few if any could have foreseen. It's also a task where a sense of humor facilitates the story while assisting in revealing the consequent truth. Perhaps no novel of Estrin's does this more obviously and with a recognizable delight than his tale of a blonde boy from Texas with the name Arnold Hitler. Titled *The Education of Arnold Hitler*, Estrin's novel begins in the small southern town of Mansfield, Texas; the town where John Howard Griffin, the author of the 1961 book *Black Like Me*, was born. For those unfamiliar with the book, it describes the experiences of the author—a white man—who has his skin darkened and passes as a Black man in a journey across the Deep South in the US. It's not something anyone would get a book contract to write today, but it was quite a sensation in the early days of the 1960s when legal apartheid described the US South.

Arnold, being blonde, is Estrin's archetypal Aryan. Of course, Arnold doesn't have a clue about Aryanism, white supremacy or Dachau. After all, he's just a white kid in white America doing white kid things. He means no harm. It's only when he goes east to college on a scholarship that he genuinely realizes that his name can be a problem. Not the Arnold part of it, mind you. Jewish students ostracize him and student Nazi clubs try to recruit him. Arnold just wants to be a college student who's interested in college things, which in the late 1960s means protests and marijuana, among other things. He could change his name, but that wouldn't address his intellectual crisis; it would only ignore it. The weight of history is carried in his name and on his shoulders as much as the weight of history is carried in the guilt of the German nation after its murderous Nazi orgy of violence and rationality. His soul-searching includes a conversation with MIT professor Noam Chomsky, a friendship with Leonard Bernstein's daughter, a kiss from the maestro, intimidation from Harvard white supremacists and a couple of women.

Estrin's work includes seventeen novels, a couple essay collections and two books he considers memoirs. Of the latter, one is a discussion of the art of writing and the other—titled *Rehearsing With Gods: Photographs and Essays on the Bread & Puppet Theater*—is a beautifully constructed reminiscence/history of the Bread and Puppet Theater, a phenomenon unique in the world. Estrin was one of the early recruits to the puppet theater group; he joined a few years after Peter and Elka Schumann introduced Bread and Puppet to the world in 1963. At the time, Estrin was working in Washington, DC's Institute for Policy Studies and had founded (with Dennis Livingston) the antiwar guerrilla theater troupe known as the American Playground Theater which was merely one element of the new left counterculture Washington Free Community in the late 1960s. The Free Community included Raymond Mungo and Allan Bloom's underground media clearinghouse Liberation News Service, draft resistance organizations and numerous other artistic and political endeavors challenging the imperial war machine at its center. Prior to his residence in DC, Estrin had been part of San Francisco's Actor's Workshop, directing Michael McClure's play *The Beard*. After turning down McClure's request to take the show on the road, he spent time in Pittsburgh's alternative drama scene. One of my favorite stories of Estrin's involves his meeting with rock music impresario Bill Graham in the then cobweb-covered, rat-infested building in San Francisco's Fillmore District that would become synonymous with the San Francisco rock scene and Graham himself—the Fillmore West. Estrin determined the building was not what he was looking for in terms of presenting plays and Graham left his job as manager of the San Francisco Mime Troupe to become the world's best (in my opinion) promoter of modern popular music.

I was part of a small collective of people publishing a local agitational newspaper called the *Old North End Rag* in Burlington, Vermont, in the late 1990s and early 2000s when Marc began sharing the draft of a novel he was writing. Although it was the second novel he had written, it would be the first to be published. And it would be published twice— once as the 2002 Putnam/Blue Hen title *Insect Dreams: The Half-Life of Gregor Samsa* and later as the 2017 release *Kafka's Roach* (Fomite). The latter version is essentially what is called the director's cut in cinema. In other words, it's the manuscript I was reading as Estrin finished each chapter back in 2000-2001. It's the same tale as *Insect Dream*s only with many details filled in and no wormholes across time..

The story begins the day Franz Kafka's human wakes up as a cockroach but with a different outcome than the one determined by Kafka. Instead of dying alone and unwanted, he remains Gregor Samsa and goes on to live a life most humans can only imagine. Gregor reads Spengler to audiences in a sideshow act as the Nazis take over Germany; he flies across the Atlantic and ends up having a dance named after him. He then goes to work for Charles Ives as a risk management genius in Ives' insurance business. There's romance and an eventual job in the FDR White House. It's a job that takes him to Los Alamos, New Mexico and the Manhattan Project's development of a nuclear weapon. Samsa's final act is to immolate himself in the first test of the discovery that changes the world, in the explosion that saw humanity become the destroyer of worlds. It's a human moment where the pursuit of science alone requires a barrage of inquiry; maybe the ultimate such moment. Is it worth planetary suicide to answer the question of nuclear fission? Is it worth planetary suicide to build a better a better bomb, especially when that bomb's purpose is the incineration of human lives?

It should be apparent from the quick plot description above that Estrin is not just interested in telling a good story. Indeed, *Insect Dreams/ Kafka's Roach* also serves as a history of the twentieth century up to the time of Samsa's death. That in itself is quite a story; a story that is certainly full of sound and fury even if we have no idea what, if anything, it signifies. Estrin's life work is one that simultaneously seeks some significant understanding that there may be none while also doing his part to give this life, these lives, this human species some meaning. I wrote this in a 2017 review of *Kafka's Roach*: "The underlying context of Marc Estrin's novel *Kafka's Roach: The Life and Times of Gregor Samsa* is the relationship of the Other to a world where its inhabitants reject, ignore and even murder those it considers different. To emphasize this, Estrin's Samsa is both a cockroach and Jewish; both of them the subject of revulsion in many circles."[1] Alienation as a way of life, in other words.

If there is one theme that runs through Estrin's major novels, it would be the one described in that quote. That's clear in his second published novel, which I refer to in my earlier paragraphs, and it is also apparent in his 2008 novel *The Annotated Nose*, a sort of metafiction of a fictional novel titled *The Nose* that exists only in the universe Estrin creates in his novel appropriately titled *The Annotated Nose*. This is at first glance a merely playful book, but with each subsequent glance (if you will) it becomes a commentary on modern disconnections and the desire to transcend them, on the nature of popular culture and the role the market plays in such culture and, one could argue, the absurdity of it all. Told with Estrin's particular humor, the reader is introduced to a cult-like sensation centered on a novel by a fictional author named Hundertwasser. This introduction is not through Hundertwasser's text, however, but through the annotated text and commentary of Estrin's fictional author Alexei Pigov, described in the book as a "premature goth." It's Pigov's descent into a certain madness that informs *The Annotated Nose* and, together with the shadowy illustrations by real-life artist Delia Robinson (who also exists as a character in Pigov's work), Estrin's novel becomes an artistic delve into the truths of the human endeavor and the rationales for its often nonsensical and tragic reality.

Estrin has several other novels—one might call them minor works, although I prefer the term slight to describe them. Not slight in terms of themes approached or in questions asked, but merely in terms of size. Like the three fictional works mentioned (discussed?) here, all of Estrin's fictions take place in a world where the fantastic never becomes commonplace. However the commonplace does become fantastic. For Estrin, life is not a joke, it has meaning, yet it is endlessly humorous. Although he might disagree, his fiction implies that it is because of that humor we humans have survived up to now, despite those whose science, politics and economics conspire to destroy us.

In 2011, Marc and his wife Donna Bister told me they were considering starting a small literary press. Estrin's experiences with the world of corporate publishing had convinced them both that too many good if not excellent writers were not getting published because of the corporate bottom line, despite the numerous imprints that existed as subsidiaries of the corporate houses at the time. I encouraged the idea. Soon thereafter, they asked if I had a manuscript that might be ready. I did. My novel *The Co-Conspirator's Tale* became the first book published by the infant Fomite Press. Since that first book, Fomite Press has published over two hundred books. Their list includes novels, short fiction, poetry, creative non-fiction, essays and a number of unique books combining text and graphics from Bread & Puppet's Peter Schumann. Since October 7, 2023 much of the press's focus has been on publishing books about Palestine and against the ongoing genocide there. I mention Fomite primarily because it is an embodiment of Estrin's ongoing project that invites and encourages the mysteries of circumstance, the pursuit of truth and the repercussions and ripples of both the pursuit and the truth itself.

In 2009, Estrin's novel *The Good Dr. Guillotin* was published by Unbridled Books. Nominally the story of the invention of the tool for execution bearing the good Doctor's name, it is also a musing on revolution, the common man(woman), science (again), and killing by the State. Around the time of the novel's release, I conducted an interview for *Counterpunch* magazine with Estrin. The 2008 election (Obama's first term) was still relatively fresh in the popular mind. Here is a brief excerpt:

Ron Jacobs: Ah, yes… the Faustian bargain. I think we've all made a few–at least at a personal level–to get a job or maintain a relationship. However, the ones I'm more interested in are those that we make in the political/economic realm as a people. Last November's election appears to me as a Faustian bargain of this type. Hell, every election is a Faustian bargain of a sort. Anyhow, back to the more general one we make as residents of the United States — we know what our government, its military and the corporate/financial monoliths do to maintain our standard of living… and we support it, if only tacitly. Keeping Nicholas Pelletier (Pelletier is the name of the first person killed by the guillotine)in mind, one could argue that it is only the criminals and others — those that Bob Dylan called "the luckless, the abandoned an' forsaked"–that do not make this bargain. But then, they probably make their own with Mephistopheles in another form. I guess my question is–can any human in our modern society avoid the Faustian deal?

Marc Estrin: Faustian bargain: Let's make some distinctions because not every bargain is a Faustian bargain. The key dynamic in the Faustian bargain is a quest — for knowledge, or power, or the establishment of some ideal — with every attainment receiving some unexpected blowback, usually a just punishment. I don't think the US elections represent a Faustian bargain: we certainly don't learn anything from them, nor do we get any power, nor do we further any ideal. Rather the opposite in each case.

I quote this section of the interview if only to illustrate a foundation of the world Estrin creates in his fiction; a world where despite a daily reality that may be a constant set of negotiations that often mean little, there are humans who still pursue a quest beyond the daily negotiating session.

In the world of Estrin's fiction, the person pursuing that quest might very well be a human sized insect.

About the Author

Ron Jacobs is the author of several books, including *The Way the Wind Blew: A History of the Weather Underground* (Verso 1997), *Daydream Sunset: 60s Counterculture in the 70s* (Counterpunch 2015), and a crime fiction trilogy published by Fomite *(All the Sinners Saints, The Co-Conspirator's Tale, Short Order Frame Up)*. His most recent book, also published by Fomite, is titled *Nowhere Land: Journeys Through a Broken Nation*. His articles, reviews, and essays have been appeared in anthologies and numerous print and online journals around the world. He lives in Winooski, Vermont.

Writing a review on social media sites for readers will help the progress of independent publishing. To submit a review, go to the book page on any of the sites and follow the links for reviews. Books from independent presses rely on reader-to-reader communications.

For more information or to order any of our books, visit:
fomitepress.com/our-books.html

More essays from Fomite...

William Benton — *Eye Contact: Writing on Art*
Marc Estrin — *Longing for the Sky: Essays on Music, Unmusic, and Antimusic*
J. Malcom Garcia — *A Different Kind of War: Uneasy Encounters
                    in Mexico and Central America*
Stephen Langfur — *Confession from a Jericho Jail*
Douglas W. Milliken — *Any Less You*
George Ovitt & Peter Nash — *Trotsky's Sink: Ninety-Eight Short
                    Essays on Literature*
Robert Sommer — *Losing Francis: Essays on the Wars at Home*

www.ingramcontent.com/pod-product-compliance
Lightning Source LLC
Chambersburg PA
CBHW030353130626
46549CB00004B/1477